SIKH *The Politics of Faith*
SEPARATISM

SIKH SEPARATISM
The Politics of Faith

Rajiv A. Kapur

London
ALLEN & UNWIN
Boston   Sydney

**Allen & Unwin (Publishers) Ltd,
40 Museum Street, London WC1A 1LU, UK**

Allen & Unwin (Publishers) Ltd,
Park Lane, Hemel Hempstead, Herts HP2 4TE, UK

Allen & Unwin Inc.,
8 Winchester Place, Winchester, Mass 01890, USA

Allen & Unwin (Australia) Ltd,
8 Napier Street, North Sydney, NSW 2060, Australia

First published in 1986

British Library Cataloguing in Publication Data

Kapur, Rajiv A.
  Sikh separatism: the politics of faith
1. Sikhism – History
I. Title
294.6'09 BL2017.6
ISBN 0-04-320179-2

Library of Congress Cataloging in Publication Data

Kapur, Rajiv A.
  Sikh separatism: the politics of faith
Bibliography: p.
Includes index.
1. Sikhs – Politics and government. 2. Sikhs – Ethnic identity. 3.
Punjab (India) – History – Autonomy and independence
movements.
I. Title.
DS485.P3K36   1986   954'.552   85-22856
ISBN 0-04-320179-2 (alk. paper)

Set in 10 on 12 point Garamond Original by
Computape (Pickering) Ltd, N. Yorkshire
and printed in Great Britain by
Anchor Brendan, Tiptree, Essex

To my great grandfather
Lala Ruchi Ram Sahni

Contents

Preface   *page* ix

Introduction   xi

1 *The Evolution of Sikh Identity*   1

2 *From Identity to Consciousness*   36

3 *Communal Consciousness and Competition*   61

4 *Solidarity and Agitation*   105

5 *Agitation Extended*   132

6 *Implications of Militancy*   173

7 *Power for the Faithful*   194

Epilogue   235

Bibliography   251

Index   265

Preface

This study is concerned with the evolution of contemporary Sikh identity and communal consciousness and its impact on the social and political activity of Sikhs. The self-perception of any group is, of course, only a factor affecting its activity in a larger arena, but in the case of the Sikhs it is believed to be an important and hitherto neglected aspect. A diverse set of developments spanning more than a century contributed to this process and have been examined. It is not, however, intended to provide a comprehensive historical account of social and political change among the Sikhs.

My interest in the Sikhs began while pursuing post-graduate work at Oxford University, and five years of research towards my doctoral dissertation, contributed to this study. At the outset, I would therefore like to express my deep gratitude to my former tutors, Professor R. E. Robinson, Dr J. M. Roberts and Dr J. R. L. Highfield, and to Mr Harry Pitt for their guidance and encouragement. My field research was assisted by grants from several sources at Oxford University, and I would also like to take this opportunity to acknowledge the financial help provided by the Warden and Fellows of Merton College, the Trustees of the Radhakrishnan Memorial Bequest and the Trustees of the Beit Fund.

The research for this book was conducted at a number of libraries in India, England and the United States, and I owe thanks for their assistance to the librarian and staff of the National Archives of India and the Nehru Memorial Library, New Delhi; the Punjab States Archives and the Punjabi University, Patiala; the Library of the Sikh Itihas Research Board (SGPC) and the Khalsa College, Amritsar; the Bodleian Library, Oxford; the India Office Library and Records and the Oriental Collection of the British Museum, London; and the Library of Congress, Washington DC.

Years of research brought me into contact with a large number of scholars and with individuals active in Sikh politics or in the British administration in the period under study. Many of them offered valuable advice or shared their recollections willingly. In particular, I would like to thank Mr Khushwant Singh, Professor N. Gerald Barrier and Sir Evan Jenkins. Grateful thanks are also due to Sardar Nahar Singh, who simply handed over to me his valuable collection of papers and Sikh political literature banned by the Government of India at the time. I would also like to take this opportunity to thank a number of friends, particularly Bonnie Bunnag, Nidhi Dalmia, Gillian Halford and Tejeshwar Singh, who helped at crucial moments in the preparation of this book.

Finally, I owe much to my parents for their patience and generosity, to my wife Lekha, who checked notes, compiled figures and provided constant encouragement through years of seemingly endless research and writing, and to little Avani, who slept through half the writing of this book and believed that I was asleep through the other half.

Rajiv A. Kapur

Introduction

If men could learn from history, what lessons it might teach us! But passion and party blind our eyes, and the light which experience gives, is a lantern on the stern, which shines only on the waves behind us!

(S. T. Coleridge, quoted in T. Allsop, *Recollections*, 1836)

The Sikhs in India are in economic terms a relatively secure community. They have a higher per capita income and a higher life expectancy than the national average. The Sikhs are about 2 per cent of the population of the country, but they constitute a considerably higher proportion of the Indian army and of all central-government employees than their numbers alone would suggest. The President of India is a Sikh. Besides, Sikhs head several national corporations and numerous private ones, and they have contributed to making the Punjab the wheat bowl of almost 700 million Indians. The Sikh homeland of Punjab is also of considerable geo-political importance as the Indian state bordering Pakistan and providing the lifeline to disputed Kashmir.

Between 1981 and 1984, Sikh political leaders led a series of mass civil-disobedience campaigns against the Indian government for fulfilment of a set of demands which included greater autonomy for the state of Punjab. As the agitation progressed, rivalry between Sikh leaders drove them further towards extremism. Sikh unrest also saw the appearance of a violent terrorist campaign for the creation of a sovereign Sikh state. Led by a militant fundamentalist Sikh preacher, Jarnail Singh Bhindranwale, the terrorist campaign resulted in considerable violence directed at the Hindu community and at moderate Sikhs. According to the government the extremist campaign also found active support among some Sikhs in Britain, the United States and Canada.

In June 1984 the Indian army launched a massive anti-terrorist operation against Sikh militants in the Punjab. Military action began with an assault on the Golden Temple in Amritsar, the bastion of Sikhism where Sikh extremists had found sanctuary, and resulted in considerable damage to sacred Sikh property. The fundamentalist leader Jarnail Singh Bhindranwale and many of his supporters were killed and Sikh political leaders arrested. For many Sikhs, this government action was an insult to their religion which could not easily be forgiven. The aftermath of this military action against Sikh extremists saw a resurgence of terrorist activity, the assassination of the Indian prime minister, and an outbreak of brutal communal violence against Sikhs. The campaign for Sikh separatism developed into a most serious threat to the unity and stability of India.

Recent demands by the Sikhs stemmed from what their leaders considered essential to safeguard and promote their interests as a separate people. But the growth of Sikh fundamentalism and the separatist demand is not as sudden as it may seem. Both have deep social and historical roots, linked to the development of a distinct Sikh identity, community and organization, which are examined in this book.

We recognize the Sikhs today as a distinct and separate people. Indeed, of the religious communities in India, the Sikhs probably possess the strongest sense of their own identity and community. This Sikh communal consciousness is the result of a social movement among the Sikhs in the last quarter of the nineteenth century and the first decades of this century which reformulated Sikh identity and established new norms for Sikh orthodoxy. Whether the Sikh gurus intended the creation of a separate faith and community for their followers is a subject of theological debate and is outside the scope of this study. Certainly, the philosophical foundations of Sikhism derive significantly from Hindu religious thought. More importantly, until recently all Sikhs or followers of the gurus did not consider themselves as a distinct group or community outside the large Hindu framework. The boundaries of Sikh identity, of what it meant to be a Sikh, were unclear and flexible and overlapped with Hindu identity. The militant Khalsa brotherhood founded by the tenth guru, Gobind Singh, shared a set of common symbols, rituals and practices which superficially set them apart from the Hindus, but Khalsa numbers were fluid, their numerical strength derived from converts from the Hindu community, and they relapsed into the

Hindu community from time to time. Besides, even as members of the Khalsa, they followed many of the practices, customs and traditions of the Hindus and continued to be bound to the Hindus by ties of kinship and marriage. Moreover, it was common for one member of a Hindu family to adopt the garb of the Khalsa without being seen by Hindus to become a lesser Hindu in the process. If few Sikhs would spurn Hindu beliefs without a heavy conscience, the Punjabi Hindus for their part paid homage to Sikh gurus in their thousands. For four hundred years, Sikh and Hindu identities remained interlinked and overlapping.

The nineteenth century saw the emergence of a number of social and religious reform movements in Indian society. In the Punjab, the Hindu Arya Samaj had much in common with the Sikh reform movement of the Singh Sabhas. They shared a concern with a need to revitalize their faith and safeguard it from growing Christian missionary influence, and they adopted similar tactics. But the Singh Sabha movement went much further than the other reformist campaigns. Led by a group of militant Tat (true) Khalsa reformers, the Singh Sabhaites reformulated Sikh identity and drew communal boundaries between the Sikhs and Hindus. In the face of accepted norms of Sikh orthodoxy they asserted that being a Sikh was limited to members of the Khalsa. Sikhs who did not observe the symbols of the Khalsa, though they might well revere the Sikh gurus and worship at Sikh shrines, were seen as apostates or as Hindus. Further, within the Khalsa brotherhood, the Tat Khalsa reformers were enormously success-ful in building a spirit of internal solidarity and consciousness. This study is initially concerned with the social, political and economic developments which led to this process of reformu-lation of Sikh identity and the emergence of Sikh consciousness and communal separatism.

The twentieth century brought the devolution of power to Indians by the British colonial authorities. English-educated Sikhs and Hindus scrambled for posts in the newly formed provincial legislative bodies. The race for political patronage and office brought with it the beginnings of communal political competition. Seen as part of a much larger Hindu community, the Sikhs and their leaders were of little political consequence, but as a distinct minority group they had a platform from which to fight. For Sikh politicians separatism from the Hindus became an issue in practical politics and they demanded recognition of the Sikhs as an independent political entity. But as a separate community the Sikhs constituted only 13 per cent of the Punjab, and Sikh politicians realized that for them to be in a position to safeguard meaningfully the interests of their community, the Sikhs would have to have political representation way out of proportion to their numbers. Hindu politicians for their part rejected Sikh claims to separate political representation on the ground that the Sikhs were Hindus. Besides, the acceptance of such a claim would only reduce Hindu political representation in the province. When Sikh aspirations were not fulfilled, traditional Sikh leaders, who had been loyal or tacit supporters of the colonial authorities, were challenged by a younger generation of educated Sikhs, who joined hands with nationalist politicians in anti-government agitation for greater Indian participation in the administration. While these Sikhs collaborated with the largely Hindu nationalist politicians in the Punjab, their participation in the nationalist campaign stemmed from a desire to promote their separate existence in what they saw as a hostile world. This process of politicization among Sikhs, the establishment of Sikh political organization and the emergence of an essentially communal, Khalsa nationalism, is further examined in this book.

But Sikh participation in nationalist politics was initially largely eclipsed by their concern over the management and control of Sikh temples or *gurdwara*. The management of these institutions had for centuries been entrusted to non-Khalsa Sikhs who nominated their own successors. Under Sikh rule in the Punjab (1801–49), the revenue derived from Sikh ecclesiastical property grew enormously with the grant of estates to Sikh shrines by the state. The annexation of the Punjab by the British in 1849 brought the compilation of elaborate land-settlement records, and in many cases Sikh religious property was registered in the name of the manager in charge. Some of these managers, safe in the belief that the civil law would safeguard their right to possession of the property they managed, misappropriated religious funds and abused their trust. The misuse of Sikh religious property became of major concern to Sikh reformers. Civil suits were instituted and petitions seeking redress were sent to the local authorities to no avail, for under British law possession constituted the deciding factor. The growth of Sikh communal consciousness and separatism introduced another element into the demand for *gurdwara* reform. The non-Khalsa Sikh managers of Sikh shrines did little to enforce strict Khalsa tenets, and militant Tat Khalsa reformers saw the presence of what they considered to be Hindu and non-Sikh practices in Sikh worship as another example of the depravation of these managers. Besides, the purging of Hindu practice from Sikh worship was an essential prerequisite for the development of a separate Sikh communal solidarity. By 1920 militant reformers had taken matters into their own hands and begun the forcible takeover of Sikh shrines. When the government attempted to enforce the law, a mass conflict between Sikh agitators and the authorities ensued. The conflict raged sporadically until 1925; in this period 30,000 Sikhs were arrested, 400 lost their lives and 2,000 were wounded.

This Sikh agitation is believed to have been of crucial significance for the Sikh community, and it is examined in depth in this book. The agitation culminated, in 1925, with the adoption of legislation relating to the management and control of Sikh shrines in the form of the Sikh Gurdwaras Act. The formulation of this legislation is reviewed in detail, for it provided an institutional framework for Sikh communal consciousness and separatism from the Hindus which continues to be valid today. The agitation also saw the geneses of two Sikh organizations, a central committee for the management of Sikh shrines, the Shiromani Gurdwara Prabhandak Committee (SGPC) and its political and agitational wing, the Akali Dal, which have continued to govern the direction of Sikh politics for the past sixty years and provided the base for recent Sikh agitation. The strategies and tactics employed by Sikh militants, the formulation of their ideology and the emergence of these Sikh organizations are examined.

The Sikh Gurdwaras Act of 1925 has undergone thirty amendments, but the basic institutions it established remain the same today. The nature of these Sikh institutions is believed to be of considerable significance. The central body for the management of Sikh shrines established under this legislation, the SGPC, rapidly became an arena and a base for Sikh politics. The control of several hundred Sikh shrines provided the SGPC with access to the enormous resources of these shrines derived from religious property and daily offerings. Indeed, the annual budget of the SGPC from these sources amounted to more than $12 million US in 1985. The utilization of these funds for any non-political purpose and the distribution of patronage in the form of a variety of jobs required for the management of Sikh shrines enabled the SGPC to gather support from strategic groups within the Sikh community. Further, control over all Sikh religious institutions gave the SGPC a quasi-religious authority, and it resorted to excommunicating its opponents from the Sikh community from time to time. Contests for control of the SGPC become primary political battles within the Sikh community, for leadership of the SGPC provided a powerful base for leadership in the Sikh community.

Since its inception the Akali Dal has controlled the SGPC. The Akali Dal's domination of this body for more than sixty years, and its association with the successful Sikh struggle for control over their shrines, have made it a formidable force in Sikh politics. Akali leaders have remained ideologically committed to a separate Sikh identity and acutely aware of the fragility of a distinct Sikh community, for once Sikhs shed the symbols of the Khalsa they become indistinguishable from a large body of Punjabi Hindus. Besides, Sikh communal separatism has provided a base and a political appeal for the Akali Dal. The Akali Dal's political and religious demands have therefore been constantly guided by a desire to maintain and develop communal boundaries with the Hindus and to seek a political base on which the Sikhs will be secure as a separate people. The tactics and strategies adopted by the Akali Dal in pursuit of these objectives have remained those developed in the 1920s. A series of demands and agitations launched by the Akali Dal in India before and after independence, and its recent demands, are examined in this light.

1

The Evolution of Sikh Identity

Guru Nanak, the founder of the Sikh faith, was born in the Punjab in 1469. Nanak rejected the idolatry of Hinduism, he challenged the authority of Brahmins, preached the equality of all men, and negated the elaborate worship of diverse gods and goddesses as a means to salvation. He propounded instead a simple and strict monotheism. God was *sat*, both truth and reality, the only one, omnipotent and omniscient reality. The divine being was formless (*nirankar*). He revealed himself through his creation. It was thus man's duty to meditate on this creation, this revelation of the divine, which was known as *nam* or the name or spirit of God. Through such meditation man could grow to be more like his creator, and through devotion could attain nirvana, a mystical union with the divine and end the cycle of transmigration. Guru Nanak's plea for meditation on God's creation was not, however, an appeal for asceticism. On the contrary, fundamental to his teachings was a pragmatic view of the physical world. The path to salvation, according to Nanak, could be pursued while living the normal life of a householder. Indeed he stressed both the spiritual and the temporal side of human existence and upheld the dignity of labour.[1]

Fundamental to Nanak's teachings was the role of the guru. The guru was a divine messenger, a guide, the indispensable path through which man could attain salvation. The guru's teachings, his word, or *gurbani*, was regarded with the same reverence as was accorded to the guru's person, and meditation on the guru's word was considered the best mode of worship. Nanak instituted a common mode of worship in the *sangat*, a religious congregation where his followers, or Sikhs, met as equals, irrespective of caste or status, sang the hymns of the guru and meditated on his teachings. This essential brotherhood of man was further given practical demonstration by the levelling of caste barriers and pollution inhibitions through the institution of *guru-ka-langar*, or a free community kitchen in which all participated.

Nanak was succeeded by a line of nine gurus, who propagated his gospel until the death of the tenth guru, Gobind Singh, in 1708. According to Sikh tradition the ten gurus are not to be seen as a succession of mystics, but as ten manifestations of the same guru propagating the faith. Thus before his death Guru Nanak superseded the claims of his sons to the guruship and appointed one of his followers to succeed him. He stressed that the guruship was conferred on the basis of merit in piety and devotion to the guru, that it was not simply hereditary, and that his successor was in fact the embodiment of the same spirit as himself. He named his successor Guru Angad or, literally, a part, or *ang*, of his own body. However, Nanak's eldest son, Sri Chand, asserted his hereditary right to the guruship and founded an order of ascetics known as Udasis.

The successors to Guru Nanak made no radical change in the fundamental precepts of his philosophy. However, the expansion of Sikh numbers necessitated clearer organization and definition within the Sikh community. The third guru, Amar Das, responded to this need by instituting a place of pilgrimage, a rallying point for the Sikhs. Ram Das, the fourth guru, founded the holy city of Amritsar, where his successor Arjun later built a *gurdwara*, or Sikh temple, and called it Harmandir. Amritsar became the religious capital of Sikhism. Guru Arjun also compiled the Guru Granth Sahib, the holy book of the Sikhs, which contains all the hymns of the Sikh gurus and those by various Hindu and Muslim mystics.

By the beginning of the seventeenth century, however, with the guruship in the hands of Hargobind, the sixth guru, a more important element had crept into the character of the Sikh community. Under a severe threat from the Mogul rulers which culminated in the martyrdom of Guru Arjun, an element of militancy had appeared among the Sikhs. Following the death of Guru Ram Das, the institution of guru had become hereditary. The spiritual authority of the guru, which also had temporal overtones for the Sikhs, was now firmly entrenched in the physical world. Guru Arjun had thus been declared the *saccha padshah* or the true or real king, both spiritual and temporal. Hargobind gave visible expression to this title. He took to arms, and himself carried two swords, *miri* and *piri*, the one representing the spiritual and the other the temporal side of his authority. He fortified Amritsar and built the Akal Takht, the throne of the timeless one, opposite the Harmandir. The complex of these two buildings later became known as the Golden Temple. From the Akal Takht he dispensed justice and temporal orders, from the Harmandir, spiritual guidance. Some of the followers of the gurus were beginning to be transformed from being pacifist members of a purely religious sect to a highly organized body, militant in spirit and oriented towards meeting any challenge to their faith. With the formation of the Khalsa brotherhood under the tenth guru, Gobind Singh, this transformation was complete.

The Sikh view of the foundation of the Khalsa is of immense significance, for it provides the basis of a martial tradition in the cause of righteousness. The ninth guru, Teg Bhadur, had met a violent death at the hands of the Moguls. His successor, Gobind Singh, reflected on the perilous situation of his followers. To instil in them a spirit of courage and brotherhood, he chose the day of the *Baisakhi*, the Hindu new year festival, when his followers had gathered in large numbers at Anandpur Sahib. The guru, having concealed himself, emerged when the fair was in full swing. With sword aloft he demanded the head of a loyal Sikh as a sacrifice to the guru. An awestruck hush fell upon the gathered Sikhs. The guru repeated his demand, and on his third call a single Sikh volunteered his life to the guru. The guru led him into a nearby tent and emerged a few moments later with blood-stained weapon. He demanded another follower to sacrifice his life similarly for the guru. Initially there was no response. On his third call, another Sikh stepped forward and was led into the tent, and once again the guru emerged with blood dripping from his sword. The process was repeated until five Sikhs had thus volunteered their lives to the guru. The guru then returned with the five Sikh volunteers and revealed the five dead goats that lay in his tent. He addressed the astonished gathering saying, 'In the time of Guru Nanak there was found one devout Sikh, namely Guru Angad. In my time there are found five Sikhs totally devoted to the guru. These shall lay anew the foundations of Sikhism.'[2]

The five chosen by the guru, the *Panj Pyaras*, were to form the nucleus of a new brotherhood, the Khalsa. Those who chose to join the brotherhood were to abandon all links with their caste, and with their old scriptures and deities, and were to follow only the one immortal God and the guru. Male converts to the Khalsa were to adopt the common surname of Singh, or lion, thereby levelling all caste distinctions and expressing their distinctiveness and solidarity. They were enjoined to wear five symbols, comprising *Kes* (uncut hair), *Kanga* (a comb), *Kara* (a steel bangle), *Kirpan* (a sword) and *Kachcha* (a type of breeches). Not only were these symbols intended as a visible identification with the Khalsa, but they had a deep symbolic significance.[3] Members of the Khalsa were, in addition, to avoid association with five groups who were followers of figures who had at some time disputed the succession of a guru. They were further prohibited the use of tobacco and of meat slaughtered in the Muslim fashion.

The guru then proceeded to administer the *pahul*, or baptism, to the *Panj Pyaras*. Sweetened water, or *amrit*, was stirred with a double-edged sword in an iron bowl and administered to the five. They in turn were then instructed to baptize the guru. Thus was the Khalsa merged with the guru and the guru with the Khalsa. The Khalsa were instructed that the divine was forever present in their midst, and that the will of the Khalsa, symbolically represented by a congregation of five of the devout, represented in fact the will and person of the guru.

To complete the tradition of the birth of the Khalsa, there was one more incident of fundamental importance. Before his death, Sikh tradition informs us, Gobind Singh announced that the line of personal gurus was at an end. Henceforth, the sacred book of the Sikhs containing the teachings of the gurus, the Guru Granth Sahib, was to be regarded as the spiritual authority, while the temporal aspects of the authority of the Guru were vested in the collective wisdom of the devout, the Khalsa *panth*, or community.

Ideologically, the creation of the Khalsa aimed at a combination of spiritual excellence and militant valour of the highest order. The Sikh conception of divinity was reinterpreted, laying stress on the martial attributes of the divine being. The supreme being was seen not only as protecting the good, but as a destroyer of evil. The Sikhs were thus exhorted to sacrifice their lives for the faith if necessary. The adoption of the name Singh, or lion, the use of the double-edged sword in the *pahul*, and the wearing of arms, or *kirpans*, were intended to stress this spirit of militancy in the cause of the faith.

Not all Sikhs, however, accepted the baptism of Gobind Singh and became Kesdhari Sikhs, that is, those having *kes*, or uncut hair, and observing the tenets of the Khalsa. Some of the Nanak-panthis (followers of Guru Nanak) continued, as did followers of various Sikh schismatic groups, or of all the gurus preceding the tenth guru, and these were known as Sahajdhari Sikhs, or the slow converters. Indeed it was common to have in a family of Sahajd-hari Sikhs a single member who took the *pahul*, and observed the *kes* and the other symbols of the Khalsa. Often a male child of Sahajdhari Sikh parents was promised to the Khalsa on recovering from a serious illness, or indeed on birth, in fulfilment of an earlier plea to the gurus for an heir. There was thus Sikhs Kesdhari and Sahajdhari.

The Sikh gurus were all Hindu *khatris* by caste, but since its inception the Sikh community contained a large proportion of Sikhs of the *jat* caste. Certainly by the time of the third guru, Amar Das, *jat* numbers among the Sikhs appear to have been increasing rapidly. The fact that the area of central Punjab where the first three gurus lived possessed a particularly high proportion of *jats*, and that the three villages of Tarn Taran, Sri Hargobind-pur and Kartarpur founded by the fifth guru were all located in *jat* territory, bears testimony to this.[4] Indeed, it has been argued that the beginning of Sikh militancy, traditionally ascribed to a decision of Guru Hargobind in direct response to Mogul persecu-tion, was in fact largely the result of growing *jat* influence among the Sikhs. The increasing number of militant *jats* among the Sikhs has been seen to have preceded, and to some extent prompted, a Mogul reaction. Further, the five symbols of the Khalsa have been linked to *jat* customs and traditions.[5]

Traditionally, *jat* willingness to adopt a set of beliefs instituted and guided by *khatri* gurus is quite understandable. The *khatris* had for centuries served as teachers of the *jats*. The *khatris* could thus be expected to dispense guidance to the *jats*, and the *jats* expected to respond. The origin of the *jats* has been traced to a pastoral people of the same name who first appear in reports dating from the seventh century. As these people moved into the

Punjab they discarded their pastoral life and took to cultivation. In doing so they advanced their economic position but retained the social stigma derived from their initial pastoral pursuits. The *jats* had originally been noted for their lack of social stratification. They were thus understandably drawn towards a community which not only shared their lack of caste consciousness but also provided them with an opportunity to move up the social scale and be rid of their social stigma.[6]

The evidence of various observers suggests that the *jats* continued to join the Khalsa in large numbers following the death of the tenth guru, and that upward social mobility was the main motive behind their adoption of Sikhism. An English observer, George Forster, writing in 1798, described the period following the death of the tenth guru as one in which Sikhism gained many proselytes. Further, he informs us that a large proportion of these converts were *jats*, particularly among the Khalsa Sikhs.[7] Similarly, W. L. Mc'Gregor, an English surgeon attached to the court of the Sikh monarch Ranjit Singh, wrote in 1846 that the lack of caste stratification, at least in theory, among the Sikhs, attracted a large number of *sudras*, the lowest caste in the Hindu hierarchy, to the Sikh fold.[8] The ritualistic simplicity of Sikhism and its pragmatism, which appealed to the simple peasant, and the fact that Sikh community already possessed a large number of *jats* makes this phenomenon quite understandable.

In the everyday socio-religious life of the Sikhs, however, the acceptance of Khalsa baptism did not set the Kesdhari Sikhs apart from the Hindu community. Even when the Khalsa Sikhs established a powerful kingdom in the Punjab, their rulers continued to observe Hindu rituals and traditions in addition to Sikh practice. Thus, an English observer noted in 1812, when the Sikhs were the rulers of the Punjab,

The Seikh converts continue, after they have quitted their original religion, all those civil usages and customs of the tribes to which they belonged, that they can practice without infringing the tenets of Nanac, or the institution of Guru Govind. They are most particular with regard to their inter-marriages, and on this point Seikhs descended from Hindoos almost invariably conform to Hindoo customs ... The Hindoo usages regarding diet [are] also held equally sacred, no Seikh de[s]cended from a Hindoo family ever violating it, except upon particular occasions ... when they are obliged ... to eat promiscuously. The strict observances of these usages [have] enabled many of the Seikh[s] ... to preserve an intimate intercourse with their original tribes, who, considering the Seikhs not as having lost caste, but as Hindoos that have joined a political association ... neither refuse to intermarry nor to eat with them.[9]

A similar opinion had been expressed earlier by George Forster. Writing of the Kesdhari Sikhs in 1798, he stated,

> Though many essential differences exist between the religious code of the Hindoos and the Siques, a large space of their groundwork exhibits similarity. The article indeed of the admission of the proselytes among the Siques, has caused an essential deviation from the Hindoo system ... Yet this indiscriminate admission, by the qualifications which have been adopted, do not widely infringe on the customs and privileges of those Hindoos who have embraced the faith of the Siques. They still preserve the distinctions which originally marked their sects and perform many of the ancient ceremonies of their nation. They form matrimonial connections only in their own tribes, and adhere implicitly to the rules prescribed by the Hindoo law, in the choice and preparation of their food.[10]

'The Sikh religion which has long since reached its zenith is now visibly on the decline. The Sikhs themselves say that the free thinking Sikhs who follow their own whims and fancies instead of the precepts of the Gurus are daily on the increase.'[11] Such was the opinion of an informed observer of the state of the Sikh religion in 1845. The distinction between Sahajdhari Sikhs and Hindus in the Punjab had always been more that of philosophical belief than visible difference; by the beginning of the nineteenth century the line between Kesdhari Sikhs and the Hindu community had also grown thin. Though a Kesdhari Sikh might observe the distinctive symbols of his community, symbols which were intended to stress an independent identity and the brotherhood of the Khalsa, these had largely become distinctions of mere form. Kesdhari Sikhs worshipped the Granth Sahib with ceremonies akin to the ritualistic worship of Hindu gods and goddesses, observed pollution inhibitions towards converts from the outcastes of the Hindu hierarchy and consulted astrologers and mystics. In the everyday socio-religious life of the Khalsa community, Hinduism had slowly come back into its own.

The Punjab was annexed by the British in 1849. Its last Sikh monarch, Maharaja Dalip Singh was removed from the province. The once proud Khalsa army was disbanded, and the military fiefs, or jagirdars, the mainstay of Khalsa power, humiliated with the abolition of all military grants. Of the fate of these jagirdars, the Governor-General of British India, Lord Dalhousie, wrote, 'let them be placed somewhere under surveillance, but attach their property till their destination is decided. If they run away our contract is void. If they are caught, I will imprison them. And if they raise tumult again, I will hang them, as sure as they now live, and I live then.'[12] Annexation was the final blow to Khalsa prestige, crumbling as it was through a decade of civil strife.

The collapse of Sikh political power in the Punjab led directly to a decrease in the numbers of Kesdhari Sikhs. During the years of Khalsa rule, large numbers of Hindus and Sahajdhari Sikhs had grown their hair and adopted the symbols of the Khalsa. Visible identification with the authority and prestige of the ruling power was understandably deemed profitable. With the collapse of Sikh political power and the annexation of the Punjab by the British, such identification with the defeated rulers gave rise to considerable apprehension. Uncertain of the British attitude towards their recent foes, those who had earlier adopted the garb of the Khalsa in their thousands, now deserted it with the same vigour. They were joined by families who had been Kesdhari Sikhs for several generations. The Governor-General in two brief visits to the Punjab in 1849, observed such a tendency and acknowledged the adverse impact that annexation seemed to be having on the strength of the Kesdhari Sikhs. The Sikhs, he wrote, are 'gradually relapsing into Hindooism, and even when they continue Sikhs, they are yearly Hindooified more and more.'[13] Sir Richard Temple, writing as secretary to the government in 1853, agreed with him:

> The Sikh faith and ecclesiastical polity is rapidly going where the Sikh political ascendancy has already gone ... The Sikhs of Nanak, a comparatively small body of peaceful habit and old family will perhaps cling to the faith of [their] fathers, but the Sikhs of Govind, who are of more recent origin, who are more specially styled the Singhs or Lion, and who embraced the faith as being the religion of warfare and conquest, no longer regard the Khalsa now that the prestige has departed from it. These men joined in thousands, and they now depart in equal numbers. They rejoin the ranks of Hinduism whence they originally came, and they bring up their children as Hindus. The sacred tank at Amritsar is less thronged than formerly, and the attendance at the annual festival is diminishing yearly. The initiation ceremony for adult persons is now rarely performed.[14]

The first census of the Punjab in 1855 enumerated Hindus and Sikhs together. In the districts of Amritsar, Gurdaspur, Sialkot, Lahore and Gujranwala, however, Sikhs were enumerated separately. The area comprised by these five districts was where Sikhism had originally found much of its support and where it retained most of its following. The census report makes no attempt to define its application of the term Sikh, that is, whether it referred to the Kesdhari Sikh population only or to both Kesdhari and Sahajdhari Sikhs. Nevertheless, the remarkably low figure of 181,172 persons returned as Sikh out of a total population of some 3.5 million persons in the area suggests that there had been a dramatic decline in the number of Sikhs.[15]

The harsh measures taken to ensure unchallenged British authority in the Punjab had meant that, a mere two years after annexation, the board of administration of the province was able to report that 'in no part of India has there been more perfect quiet than in the territories lately annexed'.[16] In addition, a highly organized system of local administration had been introduced, the Khalsa kingdom's complex and unwieldly system of taxation simplified, the rate of assessment of land revenue reduced and several new varieties of crop planted. After ten years of endemic lawlessness and of intrigue at the highest points in the Royal Court, the rule of law had been restored, and the first two years of British administration had left the government with surplus finances. The new administration, finding its authority secured, had turned its attention to programmes of public works. In the Punjab administration report of 1849–50 and 1850–1, it claimed: '1,349 miles of road have been cleared and constructed, 853 miles are under construction; 2,487 miles have been traced and 5,272 miles surveyed ...'[17] The Punjab's extensive network of canals had been cleared and extended, trees planted alongside roads and canals, and a programme of afforestation of barren lands implemented. 'In the districts of Lahore, Gurdaspur, and Gujranwala a million saplings were planted.'[18] The initial years of British administration in the Punjab were thus an unqualified success. The Punjabis saw that not only was the new administration free from the persecution and vengeance they had feared, but it had brought peace and stability, and a taste of the prosperity that was to come.

As foes the Khalsa Sikhs had won ungrudging admiration from

the British. Commenting on the Second Anglo-Sikh War (1848–9), a British commander, General Thackwell, noted: 'Seikhs caught hold of the bayonets of their assailants with their left hands and closing with their adversaries, dealt furious sword blows with their right ... This circumstance alone will suffice to demonstrate the rare species of courage possessed by these men.'[19] This opinion of Sikh valour was shared by many of his contemporaries. Admiration for Sikh courage, which had in the eyes of the British made them most worthy enemies, turned to gratitude for their loyalty in the Indian mutiny of 1857. While the rest of India seethed under various grievances, the situation in the Punjab was quite different. The Sikhs were leaderless. Moreover, they did not share many of the grievances of the Indian sepoys and harboured a deep resentment for these very soldiers, who had sided with the British against the Khalsa. When the mutiny broke out at Merrut, the Sikhs, with a few exceptions, remained loyal. They helped to maintain order in the Punjab and fought with distinction at the side of the British in defending British establishments and saving British lives. Sikh soldiers were in the vanguard of the final assault on besieged Delhi, and the triumph of British arms was theirs to share. A legend attributed to the tenth guru, Gobind Singh, which was widely circulated at the time and provided sanction for Sikh loyalty to their new rulers gives a good indication of the spirit which pervaded Anglo-Sikh relations, at least from the Sikh point of view.

The tenth guru, according to Sikh tradition, had instructed his dispirited followers thus:

> When the army of the turks cometh, my Sikhs shall strike steel on steel. The Khalsa shall then awake, and know the play of battle ... Then shall the English come, and joined by the Khalsa rule as well in the East as in the West. The holy Baba Nanak shall bestow all wealth on them. The English shall possess great power, and by the force of arms take possession of many principalities. The combined armies of the English and Sikhs shall be very powerful as long as they rule with united councils. The empire of the English shall vastly increase, and they shall in every way attain prosperity. Wherever they take their armies they shall conquer, and bestow thrones on those who assist them. Then in every house shall be wealth, in every house happiness, in every house rejoicing, in every house religion, in every house learning, and in every house a woman.[20]

The guru's prophecies had come true.

In contrast to the feeling of apprehension that pervaded Anglo-Sikh relations from the Sikh point of view at the time of the first census of the Punjab in 1855, the census year of 1868 was marked by a feeling of mutual respect and confidence between the Sikhs and their new rulers. A significant outcome of Sikh loyalty during the mutiny had been that service in the army was opened to them. The *jats'* inherent inclinations and the economic opportunity offered by the army attracted them to such service. Following the First Anglo-Sikh War in 1846, a small force commanded by British officers had been raised out of the disbanded Khalsa army. On annexation this force was increased slightly in strength. However, the British did not completely trust the Sikhs. 'I do not like to raise large bodies of old Sikhs,' wrote John Lawrence, the Chief Commissioner of the Punjab. 'I recollect their strong nationality ... and how much they have to gain by our ruin ... and though I am willing to raise Sikhs gradually and carefully, I wish to see them mixed with Mahommedans and hillmen.'[21] Though Sikhs were recruited, their numbers were limited in each regiment, and recruits had to be under 20 years of age, effectively debarring the old veterans of the Khalsa army. The regulation providing for the recruitment of Sikhs, however, had considerably significance. It stated:

> The paol, or religious pledge of Sikh fraternity, should on no account be interfered with. The Sikh should be permitted to wear his beard, and the hair of his head gathered up, as enjoined by his religion. Any invasion, however slight, of these obligations would be construed into a desire to subvert his faith, lead to evil consequences, and naturally inspire general distrust and alarm. Even those, who have assumed the outward conventional characteristics of Sikhs should not be permitted after entering the British army, to drop them.[22]

The British had, for recruitment into the army, defined Sikh as meaning Kesdhari Sikh, a member of the Khalsa. To be recruited as a Sikh, a Sikh not only had to observe the tenets of the Khalsa, but was compelled to maintain them. Though the initial recruitment of Sikhs into the army was small, this policy provided some impetus to the Kesdhari Sikhs of the community. Thus the Punjab administration report for 1856–7 reported, 'Sikhism ... which had previously fallen off so much, seems again to be slightly on the increase. During the past year the baptismal initiations at the

Table 1.1   Sikh Population in Five Selected Districts[24]

Districts	Total population		Sikh population	
	1855	1868	1855	1868
Amritsar	884,429	1,083,514	71,364	262,639
Gurdaspur	787,417	655,362	24,746	39,967
Sialkot	641,782	1,005,004	19,775	50,279
Lahore	591,683	789,666	55,709	119,268
Gujranwala	553,383	550,576	9,578	38,911
Total	3,458,694	4,084,122	181,172	511,064

Amritsar temple have been more numerous than during the preceding year. Sikhism is not dormant.'[24]

Between 1855 and the next census of the Punjab in 1868 the Sikh population increased significantly. As indicated by Table 1.1, the Sikh population in five Punjab districts rose almost three times by 1868, while the increase in the total population was 18 per cent.

The euphoria of the mutiny days and the initial burst of confidence in the new rulers was short-lived. The Sikhs, along with the other communities in the Punjab, had to face the problems of adjustment to the new administrative system. The army could offer employment initially to only a very limited number of Sikhs of the disbanded Khalsa army. The Sikh *jats*, who in particular had benefited greatly under Khalsa rule, felt the pinch most strongly. When the Khalsa was paramount in the Punjab, they as the ruling community had more than their share of power and prestige. They had dominated the army and the administrative services, and were the largest group of proprietors in possession of land. Annexation, and the introduction of a new system of administration, were a tremendous blow to them. Moreover, since they were far behind other castes in the Punjab in literacy and education they were not able to avail themselves of the opportunities provided by the new administration. The Khalsa faith had already become strongly tainted by prevalent Hindu customs; it now sank deeper into the fold of traditional Hinduism.

In the next census year of 1881, Sikhs were enumerated separately from Hindus for the province and for each district, though the application of the term 'Sikh' was again not defined.

Table 1.2 Sikh Population in Amritsar Division, Lahore and
Gujranwala Districts[25]

Area	Total poulation		Sikh population	
	1868	1881	1868	1881
Amritsar Division	2,743,880	2,729,109	352,885	328,927
Lahore District	789,666	924,106	119,268	125,591
Gujranwala District	550,576	616,892	38,911	36,159
Total	4,084,122	4,270,107	511,064	490,677

The area of the province and that of districts had, moreover, changed quite considerably. Fortunately, the limits of the Amritsar Division, that is, the districts of Amritsar, Gurdaspur and Sialkot, and the districts of Lahore and Gujranwala had not materially altered. As indicated by Table 1.2, by 1881 Sikh numbers had declined again, by some 4 per cent on their previous figure. The total population representing all communities had, however, increased by 4.5 per cent in the same area.

There is ample evidence to suggest the strong influence behavioural Hinduism exercised on Sikh practice in this period. The census of 1881 reported: 'The precepts which forbid the Sikh to venerate Brahmans or to associate himself with Hindu worship are entirely neglected, and in the matter of worship of local saints and deities and of the employment of and reverence for Brahmans there is little, while in current superstitions and superstitious practices there is no difference between the Sikh villager and his Hindu brother'.[26] Though the Sikhs were more lax than the Hindus in observing caste distinctions, the majority of them belonged to castes which even among Hindus had no restrictions between them. The Sikh converts from the outcastes of the Hindu community were treated as they would have been among Hindus and scrupulously avoided. They were in fact not even permitted into the precincts of Sikh *gurdwara*s.

Since the beginning of the nineteenth century, Sikhism as a distinct creed had for the most part been declining. To the passive influence of ever-absorbing Hinduism the advent of British rule in the Punjab added the active proselytizing practices of Christian missionaries. As early as 1835, in fact, an American Presbyterian mission had been established in the Punjab. The location of a mission in the Punjab was explained by one missionary by the fact that 'this was the land of the Sikhs ... a people of fine physique and unusually independent character, a people, moreover, who had already, in principle at least, discarded the old idolatry of Hindooism, and broken, in some measure, the bond of caste, and therefore might be considered to be in a favourable state to be influenced by the preaching of Christian Missionaries'.[27] After annexation, this mission further expanded its area of operation. It was joined in the task of spreading the gospel by the Church Missionary Society, the Salvation Army, the Methodists, the Episcopalians, the Church of Scotland and several Roman Catholic organizations. The zeal of these Christian missionaries also found active support among senior British officials in the Punjab. In 1853, only a few years after the fall of the Sikh kingdom, the missionaries won a dramatic victory. Maharaja Dalip Singh, the last Sikh monarch, converted to Christianity. With the zeal of the recent convert he offered his influence to their cause. The real success of Christian missionary activity, however, was in quite another field. They directed their efforts at the lowest outcaste and untouchable (*chuhra*) castes of the Hindu heirarchy. These castes were offered not only the true path to salvation, but an opportunity to remove the shackles of being untouchable in their everyday existence. The proselyte became simply Christian. The considerable success of Christian missionary propaganda is apparent from census figures. In 1881 there were 3,796 Christians in the Punjab. By 1891 their number had increased to 19,547, by 1901 to 37,980, by 1911 to 163,994 and by 1921 to 315,931 persons.[28] In forty years converts to the Christian faith had increased their number by more than eighty times. While the greatest success of Christian missionary propaganda remained with the outcastes, aristocratic and well-to-do Sikh families were not entirely immune to their influence. Educated Sikhs were deeply distressed at prevalent Sikh social and religious practices. For some of them the solution was to turn to Christianity. Notable among those who entered the Christian fold was Kanwar Harnam Singh, the heir apparent to the Sikh princely state of Kapurthala.

The adoption of Christianity by families of note came as a great shock to Sikhs of the aristocracy and landed gentry. The conversion of hundreds of outcastes might have meant little, but such proselytism represented deep inroads into the bastions of Sikh tradition and respectability. For this segment of Sikh society, their world was defined by their religious identity. Psychologically they drew comfort from memories of recent Khalsa greatness, within the community they drew prestige as upholders of Sikh tradition, and materially they were recipients of recognition and patronage from the British administration by virtue of their standing in a community defined by religion. While the enormous numerical success of Christian proselytism could not be ignored, the attitudes and methods of Christian missionaries contributed profoundly to raising the cry of religion in danger among the Sikhs. The missionaries introduced an aggressive brand of proselytism hitherto unknown in the Punjab. They employed professional preachers and brought in the use of the printing press for the mass dissemination of religious propaganda. One Christian missionary institution, the *zanana* mission, in itself did much to produce a Punjabi reaction. The *zanana* missions, aimed at womenfolk, carried proselytism directly into the seclusion of the home. The threat of subversion in the home was compounded by the establishment of schools and hospitals by the missionaries as vehicles to transmit their creed. English education, a vital prerequisite for success under the new administration, carried with it the danger of conversion. For aristocratic Sikhs, the advent of British rule in the Punjab had utterly altered their position in the province. The inroads of Christian missionaries threatened to tarnish their remaining prestige and influence within their own community. The reform of behavioural Sikhism to renew its vitality, the need to safeguard it from Christian inroads and the preservation of a distinct Sikh identity were for many of these Sikhs no longer a mere intellectual concern, they had become a practical necessity.

Criticism of prevalent Sikh social and religious practices and movements towards their reform had begun before the advent of British rule in the Punjab. The challenge presented by growing Christian influence only imparted greater urgency to such reforms. The Nirankari sect, descended from Baba Dyal Singh (1783–1854), had emphasized the *nirankar*, or formless nature, of the divine being. They vehemently opposed idol worship and preached the reform of elaborate rituals regarding birth, marriage and death. The impact of the Nirankari movement was limited however, to sections of the urban Sikhs. This tradition of reform was continued and elaborated by the Namdhari or Kuka sect. The founder of the Namdhari sect, Bhai Balak Singh (1799–1862) exhorted his followers to lead simple and austere lives and to do away with all religious ritual. They were simply to repeat the name, or *nam*, of God in prayer (hence Namdhari). His successor, Ram Singh, continued the crusade against elaborate rituals and ceremonies, and denounced the claims to reverence by the descendants of Guru Nanak and the assumption of superiority by high-caste Sikhs. Like the Nirankari movement, the Namdhari crusade had a limited impact. It developed into a peripheral group which owed allegiance to its own line of gurus and practised its own particular rituals. The impact of these reformers on the broad mass of the Sikh faith was more through the participation of some of their number in a later attempt at reform of Sikhism. This movement was heralded by the formation of a society in 1873 which described itself as a Singh Sabha.

The first Singh Sabha was set up in Amritsar at the instigation of prominent members of the Sikh gentry, Sikh theologians and notable members of the local intelligentsia. The conversion to Christianity of four students of the Amritsar Mission School spurred local Sikh leaders to consider the urgent need for organized reform of the Sikh faith to combat growing missionary influence. Following a series of public meetings, the principles delineating the Sabhas' activities were formulated. It was resolved that:

(1) The purpose of the Singh Sabha is to arouse love of religion among the Sikhs.

(2) The Sabha will propagate the true Sikh religion everywhere.

(3) The Sabha will print books on the greatness and truth of the Sikh religion.

(4) The Sabha will propagate the words of the Guru.

(5) The Sabha will publish periodicals to further the Punjabi language and Sikh education.

(6) Individuals who oppose Sikhism, who have been excluded from Sikh holy spots or who have associated with other religions and broken Sikh laws cannot join the Sabha. If they repent and pay a fine, they can become members.

(7) English officers interested in Sikh education and the well being of Sikhism can associate with the Sabha, also those who support the Punjabi language.

(8) The Sabha will not speak against other religions.
(9) The Sabha will not discuss matters relating to the Government.
(10) The Sabha will respect well-wishers of the community, those who love Sikhism, and those who support truth and education in Punjabi.[29]

In 1879, another Singh Sabha with a similar charter was founded in Lahore, and by 1899 some 121 Singh sabhas were operative. The Singh Sabhas organized religious meetings, or *diwans*, to preach reform, established schools and orphanages, and maintained varying numbers of *updeshaks*, or preachers, who roamed the rural areas and spread the reformist ideology. Financial support came from individual subscriptions and sporadic grants from well-to-do members of the Sikh intelligentsia. Though the charters of the Singh Sabhas were similar, the focuses of their activity differed greatly. Each Sabha developed its own personality, which was often the result of one man or group of men active in that Sabha. The Amritsar Singh Sabha was largely supported by the Maharaja of Faridkot (Bikram Singh) and by Baba Khem Singh Bedi (1832–1905), a direct descendant of Guru Nanak. Both these men contributed large sums of money to the Sabha, and the spirit behind the Sabha's activities was tainted by their essential conservatism. The Lahore Singh Sabha on the other hand had as its chief propagandist Bhai Ditt Singh (1853–1901) a low-caste Sikh leader. Ditt Singh had personally experienced the hierarchy of birth and status in the Sikh community, and he vehemently denounced the assumption of superiority by high-caste Sikhs. He launched a campaign against the claims to special reverence by the descendants of Guru Nanak, and the assumption of the role of guru sometimes adopted by the *pujaris*, or priests of Sikh shrines. His attacks on the *pujaris* and members of the Amritsar Singh Sabha led to much bitter controversy and a series of prosecutions. This bitterness finally precipitated an open breach between the two Sabhas in 1883. The programme of the Ferozepur Singh Sabha was led by Bhai Takht Singh (1860–1937), a man who devoted his energy to the cause of female education among the Sikhs. He was almost solely responsible for the development of the Ferozepur Sikh *kanya mahavidyala*, a boarding school for girls, in the 1890s, a time when the education of women was unthinkable even among educated circles. The Singh Sabha of a small village, Bhasaur, on the other hand, was transformed into a centre of Sikh militancy by Bâbu Teja Singh (1867–1933). Through short pamphlets he conducted a ceaseless campaign against prevalent Sikh practices, and encouraged Sikhs among his own community to take the *pahul* and become Khalsa Sikhs. The Karachi Singh Sabha represented another strain of opinion. It consisted of both Kesdhari and Sahajdhari Sikhs, 'who are ready to declare that they adhere to the tenents of the Gurus, do not belong to any other religious sect, and pay a subscription of at least annas four per mensem'.[30] The fifteen-man executive committee had six positions reserved for Sahajdhari Sikhs.

These men and others like them, with their abundant energy and enthusiasm, provided the day-to-day inspiration behind various Singh Sabha activities. The constant contact between them also provided an informal channel of communication between Sabhas. However, the rapid increase in the number of Singh Sabhas necessitated the formation of a central organization to coordinate activities. Thus in 1902 an organization known as the Chief Khalsa Diwan was formed to serve as a centre for communication among educated Sikhs. The Diwan held annual meetings to coordinate programmes between the various Singh Sabhas and its officials served as spokesmen of the Sikh community on theological, social and political issues. From the outset the Chief Khalsa Diwan was dominated by prominent members of the Sikh gentry and large landowners. Sunder Singh Majithia (1872–1941), a wealthy landowner and sugar magnate whose family had been notable among Sikh aristocratic circles under Maharaja Ranjit Singh, became the first secretary of the Diwan in 1902; he retained this position and domination of its proceedings until 1921.

The preoccupation with reform of behavioural Sikhism focused Sikh intellectual activity in the nineteenth century on determining what constituted tradition and orthodoxy. The Sikh scriptures could be and were interpreted in different ways. In 1877 the first English translation of the Sikh scripture the Granth Sahib appeared. The English translator, Dr Ernest Trumpp, was far from complimentary to the Sikh gurus, and suggested that the gurus had not intended the separation of the Sikh faith from the Hindu community. 'The greater part of the Granth', he wrote,

> contains a sort of devotional hymn, rather poor in conception, clumsy in style, and wearisome to read ... The writings of the old Hindu Bhagats (or devotees) are on the whole far superior to those of the Sikh Gurus themselves as regards contents and style, especially those of Kabir from whom Nanak and his successors have borrowed all they know and preach. In fact so much is clearly seen from the Granth itself that the Sikh Gurus taught nothing new whatever, and if a separate religion and a partially new nationality has in the course of time sprung from it, this was not owing in any way to the doctrine taught by them, but to their financial and political organizations which they gave their disciples.[31]

The publication of Trumpp's translation of the Granth Sahib produced a violent reaction among Sikh intellectual circles. His assertion that the separation of the Sikh faith from the Hindu religion was not intended and was a later development, in particular, evoked much interest in the interpretation of Sikh scriptures and tradition. Some Sikhs were inclined to agree, though they too resented Trumpp's remarks as to the value of the Granth Sahib. They paid homage to Sikh gurus in addition to Hindu deities, and regarded the two traditions and faiths as interlinked and overlapping. Others responded to this assertion quite violently. In 1898 the question of a separate Sikh identity again became a major public issue for educated Sikhs. Dayal Singh Majithia, an enormously wealthy Sikh aristocrat, died leaving his fortune to a trust in his name. His widow contested the will, claiming that the Hindu law of inheritance under which her husband had given his property to the trust did not apply, as he was a Sikh, not a Hindu. A prolonged legal battle ensued, and the Punjab High Court was asked to determine if Sikhs were Hindus. The decision of the court that Dyal Singh Majithia was a Hindu sparked off considerable debate. Two widely circulated pamphlets entitled *Sikh Hindu Hain* ('Sikhs are Hindus') argued that Sikhism was but a reformist strain within Hinduism. In an equally publicized rejoinder, Sardar Kahan Singh's pamphlet *Ham Hindu Nahin* ('We are not Hindus') argued the case for Sikh separateness.[32]

The controversy generated by this issue of Sikh identity was hotly debated in newspapers, journals and series of pamphlets and responses. Men such as Bhai Ditt Singh espoused the cause of a separate Sikh identity with vigour. They located and published

old texts to support their views, and by the end of the century two
societies existed which actively sponsored historical research into
Sikh tradition, the Gurmat Granth Pracharak Sabha of Amritsar,
and the Gurmat Granth Sudharak Committee of Lahore. The
work of these organizations was supplemented by the enormous
dedication of individuals. For example, between 1880 and the turn
of the century Bhai Ditt Singh himself wrote some forty books on
Sikh martyrs, history and theology. These books stressed the
distinctiveness of the Sikh community, and passionately argued
that the survival of a separate identity was dependent on a clear
demarcation of boundaries, a strong emphasis on traditions and
customs identified as Sikh, and the elimination of 'non-Sikh'
elements from the faith. The zeal of such men in espousing the
cause of Sikh distinctiveness was spurred by the emergence of a
militant Hindu ideology in the Punjab, represented by the Arya
Samaj, which had a significant impact on Punjabi Hindu
consciousness and consequently on relations between those who
advocated a separate Sikh identity and the parent Hindu community.

Swami Dayanand, a wandering ascetic from western India,
founded the Arya Samaj, or Aryan Society, at Rajkot in Gujarat in
1875 to promote a purified and revived form of Hinduism.
Dayanand denounced caste, idol worship and child marriage,
extolled the remarriage of widows and emphasized the infallible
nature of the Vedas, the ancient sacred books of the Hindus. The
Vedas, divinely inspired, were the sole source of legitimate
teaching. All scriptures compiled after the degeneration of Vedic
scholarship were regarded as unacceptable. Corruption and
superstition in post-Vedic Hindu society had brought the domination of false texts which had in turn introduced decadence into
Hindu society. Initially, Dayanand directed his energies towards
religious debates with Brahmins but met with little success. In
April 1877 he visited the Punjab, and simplified and reorganized
his creed, and it was here that his vision evoked a significant
response. Between April 1877 and July 1878 Dayanand succeeded
in establishing nine local branches of his Arya Samaj.

The appeal of the Arya Samaj proved particularly strong to the
English-educated segment of Punjabi Hindu society. Dominant
among literate Punjabis at the advent of British rule, Punjabi
Hindus had been quick to benefit from the spread of western

education. Their education opened up new opportunities for them, enhanced their social prestige within their own community, and in the eyes of fellow Punjabis made them leaders of the new world created by the British Raj. Yet exposure to English interpretations of their society, their religion and their history undermined their ability to identify with their traditions with dignity. Inevitably they turned to an appraisal of their own culture and its prevalent practices. The Arya Samaj provided a rationale to cope with their sense of alienation.

Following Dayanand's death in 1883 the Arya Samaj attracted a new generation of young, educated, Punjabi Hindus who rapidly moved into positions of leadership within the movement, provided a militant interpretation of Dayanand's philosophy, and advocated aggressive methods to propagate the faith. This generation of young Punjabi Arya Samajists was typified by two individuals, Pandit Guru Dutt and Lala Munshi Ram, later known as Swami Shradhannand. Pandit Guru Dutt, a brilliant student at the Government College at Lahore, joined the Multan Arya Samaj in June 1880. Between 1885, when he received his MA, and his death in 1890 Guru Dutt played a significant role in the reinterpretation of Dayanand. In his writings and public speeches he stressed the religious nature of Dayanand's work. Dayanand was seen not merely as a reformer but as a saint, and his writings were to be regarded as sacred texts to be followed without question. In 1889 Guru Dutt founded the *Vedic Magazine* to publicize his views, and launched a bitter attack on orthodox Hinduism and the teachings of Christian missionaries. He further instituted a paid class of professional preachers to propagate the tenets of the Samaj. The other leading young Arya Samajist, Lala Munshi Ram, was born in 1856. In 1882 he went to Lahore to study for his law examinations, was influenced by Guru Dutt's leadership and joined the Arya Samaj in 1885. He returned to his native Jullundur and became president of the local Arya Samaj. Under his leadership the Jullundur Samaj pioneered in missionary work. Fund-raising drives were conducted and Aryas began to travel to neighbouring villages in search of converts. An aggressive Arya proselytism was instituted through a revival of *shuddhi*, a traditional purification ceremony used to reclaim Hindus from Islam or Christianity.[33]

Arya Samajists and Sikh reformers shared a common concern

with the reform and revitalization of their faith and a deep-felt apprehension at growing Christian missionary influence. Initially this shared concern was reflected in active co-operation between Sikh reformers and Aryas. During the early 1890s, for example, a Shuddhi Sabha was founded in Lahore by both Sikhs and Arya Samajists. But overlapping identities between Hindus and Sikhs in the Punjab ensured that this co-operation was shortlived. In August 1896 the Lahore Shuddhi Sabha precipitated matters by purifying and reclaiming to Hinduism a group of more than two hundred outcaste Sikhs. For Sikh reformers the Arya Samaj now posed a direct and serious threat. Bitter debate between Aryas and Hindus over the demarcation of communal boundaries only added fuel to the passion with which Sikh reformers advocated the distinctiveness of Sikh identity. Indeed, within a few years Sikh reformers who espoused the cause of a separate Sikh identity, the Tat, or true, Khalsa as they came to be called, had become the dominant group among active Singh Sabhaites.

These Singh Sabhaites were quick to appreciate the necessity and potential of using the Press to disseminate their propaganda and draw public attention to the threat to their faith. One prominent Singh Sabha newspaper, the *Khalsa Akhbar* of Lahore, reported in May 1894:

> An English newspaper writes that the Christian faith is making rapid progress ... just as we do not see any Buddhists in the country except in images, in the same fashion the Sikhs, who are now, here and there, visible in their turbans and their other religious forms like wrist-bangles and swords, will be seen only in pictures in museums. Their own sons and grandsons turning Christians and clad in coats and trousers and sporting mushroom-like caps will go to see them in the museums and say in their pidgin Punjabi: 'Look, that is the picture of a Sikh – the tribe that inhabited this country once upon a time'. Efforts of those who wish to resist the onslaughts of Christianity are feeble and will prove abortive like a leper without hands and feet trying to save a boy falling off a rooftop.[34]

Similarly, a letter to the editor of the *Khalsa Akhbar* on 12 February 1897 protesting the persisting influence of Hinduism on prevalent Sikh practice, claimed:

> Near the Dukhbhanjani beri tree [in the Golden Temple precincts] there is a room on the front wall of which is painted a picture. The picture depicts a goddess and Guru Gobind Singh. The goddess stands on golden sandals and she has many hands – ten or, perhaps,

twenty. One of the hands is stretched out and in this she holds a Khanda. Guru Gobind Singh stands barefoot in front of it, with his hands folded.[35]

Singh Sabha propaganda such as this went a long way to arousing indignation at Christian and Hindu influence and fostering a separate Sikh identity. The first decades of the twentieth century, particularly, saw an upsurge in such Sikh journalism. The new newspapers, in the form of weeklies, bi-weeklies and monthlies, focused on a variety of topics and directed their appeal to varied sections of the community. The *Istri Satsang*, a Punjabi weekly from Amritsar, and the *Punjabi Bhain*, the Ferozepur Sikh *kanya mahavidyala*'s monthly publication, focused on the cause of female education; the *Khalsa Samachar* and the *Khalsa Akhbar* were dedicated to social and religious reform; while the *Sikh Sepoy*, the monthly journal of the Ferozepur Sikh recruiting committee was designed for soldiers and reproduced Sikh scriptures and sermons. In 1894, the Khalsa Tract Society was founded for the dissemination of religious propaganda. It produced short, cheap volumes on theology and social topics, and complemented the work of individual pamphleteers. In eight years it published some 192 items, and distributed more than half a million copies. It was assisted in this task by the Sikh Book Club of Peshawar. By 1911, this club and its successor, the Panch Khalsa Agency, had printed some 125 items on religious and social topics. In 1908 the Khalsa Handbill Society was founded, and it distributed as many as 20,000 free copies of a publication in rural areas relatively inaccessible to the influence of Singh Sabha newspapers.[36]

The impact of such Singh Sabha propaganda was considerable. Khalsa Sikh numbers in the third quarter of the nineteenth century and the first two decades of the twentieth increased substantially. In a surge of emotionalism and intellectual excitement, hundreds of Hindus and Sahajdhari Sikhs took the *pahul* and took considerable pride in their new-found Khalsa identity. A return to the original egalitarianism of Sikhism, particularly among the reformers, further encouraged low-caste and outcaste Hindus to take the Khalsa baptism. The Singh Sabhas directed their appeal at these lower castes, and in areas where their support was strong and vibrant the response was forthcoming. In Table 1.3, the strength of three groups regarded as outcastes and untouchables in the Hindu hierarchy, the *mazhabis*, *musallis* and

Table 1.3   Number of Mazhabis, Musallis, Chuhras, among Hindus,
Sikhs and Muslims in the Punjab[37]

Community	1911	1921	Variation
Hindu	789,915	708,686	−81,229
Muslim	393,718	374,945	−18,773
Sikh	73,160	106,709	+33,549

*chuhra*s, among Hindus, Sikhs and Muslims in the Punjab during
the period 1911–21 have been tabulated. The loss of large numbers
of these outcastes by the Hindu and Muslim communities and a
significant increase in their number among the Sikhs is immediately apparent. It can be accounted for in terms of the conversion
of many of their number to Christianity and to the Khalsa.

The substantial increase in Khalsa Sikh numbers was also due to
support from another quarter. The army had from the outset
defined Sikh to mean Kesdhari Sikhs, and had actively encouraged
the maintenance of the Kesdharis' separate identity. The regulations regarding the enlistment of Sikhs into the army announced
in 1851 were supported by an order from the Commander-in-
Chief of the Indian Army which stated: 'Every countenance and
encouragement is to be given to their comparative freedom from
the bigoted prejudices of caste, every means adopted to preserve
intact the distinctive characteristics of their race, their peculiar
convention[s] and social customs.'[38] Particular sympathy for the
Sikhs was in fact widespread in official circles. 'The Sikh', noted
Denzil Ibbetson, a prominent English administrator, 'is more
independent, more brave, more manly than the Hindu, and no
whit less industrious and thrifty, while he is less conceited than
the Musalman and not devoured by that carking discontent which
so often seems to oppress the latter'.[39] In this belief he echoed the
opinion of other civil servants. Moreover, British officials were
convinced that the valour, discipline and courage of Khalsa Sikh
soldiers derived from 'the uplift in heart and character that
Sikhism ... brought to those classes that ... embraced it'.[40] Thus
the army went to great lengths to preserve the 'purity' of faith and
tradition among Sikh soldiers and ensure that recruits possessed
the same tradition. A recruiting manual for Sikh regimental
officers suggested that, 'in judging the value of tribes, those are

considered to be Sikh tribes which supplied converts to Sikhism in the time of Guru Gobind Singh, who in fact formed the Singh people, and ... those tribes who, though they now supply converts to Sikhism, did not do so then, cannot be considered (or it is inadvisable to consider) as true Sikh tribes'.[41] Particular tribes or castes among the Sikhs and particular districts were identified as good recruiting areas while others were to be avoided. Thus the Rajput Sikh was to be avoided since he 'originally refused Sikhism, and therefore has not the original traditions of the Sikhs to inspire him'.[42] Similarly, one district was identified as being 'too far East to be desirable, the characteristics of the people being more of the Hindustani type', and another was 'too far South to be desirable'. Yet another district was seen as unsuitable for recruiting since its 'Sikhism is very diluted by Hinduism'.[43] During the third quarter of the nineteenth century Sikh recruitment into the army increased considerably, and Sikh numbers in its services became totally out of proportion to their population. At the turn of the century Sikhs provided some 10,867 men in the army out of a total contingent of 42,560 from the Punjab. Recruitment into the army provided strong encouragement for the development and maintenance of a separate Sikh identity. H. L. O. Garrett, who was stationed as a recruiting officer during the First World War reported:

> My experience during 1917 and 1918 in Ludhiana and the adjacent territories was that there were a large number of families of the Hindu Zamindar [land owning] class of which those members who had enlisted in the Army had, as a matter of course, become Sikhs. Those who in the ordinary course of events would have stayed at home did not do so, when as a result of the intensive recruiting at the later stages of the war, the latter were induced to join up they too became Sikhs. This developed into any ordinary Hindu of the Zamindar class being taken by Sikh Recruiting Officers on condition of his becoming a Sikh ... it was almost a daily occurrence for say – Ram Chand to enter our office and leave it as Ram Singh – Sikh recruit.[44]

Preference for Sikhs was not restricted to service in the army. The 1891 census report noted 'the marked preference shown for Sikhs in many branches of Government services'.[45]

In 1909 a monumental work on the Sikh religion, the result of fifteen years of labour, appeared. The author, Max Arthur Macauliffe, admitted that the work reflected the beliefs of the Sikh reformers, and made a passionate appeal for state support of the Khalsa. 'Truly wonderful are the strength and vitality of Hindusim', he wrote.

> It is like the boa constrictor of the Indian forests. When a petty enemy appears to worry it, it winds round its opponents, crushes it in its fold, and finally causes it to disappear in its capacious interior. In this way, many centuries ago, Hinduism on its own ground disposed of Bud[d]hism ... in this way it has converted uneducated Islam in India into a semi-paganism, and in this way it is disposing of the reformed and once hopeful religion of Baba Nanak. Hinduism has embraced Sikhism in its fold, the still comparatively young religion is making a vigorous struggle for life, but its ultimate destruction is, it is apprehended, inevitable without state support.[46]

Macauliffe's work became the basic text on the Sikh religion for English civil servants, and made the Sikh reformers' point of view available to a large number of sympathetic English readers.

The evolving nature of Sikh identity is apparent from an examination of Sikh population growth in the period 1881–1921. From census year to census year the census commissioners had tried to tackle the problem of definition of what a 'Sikh' was, with different results. Did it imply both Kesdhari and Sahajdhari Sikh, or should it be restricted to mean those who followed the tenets of the tenth guru, that is, Kesdhari, Khalsa Sikhs? The problem was further complicated by the fact that while some followers of the gurus considered themselves as distinct from Hindus, that is, as Sikhs, Kesdhari and Sahajdhari, others believed that Sikhism was but a sect of Hinduism and considered themselves to be Sikh-Hindus. In the 1881 census no attempt at definition of the term Sikh was made, but it was intended that only Kesdhari Sikhs be returned as Sikhs. However, in the absence of clear instructions regarding the definition of the term Sikh to be applied, large numbers of Sahajdhari Sikhs were also returned as Sikhs.[47] The 1891 census report, on the other hand, stated, 'By a true Sikh is meant a member of the Khalsa, a follower of the ordinances of Guru Gobind Singh', in other words a Kesdhari Sikh. The practical test which was to be applied in the enumeration was that 'a Sikh should be one who wears uncut hair and abstains from smoking'.[48] Sahajdhari Sikhs were thus to be returned as Hindus, though they were permitted to enter their sect as Nanakpanthi, that is, a follower of Guru Nanak, or as a follower of any other of the gurus. The 1901 census also adopted this definition of the term

Table 1.4 Sikh Population Growth in the Punjab, 1881–1921[49]

Year	Number of Sikhs	% Variation in Sikh Population	% Variation in Total Population
1881	1,706,165		
1891	1,849,371	+ 8.4	+10.1
1901	2,102,896	+13.7	+ 6.3
1911	2,883,729	+37.1	− 2.2
1921	3,110,060	+ 7.8	+ 5.7

Sikh, but sects were not enumerated. By 1911, however, the census definition of Sikh had changed. Enumerators were instructed that 'the religion to which a person claimed to belong must be accepted'.[50] The 1901 census commissioners had found that their instructions regarding the practical test to be applied so as to determine who was or was not a Sikh had been 'almost universally ignored'. Moreover, there was resentment from some Sikhs who wished to be classified as Hindus but were not permitted to do so since they met the practical test for Sikhs. Thus in 1911 'in view of the unwillingness of large numbers of Jains and Sikhs to be classed separately from Hindus permission was given to record such persons as Jain-Hindus or Sikh-Hindus'.[51] This broader definition of the term Sikh, which encompassed both Sahajdhari and Kesdhari Sikhs, was continued in the census of 1921.

In the period 1881–1921 Sikh population in the Punjab increased significantly, as indicated by Table 1.4. This increase cannot be accounted for only in terms of the natural growth in population or the changing definition of the term Sikh employed in various census years. An examination of Sikh population growth in the Punjab in the period 1901–21 is further revealing. Figures for districts and native states having a substantial Sikh population in 1901 and 1911 are provided in Table 1.5, and in 1911 and 1921 in Table 1.6. In each case, in a decade the Sikh population increased by a higher percentage than the increase in the total population. At the same time, the Hindu population in each of these areas declined or increased by a lower percentage than the total population.

It is apparent that there was between 1901 and 1921 in the Punjab considerable conversion of Hindus to the Sikh faith. This

Table 1.5   Variation Per Cent in the Sikh and Hindu Populations, 1901–11[52]

District/state	Sikhs	Hindus	Total
Jullundur	+40.0	−27.0	−12.6
Ludhiana	+25.5	−51.0	−23.0
Ferozepur	+14.9	− 1.9	+ 0.2
Gurdaspur	+31.9	−25.0	−11.0
Kapurthala State	+28.9	−34.4	−14.7

Table 1.6   Variation Per Cent in the Sikh and Hindu Populations, 1911–21[53]

District/state	Sikhs	Hindus	Total
Jullundur	+17.0	− 7.7	+ 2.5
Ludhiana	+13.9	+ 3.2	+ 9.7
Ferozepur	+15.3	+11.9	+14.4
Gurdaspur	+13.7	− 8.9	+ 1.8
Kapurthala State	+18.1	− 4.9	+ 6.0
Amritsar	+13.0	− 3.4	+ 5.5
Kalsia State	+28.1	− 6.1	+ 2.6
Faridkot State	+20.3	+ 3.3	+15.6

was certainly true of areas which possessed a substantial Sikh population, areas where Singh Sabha activity and army recruitment could be expected to be vigorous. There was in addition an economic motivation behind this movement. The last quarter of the nineteenth century brought unprecedented prosperity to the Punjab. Ambitious canal irrigation projects, the introduction of new cash crops and the establishment of a vast network of roads and railways increased the revenue from the lands considerably. The Sikh community was predominantly an agrarian one and when the Sikhs held land they usually did so as proprietors and seldom as tenants. The impact of an increase in land produce was felt by them the most, and as a community they derived the greatest benefit from it. The increase in prestige of Sikh agrarian and minor-occupational castes, such as the *jats* or *tarkhans*, in areas which contained a substantial proportion of such Sikh castes resulted in an additional motivation for Hindu *jats* or *tarkhans* to

Table 1.7 Agricultural and Occupational Castes among Hindus and Sikhs[54]

Caste/religion		1881	1891	1901	1911	1921
Jat:	Hindu	1,445,374	1,697,177	1,539,574	1,000,085	1,046,396
	Sikh	1,122,673	1,116,417	1,388,877	1,617,532	1,822,881
Tarkhan: *	Hindu	213,070	215,561	233,934	162,305	161,833
	Sikh	113,067	134,110	146,904	180,447	139,327
Darzi:†	Hindu	9,674	10,218	9,680	7,657	8,178
	Sikh	186	660	716	1,406	1,587
Chamar:‡	Hindu	931,915	1,029,335	1,089,003	909,499	968,298
	Sikh	100,014	106,328	75,753	164,110	161,862

* carpenter, † tailor, ‡ shoemaker

become Sikh *jats* or *tarkhan*s. With a few exceptions, which are explicable in terms of the changing definition of the term Sikh and inaccuracies in the enumerations, it seems that members of these agricultural and minor occupational castes in the Punjab converted in large numbers to the Sikh faith as indicated in Table 1.7.

While Sikh numbers in the last two decades of the nineteenth century and the first quarter of the twentieth century increased dramatically due to the conversion of Hindus to Sikhism, a significant change in the nature of the Sikh community had also taken place. Singh Sabha reformers had been concerned with defining the parameters of Sikh identity. In their crusade for the recognition of a distinct Sikh identity, these Sikh reformers had advocated the clear demarcation of communal boundaries with the Hindu community. For them a Sikh was synonymous with a member of the Khalsa, and Sahajdhari Sikhs were Hindus. The success of Singh Sabhaites in public advocacy of this separate Sikh identity is apparent from an examination of census figures. Punjab districts having a substantial Sikh population, both Kesdhari and Sahajdhari, in 1911 and 1921 are provided in Table 1.8. The figures indicate that the Sahajdhari Sikh population in each case had declined by 1921. The Kesdhari Sikh population on the other hand had shown a substantial increase. Sahajdhari Sikhs in these districts were taking the *pahul* in large numbers and becoming Kesdhari Sikhs.

An analysis of sect returns for the Sikhs in the Punjab in the period 1911–21, as provided in Table 1.9, is further revealing. In

Table 1.8 Numbers of Kesdhari and Sahajdhari Sikhs, 1911–21[55]

District	Sahajdhari Sikhs		Kesdhari Sikhs	
	1911	1921	1911	1921
Ambala	12,052	6,009	82,333	91,429
Hoshiarpur	48,499	23,494	85,354	109,375
Jullundur	42,177	29,282	133,718	176,838
Ludhiana	17,020	5,597	189,520	230,124
Ferozepur	15,247	5,113	246,325	297,647
Amritsar	6,140	1,568	246,757	285,436
Gurdaspur	9,674	5,460	111,383	132,092
Sialkot	16,690	6,046	65,061	68,498
Lyallpur	24,875	7,986	121,276	152,827
Kapurthala State	12,516	7,148	41,759	56,926
Malerkotla State	3,729	349	17,287	21,479
Patiala State	67,163	7,532	465,119	514,774
Jind State	1,152	85	21,414	27,932

the case of Sahajdhari Sikh sects a decline in numbers had taken place in each case. Sahajdhari Sikhs, whether they returned their sect as Hazuri, Nanakpanthi, Radha Swami, Ram Dasia, Sarwaria, Udasi, or simply Sahajdhari had declined significantly. In the case of one sect, Ram Rai, in fact the sect had disappeared altogether. In the case of Kesdhari Sikh sects, on the other hand, the number who returned themselves as Mazhabi, Ram Dasia, Tat Khalsa, or simply Kesdhari had increased significantly. Kesdhari Sikhs who returned themselves as belonging to the sects of Gobind Singh, Hazuri, Nihang, Nanakpanthi, Panj Piria, Ram Rai, Sarwaria, or Udasi, on the other hand, had declined considerably. One sect, that of Ram Rai, had in fact dropped from some 20,686 persons in 1911 to the insignificant figure of 605 persons returned in 1921.

The figures reflect the working of a complex social process and are indicative of the success of Singh Sabhaites in building a sense of internal solidarity among Sikhs. Sahajdhari Sikhs belonging to all sects had declined sharply. They were being rapidly converted to the ranks of Kesdhari Sikhs. In the case of the Kesdhari Sikhs, the idiosyncratic sects, that is, sects claiming allegiance to a particular figure while still being a part of the larger Kesdhari Sikh community, were declining rapidly in each case. All Kesdhari Sikhs believe in the tenets of Guru Gobind Singh, but those who

Table 1.9 Membership of Sikh Sects, 1911–21[56]

Sects	1911	1921	% Variation
Kesdhari			
Kesdharis	2,048,014	2,876,320	+ 19.4
Gobind Singh	107,827	42,678	− 60.4
Hazuri	287,548	246,384	− 14.3
Mazhabi	726	2,305	+217.5
Nihang	4,270	3,954	− 7.4
Nanakpanthi	99,601	22,486	− 77.4
Panj Piria	10,372	4,592	− 55.7
Ram Dasia	8,106	10,568	+ 30.4
Ram Rai	20,686	605	− 97.1
Sarwaria	53,205	14,259	− 73.2
Tat Khalsa	344,058	531,290	+ 54.4
Udasi	879	776	− 11.7
Unspecified	1,466,030	1,992,300	+ 35.9
Shajdhari			
Shajdharis	450,823	228,598	− 49.3
Hazuri	6,044	1,613	− 73.3
Nanakpanthi	176,036	14,179	− 91.9
Radha Swami	424	378	− 10.8
Ram Rai	5,890	0	−100.0
Ram Dasia	2,206	209	− 90.5
Sarwaria	25,880	2,383	− 90.8
Udasi	591	66	− 88.8
Unspecified	233,752	209,770	− 10.3

returned themselves as Gobind Singh by sect claimed special reverence for the tenth guru, though otherwise being like other Kesdhari Sikhs. Similarly all Kesdhari Sikhs also revere the memory of Guru Nanak and are in that sense Nanakpanthis, or followers of Guru Nanak. But those who returned themselves as Nanakpanthis while being Kesdhari Sikhs did so in order to claim particular regard for Guru Nanak, and so qualified their religious adherence by stating that they were Nanakpanthis though being Kesdhari Sikhs. The same is true for all the other Kesdhari Sikh sects which showed a decline in this period. The Kesdhari Sikh sects which increased significantly in this period were, on the other hand, either those of converts from outcaste Hindus, such as the Mazhabis or Ram Dasias, or else sects distinguished by a lack of any particular adherence beyond being Khalsa Sikhs. Thus

the number of Sikhs who returned themselves simply as Kesdharis and those who represented the Tat or true Khalsa had increased
considerably.

By 1921 the nature of those who regarded themselves as Sikhs
had significantly altered. For centuries, Sikh identity was diffused
between Sahajdhari and Kesdhari Sikhs and overlapped with the
Hindu community. Kesdhari Sikhs formed a distinct
brotherhood of the Khalsa, but not all Khalsa Sikhs considered
themselves as distinct from the Hindus. Khalsa numbers were
fluid and even among Khalsa members numerous divisions
between various sects and particular religious adherences existed.
By the second decade of this century, Sahajdhari Sikhs comprised
only 14 per cent of Sikhs. Influenced by the reformist Sikh
campaign, Sahajdhari Sikhs had either adopted Khalsa tenets or
chosen to be regarded as Hindus. Being a Sikh was becoming
synonomous with being a member of the Khalsa. Further, among
Khalsa Sikhs there was a movement away from individual sect
distinctions and towards the development of one common and
distinct Sikh identity. Among those who chose to be identified
with a particular group within the brotherhood, Sikhs who
expressed adherence to the views of the radical Tat, or true Khalsa
had emerged as the dominant group.

Notes to Chapter 1

1 Authorities are divided as to the influences which contributed to the
development of the religious thought of Guru Nanak. According to
some scholars, Sikhism was the result of a synthesis between Hinduism and Islam. See, for example, Khushwant Singh, *History of the
Sikhs* (Princeton, NJ, 1966), vol. 1, p. 17, Darshan Singh Mani in
the Introduction to Fauja Singh *et al*, *Sikhism* (Patiala, 1969), p. xiv.
Others see Sikhism as a reform movement within the fold of
Hinduism. See, for example, Gokul Chand Narang, *Transformation
of Sikhism* (Lahore, 1946), pp. 38, 346, 356; Dharam Pal Ashta,
'Sikhism as an off-shoot of traditional Hinduism and a response to the
challenge of Islam', *Sikhism and Indian Society, Transactions of the
Indian Institute of Advanced Study* (Simla, 1967), vol. 1, no. 5,
p. 242. Still other scholars argue that it is misleading to consider Guru
Nanak as the founder of the Sikh faith since his religious thought was
only an articulate expression of the well-defined contemporary Sant

tradition of northern India. See W. H. McLeod, *The Evolution of the Sikh Community* (Delhi, 1975), p. 5.

2 M. A. Macauliffe, *The Sikh Religion* (Oxford, 1909), vol. 5, p. 93. Similar accounts of the foundation of the Khalsa are given by many scholars. See, for example, Teja Singh and Ganda Singh, *A Short History of the Sikhs* (Bombay, 1950), pp. 68–72; Narang, *Transformation*, pp. 131–3; McLeod, *Evolution*, pp. 14–15.

3 See J. P. Singh Uberoi, 'The Five Symbols of Sikhism', in Fauja Singh *et al.*, *Sikhism*, pp. 123–38, and 'On being unshorn', in *Sikhism and Indian Society*, pp. 87–100.

4 McLeod, *Evolution*, pp. 9–10.

5 McLeod, *Evolution*, pp. 12–13, 51–3. See also Indubhushan Bannerjee, *Evolution of the Khalsa* (Calcutta, 1972), vol. 2, pp. 31–46; Fauja Singh, 'Development of Sikhism under the gurus', in *Sikhism*, pp. 9, 17–18.

6 Irfan Habib in the *Proceedings of the Punjab History Conference 1971* (Patiala, 1972), pp. 49–54.

7 George Forster, *A Journey from Bengal to England* (London, 1798), pp. 270–1.

8 W. L. Mc'Gregor, *A History of the Sikhs* (London, 1846), vol. 1, pp. 73–4.

9 John Malcolm, 'Sketch of the Seikhs' (London, 1812), quoted in Lt.-Col. Steinbach, *The Punjab, Being a Brief Account of the the Country of the Sikhs* (London, 1846), pp. 123–4. This view was supported by other observers. Describing the Sikhs in 1828, E. C. Archer wrote, 'though there are many *aberrations* from the religion of Brahman, the beliefs in most of the superstitions of that religion continue strong and prevailing' (my italics), *Tours in Upper India*, London, 1883, vol. 1, pp. 174–9. See also Col. A. L. H. Polier, 'The Siques or history of the Sique', paper read at the Asiatic Society, Bengal, 20 Dec. 1787, reprinted in *Punjab Past and Present*, vol. 4, no. 2 (Patiala, 1970), pp. 245–6.

10 Forster, *Journey*, pp. 225, 256.

11 Maj. R. Leech, 'Notes on the religion of the Sikhs and other sects inhabiting the Punjab', Government of India Foreign (Secret) Proceeding no. 144 of Dec. 1845. See also Capt. W. Murray, 'On the Manners, rules and customs of the Sikhs', 1830, in Henry T. Prinsep, *Origin of the Sikh Power in the Punjab and Political Life of Muha-Raja Ranjeet Singh* (Calcutta, 1834), pp. 191–215.

12 W. W. Hunter, *The Marquess of Dalhousie* (Oxford, 1895), p. 99.

13 J. G. A. Baird (ed.), *Private Letters of the Marquess of Dalhousie* (Edinburgh, 1911), p. 69.

14 Quoted in Government of India, Census of India, 1881, *Report on the Census of the Punjab*, report by Denzil Ibbetson (Calcutta, 1883),

vol. 1, p. 140. Similarly, Lord Dalhousie wrote, 'with the disappearance of the Khalsa prestige these votaries have fallen off, they joined in hundreds and have deserted in thousands. The ranks of Hindooism receives them again, and their children will never drink the pahul at Amritsar' (E. Arnold, *The Marquess of Dalhousie's Administration of British India*, London, 1862–5, vol. 1, p. 386.

15 GOI, *1881 Census Report, Punjab*, vol. 1, p. 140.

16 Quoted in Khushwant Singh, *History of the Sikhs*, vol. 2, p. 94.

17 Kushwant Singh, *History of the Sikhs*, p. 91.

18 Kushwant Singh, *History of the Sikhs*, p. 91.

19 E. J. Thackwell, *Narrative of the Second Sikh War, 1848–1849* (London, 1851), p. 213.

20 M. A. Macauliffe, *The Sikh Religion*, vol. 5, pp. 156–7.

21 R. Bosworth-Smith, *Life of Lord Lawrence* (London, 1883), vol. 2, p. 53.

22 Quoted in Khushwant Singh, *History of the Sikhs*, vol. 2, pp. 112–13.

23 GOI, *1881 Census Report, Punjab*, vol. 1, p. 140.

24 GOI, *1881 Census Report, Punjab*, vol. 1, p. 140.

25 GOI, *1881 Census Report, Punjab*, vol. 1, p. 140.

26 GOI, *1881 Census Report, Punjab*. Vol. 1, p. 140. See also Narang, *Transformation*, pp. 162, 362; Niharranjan Ray, *The Sikh Gurus and the Sikh Society* (New Delhi, 1975), pp. 19, 116–17; M. A. Macauliffe, *The Sikh Religion*, pp. xx-xxi.

27 J. Newton, 'History of the American Presbyterian Mission in India', 1886, quoted in C. H. Loehlin, 'The History of Christianity in the Punjab', *Punjab Past and Present*, vol. 7, no. 1 (Patiala, 1973), p. 180.

28 GOI, Census of India, 1891, vol. 20, *The Punjab and its Feudatories*, report by E. D. Maclagan (Calcutta, 1892), pt 1, p. 93; GOI, Census of India, 1901, vol. 17, *The Punjab and its Feudatories and the North-West Frontier Province*, report by H. A. Rose (Simla, 1902), pt 1, p. 169; GOI, Census of India, 1911, vol. 14, *Punjab*, report by Harkishan Kaul (Lahore, 1912), pt 1, p. 97; GOI, Census of India, 1921, vol. 15, *Punjab and Delhi*, report by L. Middleton (Lahore, 1923), pt 1, pp. 34–42. Punjab figures include Delhi district and exclude the North-West Frontier Province.

29 Quoted in N. Gerald Barrier, *The Sikhs and their Literature* (Delhi, 1970), pp. xxiv–xxv.

30 Barrier, *Sikh Literature*, p. xxv. See also pp. xxvi–xxvii.

31 E. Trumpp to the Sec. of State for India, 13 Jan. 1874, GOI, Foreign (General) Proceeding, no. 34–37A of July 1873.

32 Thakur Das, *Sikh Hindu Hain* (Hoshiarpur, 1899), Bawa Narain Singh, *Sikh Hindu Hain* (Amritsar, 1899), Kahn Singh, *Ham Hindu Nahin* (Amritsar, 1899).

33 Kenneth W. Jones, 'Communalism in the Punjab, the Arya Samaj

contribution', *Journal of Asian Studies*, vol. 28, no. 1 (1968) p. 28; *Arya Dharma* (New Delhi, 1976), pp. 50–6, 134–9, 313–15.

34 *Khalsa Akhbar* (25 May 1894) quoted in Harbans Singh, 'Origin of the Singh Sabha', *Punjab Past and Present*, vol. 7, no. 1, (Patiala, 1973), pp. 21–22. Begun by the Lahore Singh Sabha in 1889, the *Khalsa Akhbar* increased in its circulation from 275 in 1889 to 1,000 in 1905 (N. Gerald Barrier and Paul Wallace, *The Punjab Press 1880–1905*, Mich., 1970), p. 73.

35 *Khalsa Akhbar*, 12 Feb. 1897, quoted in Harbans Singh, 'Origin', p. 22.

36 Barrier, *Sikh Literature*, pp. 87, xxxi–xxxii. The *Khalsa Samachar*, a weekly paper, was begun in 1899. Its circulation rose from 500 in 1899 to 3,000 in 1905 (Barrier and Wallace, *Punjab Press*), pp. 75–6.

37 GOI, *1921 Census Report, Punjab*, pt 1, p. 178.

38 Quoted in Khushwant Singh, *The Sikhs* (London, 1953), p. 83.

39 GOI, *1881 Census Report, Punjab*, vol. 1, p. 103.

40 George MacMunn, *The Martial Races of India* (London, 1938), p. 82.

41 R. W. Falcon, *Handbook on Sikhs for the use of Regimental Officers* (Allahabad, 1896), pp. 61–2.

42 Falcon, *Handbook*, p. 79.

43 Falcon, *Handbook*, pp. 71–2, 98, 102. For similar views see also A. H. Bingley, *Handbook on the Sikhs* (Simla, 1899) and *Handbook for the Indian Army* (Calcutta, 1899).

44 GOI, *1921 Census Report, Punjab*, pt 1, p. 179.

45 GOI, *1891 Census Report, Punjab*, pt 1, p. 96.

46 Macauliffe, *Sikh Religion*, vol. 1, p. lvii.

47 GOI, *1891 Census Report, Punjab*, pt 1, pp. 94–5.

48 GOI, *1891 Census Report, Punjab*, pt 1, p. 91.

49 GOI, *1921 Census Report, Punjab*, pt 1, p. 184.

50 GOI, *1921 Census Report, Punjab*, pt 1, p. 171.

51 GOI, *1921 Census Report, Punjab*, pt 1, p. 171.

52 GOI, *1911 Census Report, Punjab*, pt 2, pp. 438–9.

53 GOI, *1921 Census Report, Punjab*, pt 1, p. 184.

54 GOI, Census of India, 1931, vol 17, *Punjab*, report by Khan Ahmad Hasan Khan (Lahore, 1933), pt 1, p. 308.

55 GOI, *1921 Census Report, Punjab*, pt 1, p. 186.

56 GOI, *1921 Census Report, Punjab*, pt 1, p. 186.

2

From Identity to Consciousness

'All religious movements in India are political', wrote a senior British official in 1863.

> The people have not yet learned to sever religious faith from civil Government. Hence the constant fear that the British Government is aiming directly at the conversion of the people to Christianity. Hence also the fact that every attempt to establish a new creed takes, more or less avowedly, the form of an attempt to establish a new Government.[1]

In the Punjab, the government was particularly wary of activities aimed at arousing popular Sikh opinion. Constantly watchful of troop activities and wandering messiahs, the provincial authorities were keenly alert to any attempt to resurrect the lost Khalsa kingdom. The violent propaganda of the Namdhari (Kuka) sect, often political in its overtones in the 1860s and early 1870s, reinforced this apprehension. Namdhari propagandists stressed the debasement of contemporary Sikh society and compared it unfavourably with the prestige of the Sikhs a few decades earlier. Their present condition was implicitly linked to their political domination by the British, when it was not clearly spelt out. A campaign for the abolition of cow slaughter championed by the Namdhari guru Ram Singh gave frequent expression to thinly veiled incitements to violence. A popular couplet portrayed their sentiments succinctly,

> London se malechh char ae,
> Inhan ne ghar ghar bucher khane pae,
> Guron [sic] de inhan ghat karae,
> Sannu hun Sir dene ae.

> The unclean have come from London, and have established slaughter houses in every place. They have killed our gurus and we must now sacrifice ourselves.[2]

Fed on imaginative propaganda and prophecies of a return to Sikh rule, Namdhari fanaticism resulted in the murder of Muslim butchers in Amritsar and Ludhiana, while a group of Namdharis unilaterally declared Khalsa rule in a village in Ferozepur District. In 1872 the increasing militancy of Namdhari zealots culminated in an attempt to seize arms in Malerkotla State. It provided an opportunity for decisive action. Sixty-eight members of the gang were rounded up, tied to the mouths of cannons and blown to pieces. The Namdhari guru and eleven of his lieutenants were deported to Burma.

The first Singh Sabha was founded a year after the executions at Malerkotla. With the Namdhari outbreak still fresh in official memory, Singh Sabha reformers were anxious to steer clear of politics. Thus the discussion of political questions, of 'matters relating to Government', was not permitted in the Sabhas' meetings. Moreover, Singh Sabha reformers believed that the interests of their educationally backward, minority community, could best be safeguarded and furthered by securing the active interest of the government with their programme. The association with the Sabha, and later with the Chief Khalsa Diwan, of leading Sikh gentry dependent upon government patronage and good will for their influence brought a further emphasis on this theme of loyalty. The religious zeal of Singh Sabhaites was tempered by the political interest of the landed gentry which directed their proceedings. Thus the Sabha resolved to 'interest high placed Englishman in, and assure their association with, the educational programme of the Singh Sabha', and pledged to 'cultivate loyalty to the crown'.[3] The Sabhas' proclamations of loyalty and avowed policy of co-operation with the government brought a prompt response. Government support and encouragement for the development of a separate Sikh community was politic. It would ensure the loyalty of the reformers and keep them within bounds, and conformed to British concern with the maintenance of the 'purity' of the Sikh faith. In 1881, Sir Robert Egerton, the Lieutenant-Governor of the Punjab, accepted the office of patron of the Lahore Singh Sabha. A few years later, in 1890, the Viceroy, Lord Lansdowne, commenting on the Singh Sabha movement, stated:

With this movement the Government of India is in hearty sympathy. We appreciate the many admirable qualities of the Sikh nation, and it is a pleasure to us to know that, while in days gone by we recognised in them a gallant and formidable foe, we are today able to give them a foremost place amongst the true and loyal subjects of Her Majesty the Queen Empress.[4]

Yet government association and concern with Sikh organizations was not new. Following the introduction of British administration in the Punjab, leading Sikh gentry and important religious figures had been given rent-free land grants and accorded recognition and patronage by the government, in an attempt to maintain an indirect channel of control over the community through these 'natural' leaders. In pursuance of a similar policy, the Punjab government had been intimately concerned with the management of the Golden Temple in Amritsar and its five associated shrines. Soon after the second Anglo-Sikh War a judicial officer was appointed to deal with all cases relating to the temple. In 1859 a dispute regarding the remuneration of attendants at the temple brought up the question of its management, and a committee of local Sikh gentry was appointed to deal with the management of the *gurdwara*. Effective control, however, soon passed into the hands of a manager responsible to the Deputy Commissioner of Amritsar. Henceforth the manager was an official nominee. Government policy regarding the management and control of the Golden Temple was motivated by an explicit objective. The office of the manager of the Golden Temple, with its considerable religious influence and social prestige, was used effectively to steer popular Sikh opinion. Moreover, the manager, being responsible to the government, needed little encouragement and voiced loudly the fervent loyalty of the Sikh community. A farewell message to the Viceroy Lord Ripon by the management of the Golden Temple in 1889 typified such proclamations:

> Our bodies are the exclusive possession of the British. Moreover, that we are solemnly and religiously bound to serve Her Majesty, that in discharging this duty we act according to the wishes of our Great Guru, the ever living God and that whenever and wherever need be felt for us, we wish to be the foremost of all Her Majesty's subjects, to move and uphold the honour of the crown, that we reckon ourselves as the favourite sons of our Empress-Mother, although living far distant from Her Majesty's feet and that we regard the people of England as our kindred brethren.[5]

This relationship of mutual dependence and good will between the government and Sikh leadership in the form of leading Sikh gentry, the custodians of important Sikh *gurdwaras* and the spokesmen of the Chief Khalsa Diwan worked admirably well. Sikh politicians largely accepted the structure of British administration and assumed benevolent and paternalistic good government. The distribution of government patronage, demands for the development of education in the Sikh script of *gurumukhi* and other such issues affecting the community sporadically brought forth petitions and memorandums to the government for redress. However, such petitions were couched in respectful terms and constantly stressed the humility and passionate loyalty of the petitioners. Beneath the surface, Anglo-Sikh relations began to shift during the first two decades of this century. The growth of a class of educated professional men among the Sikhs began to challenge the hegemony of the loyalist landed gentry in the community, and their fanatical sense of Tat Khalsa identity brought an assertion of Sikh communal consciousness over a series of issues. The government remained insensitive to the changing mood and clung tenaciously to assumptions of basic Sikh loyalty. As these issues brought influential new figures into the political arena, they also demonstrated the ineffectiveness of established norms of Sikh leadership.

British administration in India rested ultimately on the services of a vast pool of educated and trained men, the Indian clerks. Since Bengal was the first major area to be conquered and brought under British administration, it also became the first to possess a pool of such men. These Bengali clerks followed in the wake of British conquests, fulfiling the demand for their skills in both the expanding British administration and the growing tentacles of the Christian missionary organization. The annexation of the Punjab created an immediate demand for such men to support the functioning of the new provincial government, and initially this need was largely met by men from Bengal. The staffing of the Punjabi administration by men from beyond the Punjab was, however, only a temporary solution. The new administration quickly sought, through its educational policies, to create a breed of Punjabi clerks to meet the needs of its expanding bureaucracy. The government's encouragement of secondary and higher education and the consequent increase in locally educated manpower was reflected clearly in changing official qualifications for employees. In 1865 qualifications for any middle-level government position, paying Rs20 a month, were 'a broad vernacular education', but by 1874 qualification in a middle school examination had become mandatory for promotion to positions carrying a salary of Rs25 a month.[6] For some senior positions in government service, literacy in English and a university education had become essential.

Initially, the Hindu community greatly outstripped the Sikhs and Muslims in its ability to adapt to the new opportunities of employment, in its zeal for education and consequently in appointments to government service, particularly at the middle and upper levels. By the 1870s the Hindus held more than 80 per cent of the 'superior appointments' in government service and extended this domination into the professions of law, medicine and engineering.[7] During the next three decades, however, there was a marked increase in the number of educated and literate Punjabis as a whole. By 1891 the census enumerators reported that 819,383 Punjabis were literate, and of these 45,446 were literate in English.[8] The incentive to be educated offered by opportunities for employment in the government coupled with the educational efforts of the Christian missionaries and the programmes of various native reform societies, such as the Singh Sabhas, saw a dramatic increase in the number of educated and literate Punjabis during the first two decades of this century. The number of students under instruction at all levels increased from 248,123, including both males and females, in 1901 to 329,466 in 1909–10.[9] In 1901 census enumerators recorded 976,663 Punjabis as literate; by 1921 their number had gone up to 1,020,401 in spite of a more rigid definition of the term literate applied. The number of Punjabis literate in English increased from 98,831 in 1901 to 168,759 in 1921. The number of students under instruction had risen to 556,989 by 1921, an increase of some 124 per cent on their number at the turn of the century.[10]

Though the Sikhs were initially slow to benefit from the spread of education and literacy, the recruitment of large numbers of them into the army and the 'marked preference shown for Sikhs in many branches of Government service' reported in 1891 contributed to a rapid spread of literacy in their ranks.[11] By 1901, some 100,859 Sikhs were reported as literate. Moreover, by the first decade of this century the concerted efforts of some 123 Singh Sabhas operative in the Punjab was leading to the escalating formation of a Sikh educated elite. Indeed by 1911 literacy was spreading more quickly among the Sikhs than among Punjabis as a whole, and the census commissioners were able to report that 9.4 per cent of all Sikh males were literate compared with only 6.3 per cent of all Punjabi males who could read and write.[12] During the next decade (1911–21) too Sikh males maintained this lead in education as compared with the average Punjabi, and the census of 1921 reported that 9.3 per cent of Sikh males were literate as compared with a proportion of 7.4 per cent of the province as a whole.[13] In fact these figures are indicative of a more dramatic increase in education among the Sikhs than is at first apparent considering the large number of illiterate outcaste converts to the Sikh faith in this period. Singh Sabha emphasis on female education among Sikhs ensured an even higher proportion of females literate among the Sikhs than among the other communities in the Punjab.

As education and literacy grew among the Sikhs so too did the demand for qualified teachers to staff the various government-supported Sikh educational institutions and the ambitious educational projects of the Singh Sabhas. The Khalsa College, at Amritsar, founded in 1892, grew rapidly in its enrolment and produced increasing numbers of Sikh graduates, while generating employment exclusively for Sikhs in higher education. By 1921 the census reported a population of 4,041 Sikh instructors and clerks attached to educational institutions at all levels and their dependents.[14] The development of education in the Punjab also saw an increase in the provision of training for professional occupations in law, medicine and engineering. Beginning with a single institution for professional studies with some 106 students in 1889, there were seven such institutions with a total student body of 634 by 1910, which further increased to ten institutions and 1,711 students in all by 1921. Sikh students entering these professions also increased sharply, and by 1921 the legal profession at all levels was reported to be supporting a Sikh population of 1,704 (workers and dependents), while medicine of all kinds supported a population of 2,557. In 1921 the census commissioners reported in all 24,532 Sikhs, workers and dependents, occupied in the professions, including religious ones.[15]

The modernization of trade and agriculture in the Punjab and the creation of an efficient network of communications within the province and the country as a whole resulted in an impetus to industry and an expansion of the trading classes. By 1911, 9 per cent of all Punjabis were occupied in trade, and about 20 per cent earned a living in industry, in the widest sense of the term.[16] Though the number of Sikhs involved in trade or industry remained small in proportion to their total strength, their number also crept upwards. By 1921 industry supported a Sikh population of 356,641, and 156,408 Sikhs relied on trade for a living.[17]

The industrialization of the Punjab was, however, largely in the processing of agricultural produce for local consumption, and though the British commercialized the provincial economy it remained basically an agricultural, rural-based one. This limited industrialization of the province was reflected in the lack of urbanization and the absence of large-scale immigration from the rural areas. The proportion of the provincial population living in urban areas remained at 9.5 per cent of the total population between 1891 and 1921.[18] What was true of Punjabis as a whole was even more so as far as the Sikh community was concerned. In 1921 only 5.4 per cent of Sikhs inhabited the urban areas, and the 16.4 per cent of them occupied in trade or industry were largely working in small-scale endeavours as grocers, carpenters, tailors and so on in villages and small market towns.[19] The vast majority of the Sikh population was still occupied in agricultural or pastoral pursuits. Nevertheless, the increase in the number of Sikh instructors attached to various education institutions, and of Sikhs employed in government service and in the professions, trade and industry, represented the emergence of a distinct, educated Sikh elite.

This educated Sikh elite which grew up in the late 1890s and the first two decades of this century was deeply affected by and contributed to the environment produced by militant Singh Sabha reformers in their concern with the clear demarcation of Sikh communal boundaries, and an emphasis on Sikh customs and Sikh traditions. This was a period which saw a flurry of activity in the definition of Sikh identity and the purging of 'non-Sikh' elements from the faith. The educated and literate were exposed to the activities of the Khalsa Tract Society, the Panch Khalsa Agency, and the Khalsa Handbill Society; contributed to the feverish debates of the Gurmat Granth Pracharak Sabha and the Gurmat Granth Sudharak Committee; and swelled the ranks of committed Singh Sabhaites. Through the forums of local Singh Sabhas and the columns of an expanding Sikh press they joined in the Tat Khalsa crusade, were moulded by it, urged militancy in its name, and cast a deep impression on others among their contemporaries. Thus one Mahtab Singh, the son of a tailor, who was employed as a bookseller in Amritsar, published a monthly *gurumukhi* newspaper, the *Vir*, to propagate the cause of the Tat Khalsa movement; the *Khalsa Sewak*, a monthly newspaper in *gurumukhi* owned by Jiwan Singh, a shopkeeper of Amritsar, reprinted the proceedings of various Singh Sabhas; Rajinder Singh, a carpenter, was a proprietor of a weekly Urdu newspaper, the *Khalsa Bhadur*, published from Lahore, which provided a Sikh interpretation of political, social and religious events; and Bhai Gurmukh Singh and Harsha Singh, who taught at the Panjab University, owned and edited a newspaper, the *Gurmukhi Akhbar*, which represented the views of the Lahore Singh Sabha.[20] Such Sikh journalism was sporadic, varied in its appeal, and often tainted by the idiosyncracies of proprietors and editors, but it mirrored the changes in Sikh society.

Interest in social and religious reform fostered by Singh Sabha propaganda focused on the management of Sikh *gurdwaras*, the nuclei of community activity. Since the eighteenth century the management of these *gurdwaras* had passed into the hands of members of the Udasi sect founded by Guru Nanak's eldest son, Sri Chand. The bitter persecution of the Sikh community by the Muslim emperors of Delhi had forced large numbers of Kesdhari Sikhs into exile and made the jobs of *granthi* (scripture reader) and *mahant* (manager) of the *gurdwaras* an extremely hazardous one. Sahajdhari Sikh members of the Udasi sect were learned in Sikh scriptures and yet, being indistinguishable from their traditional Hindu counterparts, were likely to escape persecution aimed at the Khalsa. The Udasi sect was renowned and revered for its asceticism and devotion to religious tenets, and the arrangement worked well. During Sikh rule in the Punjab the Udasis continued to serve as *granthis* and *mahants* to Sikh *gurdwaras*, and since no rules had been laid down for the management of Sikh religious institutions, they admitted disciples and nominated their successors. The influence of their office was further significantly increased by grants of large revenue-free estates to the *gurdwaras* by the state. With the introduction of canal irrigation under

British administration the revenue derived from *gurdwara* property increased enormously. Simultaneously with the dramatic
increase in *gurdwara* revenue, the conduct of some *mahant*s
deteriorated. They began to look upon *gurdwara* lands and
revenue as their personal property, and dealt out patronage
associated with their office to men of dubious reputation. In some
instances the *gurdwara*s became resorts of bad characters who
kept concubines and indulged in drinking and gambling on the
strength of *gurdwara* income. The Sikhs were disoriented and
suffering from a mass crisis of identity, and initially little vigilance
was exercised over the conduct of such *mahant*s. When local
congregations did exercise a measure of vigilance, it proved
extremely difficult to enforce their will on the *mahant*s. In 1895,
for example, a group of conscientious Sikhs in Lahore District
marshalled popular opinion against the *mahant* of an important
gurdwara at Nankana, and negotiated with him in an attempt to
transfer the management of the *gurdwara* to a representative
committee of local Sikhs. In the face of this concerted effort the
mahant seemed to acquiesce, but once popular sentiment had
subsided he refused to relinquish control. The *mahant*s were in a
powerful position to resist such popular pressure. The large
revenue derived from *gurdwara* estates enabled them to act with a
considerable degree of independence and provided them with
effective immunity against attempts to boycott their shrines.

By 1905 prominent reformist Sikh newspapers such as the
Khalsa Advocate, the *Khalsa Samachar* and the *Khalsa Sewak* had
taken up the cause of *gurdwara* mismanagement with vigour.
Allegations of licentious living, misappropriation of funds,
debauchery, rape and sacrilege were made against the *mahant*s of
several *gurdwara*s. The *mahant*s remained unrepentant. An alternative to marshalling public opinion against disreputable *mahant*s
was to seek redress in a court of law. Such litigation, however, was
lengthy and could prove extremely expensive. The law provided
for a congregation to take legal action against the conduct of a
particular *mahant*, but first the approval of the local deputy
commissioner had to be sought. When public opinion could be
marshalled and sustained, and the deputy commissioner's
approval obtained, enormous legal fees usually brought an end to
the litigation. An attempt to remove the *mahant* of the Panja
Sahib *gurdwara* was thus abandoned due to court fees amounting

to Rs50,000. The *mahant* in question on the other hand usually had ample resources to prolong and combat such litigation effectively. Moreover, as the reformers found to their dismay, not infrequently legal decisions went in favour of the *mahant*. The establishment of British administration in the Punjab had brought new land-settlement records, and in many instances *gurdwara* property had been registered in the name of the *mahant* in charge. In the face of a *mahant*'s claim to private ownership, legal decisions upheld his right to utilize and to alienate the property concerned as he wished.[21]

The emergence of the Tat Khalsa introduced another element into the demand for *gurdwara* reform. Overlapping identities between Hindus and Sikhs meant that Hindu customs, Hindu rituals and even Hindu idols were prevalent in Sikh worship. Sahajdhari Sikh *mahant*s did little to enforce strict Khalsa tenets. Tat Khalsa reformers vehemently denounced the presence of what they considered to be non-Sikh practices in Sikh ceremony and saw them as an attempt to pervert the Sikh faith. The 'Hinduization' of their creed was yet another abuse attributed to unscrupulous *mahant*s and seen as another demonstration of their depravation. Thus a correspondent denounced in the *Khalsa Akhbar* the presence of Hindu idols in the precincts of the Golden Temple, and another claimed that the *mahant* of a *gurdwara* at Tarn Taran had committed a similar sacrilege.[22]

Tat Khalsa concern with the abolition of caste distinctions among Sikhs brought a further point of conflict with the custodians of Sikh *gurdwara*s. Low-caste Singh Sabha leaders such as Bhai Ditt Singh attacked discriminatory practices against their fellow Sikh outcastes and opposed restrictions prohibiting them from entering the precincts of *gurdwara*s. The significant inroads made by Hindu religious reform organizations such as the Arya Samaj in converting low-caste Sikhs added greater urgency to the need for the abolition of such discrimination. In 1907 an organization known as the Khalsa *Biradri* was founded at Amritsar with the object of removing caste distinctions among Sikhs. The society itself was initially led by low-caste Sikhs of little influence, but they had the moral support of powerful Chief Khalsa Diwan spokesmen and their objective soon became the policy of the Diwan. Members of the Khalsa *Biradri* and those of the Arya Samaj vied with one another in claiming low-caste converts to their faith. Resolutions were passed advocating the general admission of low-caste Sikhs into the faith, mass inter-caste dining was conducted and in some instances inter-caste marriages performed with much enthusiasm and publicity. The flagrant abuse of caste taboos by the reformers, and their challenge of established norms restricting the entrance of low-caste men into Sikh shrines, precipitated a conflict with the custodians of Sikh religious institutions. The *mahants* of Hazure Sahib *gurdwara* in Hyderabad State retaliated against the local Singh Sabha reformers by refusing them admission into *gurdwaras* and rejecting their offerings. Similarly an attempt by the Khalsa *Biradri* to hold a meeting at the Golden Temple in 1910 brought strong protests from the custodians of the shrine.[23]

Tat Khalsa denunciation of the 'perversion' of the Sikh faith developed into a subject of considerable controversy, for there were Sahajdhari Sikhs and even Kesdhari groups who insisted that no such debasement of their faith existed. Sikhs, they claimed, were Hindus. Prominent among them was Baba Gurbaksh Singh Bedi, a Sikh religious leader with considerable following in the north-west of the province. The Baba, a lineal descendant of Guru Nanak, claimed privilege on the ground of his ancestry. The Tat Khalsa movement threatened to undermine the basis of his authority and he reacted strongly against it. In this he was supported by prominent Hindu leaders. In 1910 Baba Gurbaksh Singh Bedi presided at the annual Punjab Hindu Conference and in his presidential address clearly enunciated his creed, stating, 'In my eyes a Hindu is a Hindu, whether he be a Sikh or an Arya or a Brahmo [Hindu reformist groups]. Whatever difference there may be between these faiths, on the main points they all agree.'[24] The *Punjabee*, a prominent Hindu newspaper, reported, 'The Baba Saheb in the several memorable sermons he delivered in the principal Sikh temples in the city, as well as in his presidential address proved from texts in the Granth Saheb that Sikhism was a vigorous off-shoot of Hinduism and the Sikh scriptures embodied the cardinal principles of Hindu Dharam [religion].'[25] Moreover, stated *The Punjabee*, 'one of the great internal dangers threatening Hindu society in the Punjab is an attempt (at first insidious but now open) in progress to create a schism by drawing away from its fold the Tatta [Tat] Khalsa, i.e. the few Sikhs who do not subscribe to the orthodox articles of faith and social ordinances of the Hindus'.[26] The rebuttal of Tat Khalsa emphasis on separatism from the Hindu community was continued at the next Punjab Hindu Conference in 1911. In an attempt to conciliate Sikh opinion the conference was held at Amritsar. In his address the president emphasized the importance of the venue of the conference and referred to the city as 'sacred to the memory of Great Sikh Gurus, who are respected and venerated by the Hindu community irrespective of the circumstances whether they all fully accept or not their particular doctrines of faith'.[27] Among the prominent figures who attended the conference was Sardar Arur Singh, manager of the Golden Temple.

As was to be expected, Tat Khalsa reformers reacted strongly to the suggestion that Sikhism was a sect of Hinduism. The conduct of Baba Gurbaksh Singh Bedi in particular was severely attacked. The *Khalsa Advocate* asserted that the Baba was neither an authority on Sikhism nor an acknowledged leader of the Sikhs. The Singh Sabha of Rawalpindi passed a resolution accusing him of 'perverting the Sikh scriptures and playing into the hands of the anti-Sikh Hindu party'.[28] For the next decade the controversy persisted with increasing bitterness, and though little material change was effected in the management of Sikh *gurdwaras*, the lines of a battle to come were being clearly drawn.

The government maintained a posture of neutrality and non-interference in religious affairs regarding the recurring demand for *gurdwara* reform. It remained insensitive to growing frustration among Singh Sabha reformers at their inability to achieve effective redress and insisted that the executive government had no role to play in such religious concerns. Yet its policy was also based on sound political strategy. In 1906, under pressure from Singh Sabha militants, the Chief Khalsa Diwan passed a resolution appealing for the management of the Golden Temple to be transferred to the control of a representative committee. Government control of the temple was considered a political necessity and the resolution was ignored. As early as 1881 a senior British administrator in a letter to the Viceroy Lord Ripon had suggested the basis for the maintenance of government control of important Sikh shrines. 'I think it would be politically dangerous', he wrote, 'to allow the management of the Sikh temples to fall into the hands of a committee emancipated from Government control and I trust your Excellency will assist to pass such orders in the case as will enable to continue the system which has worked successfully for more than thirty years.'[29] Twenty-five years later official control was still deemed expedient. The Chief Khalsa Diwan did not press the matter further.

In 1907 widespread agrarian disaffection surfaced violently. The immediate cause of the unrest was a proposed amendment of the 1893 Punjab Colonization of Land Act affecting the Chenab canal colony. Begun in 1887, this colony was to be a model farm for the rest of the province. Inhabited by carefully selected agriculturalists of 'proven loyalty' and kept under strict supervision, it was a social and economic experiment to demonstrate how careful planning and co-operation with the government could result in the welfare of all concerned. Peasant grantees were given occupancy rights in the colony which they held as long as they paid land revenue and fulfilled the other conditions of their contract. The terms of their contract made it mandatory for them to live on their land, to cut wood only from designated areas, and to ensure the cleanliness of their compound. Though the colony was initially a tremendous success, it quickly ran into trouble. To begin with, the irrigation department, having exhausted choice plots, distributed land relatively inaccessible from canal branches. From 1902 complaints from colonists in possession of inferior land multiplied. Moreover, with the sub-division of landholdings among sons the original allotments became fragmented and less productive. Further, the colonization staff found it increasingly difficult to maintain discipline: colonists evaded residency and sanitary requirements. When threats of confiscation of land grants proved ineffective, an informal system of fines was introduced to check offenders. By 1903, however, colonists were contesting the extra-legal system of fines in the civil courts, and not infrequently legal decisions went against the canal officer. The exemplary model was beginning to disintegrate at the seams.

In 1906 the Punjab government passed a bill to amend the Punjab Colonization of Land Act with many of its provisions made retroactive and contrary to the original conditions of the grants. The bill forbade the transfer of property at will, permitting only strict primogeniture and then only with the approval of the canal officer. Failing a legal heir, the landholding was to revert to the government. The fines system was accorded legal sanction and civil courts excluded from interference with executive orders concerning the colony. The bill was only an extension of earlier paternalistic legislation, and as such the government believed it would be accepted without much ado. However, the authorities failed to appreciate growing discontent among colonists. The extra-legal system of fines generated strong resentment. The enforcement of residency requirements, sanitation standards and other regulations further provided an opportunity for rampant corruption among subordinate colonization staff. Economic pressures and the high-handedness of officials had brought popular sentiment to boiling point. With the widespread destruction of the chief crop in 1905 and 1906, agrarian disaffection spilled over.[30]

For the Chenab colonists the bill was an affront to their honour. The provision restricting their right to transfer landholdings at will went contrary to accepted notions of peasant-proprietorship, while those enabling the government to resume the title of a grant in case of default on sanitation standards were regarded as an intrusion into their private lives. The legalization of the fines system enhanced opportunities for corruption and was bitterly resented. Mass rural unrest ensued. Colonists organized meetings, passed resolutions and signed memorandums vehemently attacking the bill. Nor was the agitation limited to the canal colony. It spread to the central districts from which most colonists had been derived. Unfortunately, the government also chose 1906 to announce an increase in the water rate on the Bari Doab Canal. The increase, averaging 25 per cent and rising as high as 50 per cent in the case of cash crops, was the final blow to an already disaffected local Sikh *jat* peasantry, and they added their voice to the protest.

Urban politicians and organizations took up the cause. Lajpat Rai, a Punjabi Arya Samaj leader, and Ajit Singh, a revolutionary *jat* leader from Lahore, drummed up popular sentiment and accused the government of treachery. A local editor coined a slogan – *Pagri Sambhal Jatta* ('Oh Jat! guard your turban!') – which epitomized a campaign of emotional appeals to an enraged and fiercely proud peasantry. Ajit Singh and other militant politicians appealed to the militarism of the Khalsa. In a widely circulated pamphlet he stated:

> The English have treacherously robbed the Sikhs of their King and have thus reduced them to live the lives of slaves in their own land.

The best part of their lives, of their property and honour has been confiscated by the English. The little that has been left to them will soon be taken away and then the English will look down on the natives as black dogs. Oh! Brave soldiers of the Khalsa you are lost to all sense of national honour. Give up the British service and permit the *Feringhees* [foreigners] no more to disgrace you. If you are brave enough, expel the English from your land.[31]

Local Singh Sabhas with their strong rural membership provided an appropriate forum for such appeals, and Sikh militants exhorted their co-religionists in the name of their guru. At one such secret meeting in 1907, at the tomb of the martyred ninth guru, Tegh Bhadur, a local priest counselled a group of Sikhs, stating,

The Khalsa turned itself to the service of the Goras (English soldiers) and for them cut the throats of their brethren. Has all this pleased our Guru? No, No, Never. It is our duty to help those who want to take back the land of their forefathers from the English. Brethren, here is Granth Sahib. Now you must swear by it that you will carry out the work of the Guru.[32]

Many of those attending the meeting, noted an intelligence report, were moved to tears.

The role played by urban politicians convinced the government that they had engineered the entire agitation and that, free from their influence, the inherently loyal *jats* would see reason. Strong measures were taken to remove the contagion of these 'fomentors of unrest', while the government pressed ahead with the legislation. Public meetings were prohibited in some districts and dispersed by force in others; newspapers prominent in the agitational campaign were sued for sedition; Lajpat Rai and Ajit Singh were deported to Burma. Despite severe repression, the agitation continued unabated. There were indications of disaffection spreading to the army and rumours of an imminent revolt. The government was forced to yield. The Governor-General, Lord Minto, vetoed the colonization bill, and the water rate was reduced.

The agrarian agitation of 1907 was of some significance. For the first time in the Punjab, the government had aggrieved a considerable portion of the rural population, and it was leading agriculturalists, pensioned government servants and retired army men who led local agitation. Many Sikhs who played a significant role in organizing rural dissent in 1907 entered a political arena in which they were to later play an increasingly vital role. The Sikh *jat* peasantry, hitherto known for its staunch loyalty to the government and apolitical stance, was politicized in a short but violent anti government campaign. Militant self-assuredness grew slowly, but the seeds had been sown. Moreover, while the agitation built reputations and created influential figures, it also brought discredit upon leadership which remained aloof and urged loyalty to bitter agriculturalists. The management of the Golden Temple emerged on the wrong side of the line of battle. In May 1907 the manager issued a proclamation stating:

> As representative of Sri Darbar Sahibji I hereby declare that I and my followers regard these undesirable movements and disturbances with complete hatred, that we are no party to these, and that we are the loyal and faithful subjects to our just and impartial British Government. I am prepared to give to my race the useful advice. 'Not only avoid yourselves from all political parties and gatherings but also your children, and always bearing in mind the good deeds of Government, be loyal and faithful, and value this peaceful Government where tiger and goat drink water in the same ghat [bank]'.[33]

A sequel to the unrest of 1907 was an agitation concerning a central Sikh institution, the Khalsa College at Amritsar. Singh Sabha interest in the development of adequate educational facilities for the Sikh community had led to the foundation of the college in 1892. The movement for the establishment of a Sikh college was equally indicative of Tat Khalsa preoccupation with 'ensuring that Sikh youths should receive such moral and religious instruction as would mould them into true Sikhs'.[34] Understandably, from the outset the scheme received enthusiastic support from the government, and contributions were made by the Viceroy, the Commander-in-Chief of the Indian Army, and Sir James Lyall, the Lieutenant-Governor of the Punjab. For their part, Sikh leaders expressed their gratitude by suggesting that the college be named Lyall Khalsa College in honour of the Lieutenant-Governor.[35] An Englishman was appointed principal of the college, and Sir William Rattigan, Chief Justice of the Punjab High Court, became president of the college establishment committee.

Born out of much good will and co-operation between the government and Sikh leaders, the college would, it was hoped, cast Sikh youth into 'true Khalsa Sikhs' much as it would mould them into 'loyal' ones. By 1907, however, the financial stability and administration of the college had begun to deteriorate. Moreover, the prevalent spirit of unrest had permeated the student body. Students invited a prominent nationalist politician to address the college and accorded him an enthusiastic welcome. A farewell visit to the college by the outgoing Lieutenent-Governor, Sir Charles Rivaz, brought hostile demonstrations. In 1908 the government abolished the existing constitution of the college and a new scheme of management was introduced. Under the new arrangement, the college council had fifty-eight members, of whom five were official nominees, twenty-six were drawn from districts of the Punjab, and twenty-five from the Sikh princely states, and two were to be elected by Sikh graduates. Government control of the Sikh states' representative ensured official supervision of the council. A similar change was affected in the college management committee, which was comprised of fifteen members, including six from the Punjab districts, six from the Sikh princely states, and three government nominees. The Commissioner of Lahore and the Deputy Commissioner of Amritsar were to be ex-officio chairman and vice-chairman of the committee, while the former also held the presidentship of the college council. Further, the college was to receive an annual grant of Rs10,000 from the government 'on condition that the status and the constitution of the managing bodies are maintained in accordance with the wishes of Government'.[36]

The changes introduced in the college management brought a strong reaction. There were threats of boycotts and bitter allegations of official attempts to dominate the college. A pamphlet entitled *Ki Khalsa Kalaj Sikhan da Hai?* ('Does the Khalsa College belong to the Sikhs?') accused the government of having 'robbed the Sikhs of their college, just as they had by gross breach of faith previously swallowed up the Punjab', and reminded the Sikhs that 'it was merely under the pretence of supervision that the British Government took possession of the Punjab'.[37] Ajit Singh published an appeal against the new management of the college and warned that the people must be ready to make sacrifices, and the editor of the *Punjab Akhbar* sarcastically suggested that the college ought now to be called 'College of Flatterers'.[38] With the resignation of militant members of the college staff the agitation subsided, but the management of the college remained a contentious issue and once again Anglo-Sikh relations had suffered.

Increasingly aware of a growing sense of distinct communal identity, the Sikhs reacted strongly to issues which might earlier have elicited little response. Thus the treatment of Sikh immigrants overseas, particularly in North America, developed into an issue which also had a significant impact on Anglo-Sikh relations. Around the beginning of this century a small number of Sikh peasants had emigrated to Canada. Within a few years the number of immigrants from the Indian sub-continent, the vast majority of them Sikhs, had risen to more than five thousand. The influx of a significant number of Indian immigrants in addition to an already large Chinese and Japanese immigrant community created strong resentment among Canadians. By 1906 popular sentiment against Asian immigrants was being actively expressed. In 1910 the Canadian government passed legislation severely restricting the entry of Asians into the country. The law stipulated that intending immigrants must travel by 'continuous journey' from their home country to Canada; further, the minimum sum of money would be immigrants were required to possess on arrival was raised from $25 Canadian to $200 Canadian. Both these provisions were in fact directed at stopping further Indian immigration since there were no ships running directly from India to Canada. Moreover, Chinese and Japanese immigrants were exempted from the provision requiring possession of $200 Canadian. Stricter immigration control in Canada resulted in increased emigration to the United States. By 1910 there were almost six thousand Indians in California. Americans reacted equally violently to growing Indian immigration. There were race riots directed at Asians and by 1908 an organization known as the Asian Exclusion League effectively organized anti-immigrant sentiment.[39]

Initially, immigrant organizations such as the Khalsa Diwan Society, founded in 1907, certred around Sikh *gurdwaras* and concerned themselves with educational and religious problems confronting the community. However, cases of discrimination against immigrants and anti-immigration laws soon began to dominate their proceedings. The Khalsa Diwan Society and other similar organizations became centres of immigrant political activity. A large number of Sikh immigrants were ex-soldiers and retired policemen, and loyalty to the British government was essential to their creed. However, vain attempts to seek redress through petitions and memorials to Whitehall and to the government of India generated frustration, while growing racial discrimination and laws preventing wives and families from joining their husbands provoked increasing militancy. In October 1909, for example, the executive committee of the Sikh temple in Vancouver passed a resolution which stated that 'no member of the Executive Committee of the Sikh Temple should wear any kinds of medals, buttons, uniforms or insignias which may signify that the position of the party wearing the articles is nothing but a slave to British supremacy'.[40] The immigrant societies began to publish journals publicizing their cause, and through them mounted a campaign to drum up support in India. The *Aryan*, one such journal, published in English, reprinted violently anti-Indian extracts from newspapers in Canada and sent copies by post to students at the Khalsa College and sympathetic editors for distribution. In its issue of March–April 1912 it quoted an extract from a Canadian newspaper which stated,

> The smoke-coloured Hindu, exotic, unmixable, picturesque, a languid worker and a refuge for fleas, we will always have with us, but we don't want any more of him. We don't want any Hindu women. We don't want any Hindu children. It's nonsense to talk about Hindu assimilation. The Sikh may be of Aryan stock, I always thought he was of Jewish extraction. He may be near-white though he does not look it. British Columbia cannot allow any more of the dark meat of the world to come to this province.[41]

Similarly in another issue it noted that the *Vancouver Sunset* had referred to the Sikhs as 'part of the innumerable spawn which the hell muck of India has produced'.[42]

Accounts of discrimination against Sikh immigrants evoked considerable resentment in the Punjab. Tat Khalsa militants, fervent in their sense of communal identity and bristling from reports of harsh treatment of their 'brethren' attempted to arouse Sikh opinion through mass meetings and strongly worded appeals for solidarity against white oppression. The government of India's inaction in safeguarding the interests of its subjects abroad provided a foe closer to home. New links were forged between disgruntled immigrants in North America and Sikh activists at home. Thus the Pacific Coast Khalsa Diwan, based in California, offered to help pay the security deposit demanded by the government from the *Khalsa Sewak* for provocative writing, and the secretary of the Diwan wrote, 'As long as there is life in the nation no one can stop the publication of your paper. Let them demand security not once but a thousand times, by the grace of God the nation will pay it. This security has been taken not from the paper but from the (Sikh) nation'.[43]

The foundation of a revolutionary organization known as the Hindustani Workers of the Pacific Coast added another dimension to Indian immigrant activity in North America. Led by Lala Hardayal, a revolutionary intellectual, the organization began to publish a weekly paper called the *Ghadr* [Revolution] and advocated a campaign of violence in India. The first issue of the *Ghadr*, published in November 1913, stated the party's objectives clearly:

Today, there begins in foreign lands, but in our country's language, a war against the British Raj. What is our name? Ghadr. What is our work? Ghadr. Where will Ghadr break out? In India. The time will soon come when rifles and blood will take the place of pen and ink.[44]

The Ghadr party, as the organization came to be called, added to the propaganda campaign aimed at the Punjab already being conducted by various immigrant organizations. Hundreds of copies of the *Ghadr* and numerous other revolutionary pamphlets exhorting the people to overthrow the tyrannical government were distributed in the Punjab.

In May 1914 the arrival in Canadian waters of the SS *Komagata Maru* carrying 376 prospective Indian immigrants, of whom 346 were Sikhs, precipitated an incident which dramatically illustrated the contentious issues in the debate on immigration control. The vessel had been chartered by Gurdit Singh, a prosperous businessman from Singapore, who sailed from India to Vancouver and thus hoped to secure the admission of his passengers into Canada by circumventing Canadian immigration regulations. The progress of the ship was followed closely in the Canadian Press with dire warnings of the 'oriental invasion'. When the ship arrived in Canadian waters, it was cordoned off and refused permission to dock. A few men who could prove Canadian domicile were permitted entry and the vessel was ordered to leave. Sikh organizations in Canada mounted a concerted effort against the immigration authorities. Public meetings were held expressing sympathy with the passengers of the *Komagata Maru*, and appeals were made to the Canadian government, the Viceroy in India and to the King to intervene. A shore committee in Vancouver took the case to the supreme court, with no success. There was a similar campaign in the Punjab, where the crisis elicited considerable interest. The Canadian government remained steadfast. Meanwhile, an abortive attempt by immigration officials to board the ship forcibly fuelled greater public passion on both sides.

After two months, under threat from a naval vessel, the *Komagata Maru* began its journey homewards. Its desperate and bitter passengers, many of whom had staked all their possessions on this venture, provided an appropriate forum for the dissemination of revolutionary propaganda. Copies of the *Ghadr* were distributed among passengers at Vancouver, and revolutionaries who boarded the ship at Yokohama exhorted them to rebel against the tyrannical government which was responsible for their plight. Reports of violently disaffected passengers and of arms being smuggled on board and a lurking suspicion of German intrigue (war had broken out while the ship was at sea) convinced the government of India that stringent measures were called for in preparation for the *Komagata Maru*'s arrival. When the ship finally arrived near Calcutta in September 1914, it was met by a strong contingent of police and ordered to land its passengers at Budge-Budge. The ship was searched and the passengers instructed to board a special train which was to take them directly to the Punjab. The Sikhs refused to obey, a fracas ensued and the police opened fire, killing eighteen men and wounding twenty-five others. Gurdit Singh and some of his companions escaped. The rest were sent to the Punjab, where more than two hundred of them were interned.[45]

The Budge-Budge riot brought a storm of protest in the Punjab. The militant Sikh Press laid the blame squarely on the government. Public meetings were held and the hardship of the passengers described graphically. The local authorities responded by warning the Press severely against incitement and banning public gatherings. The management of the Golden Temple for its part organized a meeting at Amritsar, disassociated itself from the 'rioters' and reaffirmed its loyalty to the government. Describing the meeting, the Deputy Commissioner of Amritsar reported,

'Government must be aware that there was nothing spontaneous about this meeting. There was an attempt to question the resolution, but the questioners were silenced and the meeting was closed. Many people, however, stayed on and expressed dissatisfaction at what had been done. The meeting can only be regarded as a sort of signpost pointing the general body of Sikhs to the direction in which it should go. It is in *no* sense an indication of the feeling of Sikhs on the subject.'[46]

The Punjab government was not unaware of the political implications of the Tat Khalsa movement and its increasing militancy. A confidential memorandum on Sikh politics prepared by the assistant director of criminal intelligence, commented in 1911,

The most fundamental and immediate of the evils which the present situation seems likely to produce is the dismantling of the fabric of the orthodox Sikh faith, with a consequent disregard of the loyal traditions which have hitherto powerfully affected the character of the Sikh attitude towards the British administration. There need be no hesitation in predicting that those Sikhs who affect the new faith will inevitably tend to become less and less reliable an asset as regards their loyalty to the Crown. The British Government, more particularly the military administration, has put itself in a queer position as regards the Sikhs, who have been fostered and petted and taught to regard themselves as a great nation with great national traditions. The glorification of the Sikhs has been productive of curious results, because, while it has kept the banner of Sikhism flying to the great advantage of the Government, it now appears to be likely to be used as an instrument to scourge us by a section of those for whose good it was primarily undertaken.[47]

Yet Sikh politics presented a constantly fluctuating variety of expression. Government played safe. It clung to its belief in the intrinsic loyalty of the rural Sikh population, and continued its backing of Sikh landed gentry considered reliable and loyal to the British Raj.

Notes to Chapter 2

1 GOI Foreign (Political) Proceedings, A, no. 154–6 of July 1863.
2 Quoted in K. S. Talwar, 'Early phases of the Sikh renaissance and struggle for freedom' *Punjab Past and Present*, vol. 4, no. 2 (Patiala, 1970), p. 291. The word *Guron* was probably intended to be *gaoan*, or cows.

3 Quoted in Khushwant Singh, *History of the Sikhs*, vol. 2, pp. 141–2.

4 *Tribune* (23 Oct. 1890).

5 *Tribune* (23 Oct. 1890). See also *Tribune*, 15 Nov. 1889.

6 N. Gerald Barrier, 'Punjab Politics and the Disturbances of 1907', PhD dissertation, Duke University, 1966, pp. 12–13.

7 Barrier, 'Punjab Politics', pp. 17–18.

8 GOI, *1901 Census Report, Punjab*, pt 1, pp. 263–4, pt 2, pp. 102–3.

9 GOI, *1921 Census Report, Punjab*, pt 1, pp. 305–6.

10 GOI, *1901 Census Report, Punjab*, pt 1, p. 268; GOI, *1921 Census Report, Punjab*, pt 1, pp. 78, 82, 305–6.

11 GOI, *1891 Census Report, Punjab*, pt 1, p. 96.

12 GOI, *1911 Census Report, Punjab*, pt 1, p. 292.

13 GOI, *1911 Census Report, Punjab*, pt 1, p. 292.

14 GOI, *1921 Census Report, Punjab*, pt 2, pp. 376–7.

15 GOI, *1921 Census Report, Punjab*, pt 1, pp. 304–5, pt 2, pp. 365–77.

16 GOI, *1911 Census Report, Punjab*, pt 1, p. 9.

17 GOI, *1921 Census Report, Punjab*, pt 2, pp. 365–77.

18 GOI, *1921 Census Report, Punjab*, pt 1, p. 107.

19 GOI, *1921 Census Report, Punjab*, pt 2, p. 365.

20 Barrier, *Sikh Literature*, p. 77; Barrier and Wallace, *Punjab Press*, pp. 52, 73, 76.

21 Teja Singh, *Gurdwara Reform Movement and the Sikh Awakening* (Jullunder, 1922), p. 92. The *Khalsa Advocate*, begun in 1903, became the leading English-language newspaper espousing the cause of the Singh Sabhas.

22 *Khalsa Akhbar*, 12 Feb. 1897, 8 Oct. 1897, quoted in Harbans Singh, 'Origin', p. 22.

23 Based on D. Petrie, *Confidential Report on Developments in Sikh Politics, 1900–1911* (Simla, 1911), pp. 20, 24, 27; Weekly Report of the Director of Criminal Intelligence (DCI), 5 Oct. 1907, GOI, Home (Political) proceedings B, nos 80–7 of Oct. 1907; Weekly Report, DCI, 16 Nov. 1907, GOI, Home (Political) proceedings B, nos 2–9 of Dec. 1907; Weekly Report of DCI, 7 June 1910, GOI, Home (Political) proceedings B, nos 10–17 of Aug. 1910; Weekly Report of DCI, 7 Nov. 1911, GOI, Home (Political) proceedings B, nos 121–3 of Jan. 1912; Weekly Report of DCI, 15 Feb. 1908, GOI, Home (Political) proceedings B, nos 105–12 of Feb. 1908; Weekly Report of DCI, 7 Aug. 1909, GOI, Home (Political) proceedings B, nos 47–54 of Sept. 1909.

24 Quoted in Weekly Report of DCI, 25 Oct. 1910, GOI, Home (Political) proceedings B, nos 17–24 of Nov. 1910; Weekly Report of DCI, 8 Nov. 1910, GOI, Home (Political) proceedings B, nos 7–10 of Dec. 1910.

25 Quoted in Weekly Report of DCI, 25 Oct. 1910, GOI, Home (Political) proceedings B, nos 17–24 of Nov. 1910.

26 Weekly Report of DCI, 25 Oct. 1910.

27 Quoted in Weekly Report of DCI, 3 Oct. 1911, GOI, Home (Political) proceedings B, nos 61–4 of Nov. 1910.

28 Quoted in Weekly Report of DCI, 1 Nov. 1910, GOI, Home (Political) proceedings B, nos 7–10 of Dec. 1910.

29 Quoted in Kirpal Singh, 'Some new light on the gurdwara reform movement', *Sikh Review*, vol. 13 (Calcutta, 1965), p. 142.

30 N. Gerald Barrier, 'The Punjab disturbances of 1907; the Response of the British government in India to agrarian unrest', in *Modern Asian Studies* (Cambridge, 1967), vol. 1, no. 4, pp. 355–6, 358–60. See also H. Calvert, *The Wealth and Welfare of the Punjab* (Lahore, 1927); C. J. O'Donnel, *The Causes of Present Discontent in India* (London, 1908); M. L. Darling, *The Punjab Peasant in Prosperity and Debt* (Bombay, 1925).

31 Quoted in Daily Report of DCI, 10 July 1907, GOI, Home (Political) proceedings B, nos. 5–90 of Aug. 1907.

32 Quoted in Daily Report of DCI, 20 June 1907, GOI, Home (Political) proceedings B, nos 39–177 of July 1907.

33 Quoted in J. R. Dunlop-Smith, Private Sec. to the Viceroy, to Herbert Risley, Sec. GOI Home Dept, 17 May 1907, GOI, Home (Political) proceedings B, nos 39–177 of July 1907.

34 Petrie, *Confidential Report*, p. 16.

35 Khushwant Singh, *History of the Sikhs*, vol. 2, p. 144.

36 Petrie, *Confidential Report*, pp. 17, 20.

37 Quoted in Weekly Report of DCI, 11 Sept. 1909, GOI, Home (Political) proceedings B, nos 110–17 of Oct. 1909; Petrie, *Confidential Report*, p. 17.

38 Based on Weekly Report of DCI, 20 June 1908, GOI, Home (Political) proceedings B, nos 72–81 of July 1908; Weekly Report of DCI, 11 July 1908, GOI, Home (Political) proceedings B, nos 1–8 of Aug. 1908.

39 Khushwant Singh, *History of the Sikhs*, vol. 2, pp. 168–74.

40 *Free Hindustan*, Sept.–Oct. 1909, quoted in James Campbell Ker, *Political Trouble in India, 1907–1917* (Simla, 1917), p. 209.

41 Quoted in Weekly Report of DCI, 9 July 1912, GOI, Home (Political) proceedings B, nos 26–30 of Aug. 1912.

42 Weekly Report of DCI, 6 Aug. 1912, GOI, Home (Political) proceedings B, nos 21–4 of Sept. 1912.

43 Weekly Report of DCI, 17 Sept. 1912, GOI, Home (Political) proceedings B, nos 7–10 of Oct. 1912. See also Weekly Report of DCI, 18 June 1912, GOI, Home (Political) proceedings B, nos 1–4 of July 1912.

44 Quoted in Khushwant Singh, *History of the Sikhs*, vol. 2, pp. 176–7. See also F. C. Isemonger and J. Slattery, *An Account of the Ghadr Conspiracy* (Lahore, 1921); Khushwant Singh and Satinder Singh, *Ghadr, 1915* (New Delhi, 1965).

45 Report of the *Komagata Maru Enquiry Committee*, GOI, Home (Political) proceedings A, nos 1–13 of Mar. 1915. See also Sohan Singh Josh, *Tragedy of Komagata Maru* (New Delhi, 1975).

46 Fortnightly Report on the Political Situation in the Punjab, 15 Oct. 1914, GOI, Home (Political), Deposit, no. 30, Dec. 1914.

47 Petrie, *Confidential Report*, pp. 51–2.

3

Communal Consciousness and Competition

The outbreak of the First World War was of considerable significance in the Punjab. At the beginning of the war, the Punjab provided some 100,000 men to the Indian army, roughly half of its total strength. As the single most important source of manpower for the army, the province was inevitably crucial to the war effort. By the end of 1918, one in twenty-eight male Punjabis had been mobilized. Within the province this contribution was distributed unevenly. The Sikh community, in particular, provided an altogether disproportionate share of the demand for men. Though the Sikhs were 12 per cent of the population of the province, they contributed 22 per cent of the combatants recruited in the Punjab during the war. In January 1915 there were some 35,000 Sikh combatants in the army, by the end of the war their number had risen to almost 100,000.

Initially, traditional channels of recruitment into the army were maintained. Recruiting officers focused on recognized 'classes' and castes in areas with an established reputation for their connection with the army. Though efforts to obtain recruits were intensified, the existing system of recruitment through touring regimental recruiting parties and regional recruiting offices, and the reliance on informal and individual contacts, remained. By 1917, however, the supply of recruits from the traditional recruiting areas was beginning to wane and a new system of recruitment was introduced. A recruiting organization was set up to parallel the civil administration and each territorial unit was accorded a quota of recruits based on an assessment of the number of men 'it could reasonably be expected to contribute'.[1]

Though recruitment was still limited to particular 'classes' of men deemed 'martial', the quota system was justified as an equitable distribution of demand. However, the desperate trench battles of the war produced devastating losses on all sides. While the casualty rate on fronts in which the Indian army was involved was not enormously high, strategic consideration increasingly demanded more Indian manpower. As British resources were concentrated on the European fronts, that invaluable imperial asset the Indian army was called upon to play an increasingly vital role in Africa, Mesopotamia and the Middle East. In May 1918, in response to a frantic appeal for a further increase in the strength of the Indian army, the Punjab government announced its resolve to increase drastically the provincial contribution to the war effort. The number of recruits to be supplied annually by the province was doubled, an increase of 100,000 men, nine-tenths of whom were to be combatants. Between June and November 1918, 98,869 men were enlisted. Nor was the provincial contribution limited to the enlistment of men. The British districts of the Punjab alone subscribed more than Rs86 million to various war loans. The Punjab, as a major producer of wheat, also provided an inordinate share of the demand for food grains. In 1918 the Lieutenant-Governor of the Punjab estimated that the province would supply 1.25 million tons of wheat to the war effort.[2] Indeed, the demand for men and the demand for wheat produced a conflict of needs in the province. In 1914 the Punjab government had informed the government of India of reports of disquiet from all district officers at the sudden increases in the prices of wheat and flour. Confronted with dire warnings that the stability of India was in jeopardy, the Viceroy, supported by the Commander-in-Chief of the Indian Army, resisted the increasing demand for more. For imperial strategists in London, however, Indian concerns were clearly of secondary importance and the Secretary of State insisted that India meet the additional requirements.

The declaration of war by England in August 1914 lulled local agitation in the Punjab and brought assertions of loyalty from diverse species of influential men. The Indian army was rapidly brought into the conflict with the dispatch of the first Indian troops, including two regiments of Sikhs, to Marseilles three weeks later. The substantial proportion of Sikhs already in the army ensured the identification of the interests of that community with the progress of the war. The Sikh princely states, influential Sikh gentry and Chief Khalsa Diwan spokesmen contributed to the war effort with gusto. War leagues, recruiting committees, publicity committees and Red Cross societies were formed in virtually every district with the collaboration of influential local men. In 1915, the Punjab War News Association was founded in Lahore with the support of members of the local intelligentsia, and by June 1918 an official publicity committee disseminated propaganda through several local branches. Two notable Chief Khalsa Diwan leaders, Sardar Gajjan Singh, a prominent lawyer of Ludhiana, and Sardar Raghbir Singh Sindhanwala, of Raja Sansi, Amritsar, served on the provincial recruiting board, founded in 1917, which allocated local quotas for enlistment. The endeavours of these official organizations were supplemented by the efforts of individuals and private institutions. In Ferozepur, for example, Bhai Takht Singh, the influential Singh Sabha reformer, played a significant role in the local war effort, and the Ferozepur Sikh *kanya mahavidyala*'s journal, the *Punjabi Bhain* made appeals to the patriotism of women. The Malwa Khalsa High School, Ludhiana, enlisted a sixth of its students, and the Khalsa High School, Lyallpur, and the Khalsa Anglo-Vernacular Middle School, Mahilpur, were notable for their contribution.[3] The management of the Golden Temple, the *mahant*s of several *gurdwaras*, as well as Sikh religious leaders like Bhai Arjan Singh of Bagrian, Bawa Gurbaksh Singh Bedi and Bawa Ujagar Singh Bedi of Rawalpindi appealed for greater effort.

The war years were for such men of influence a time to stand up and be noticed, for with significant individual contributions went the fruits of considerable government patronage. The government had made it clear from the outset that conspicuous service in the war effort would not go unrewarded and for the faithful there were Landed Gentry Grants in 1915 and various post-war rewards in the form of titles, land grants and official contracts, besides the more intangible benefits of being in official favour. Thus, Baba Gurbaksh Singh Bedi of Rawalpindi was awarded a title of Raja, a Sword of Honour, and a land grant of some 400 acres besides being knighted for his services; and Sardar Buta Singh, contractor of Rawalpindi, was awarded an OBE, a Sword of Honour, and a land grant to the value of Rs1,000 per annum for his pains.[4] Individuals also received the right to land revenue from designated areas, and villages with a good record had their land revenue remitted to a substantial extent. In addition there were grants amounting to 178,000 acres of irrigated land for war veterans.

The official publicity campaign in support of recruitment was vigorous and initially effective. An official periodical, the *Haq*, established for this purpose and published locally in English, Hindi and *gurumukhi*, achieved a record circulation for India. Tat Khalsa emphasis on Sikh traditions of valour and militarism had created an atmosphere conducive to recruitment, and the Sikhs responded to appeals to their loyalty and courage. The economic opportunity offered by service in the army, which was customary and even prestigious in the traditional recruiting grounds, provided an added incentive. The precise relationship between the rate of enlistment and rural poverty would be difficult to gauge, but clearly the link existed. Thus the Commissioner of Jullunder Division reported in 1915 that better results in the recruitment of Sikhs were hindered by the fact that 'in certain tracts the peasantry are too prosperous to be attracted to the army'.[5] While local influentials prodded the peasantry towards enlistment, some district officers did not hesitate to use their authority to further recruitment whenever the opportunity arose. Harkishan Kaul, the District Commissioner of Montgomery, was able to exercise his influence effectively to persuade reluctant groups to provide recruits in 1915 by taking advantage of the expiry of certain temporary cultivation leases of crown wastelands.

Though instances of official pressure were initially infrequent, the introduction of the territorial-quota system brought with it a systematic campaign of coercion which the government tolerated and sanctioned. From the outset of the new system of recruitment the Punjab government had stated:

> We shall fix quotas for each District, Tahsil [sub-division of a district] or village with reference to the material which is available, and shall in the great majority of cases obtain the number of men we require without resort to compulsion. But in order to be fair to those who come forward at the call of duty we must forthwith be armed with authority. We must be able to say that when there has been a failure on the part of the people to choose their champions for the areas, Government will step in and make the choice for them.[6]

Local quotas were fulfilled through the delegation of the demand for men to rural government officials who were made personally responsible for achieving the number of recruits required of them.

Faced with an ultimatum, rural officials hastened to prove their good faith and employed various forms and degrees of pressure to meet this requirement. As a rural official passed on his demand to a subordinate and he further parcelled out the requirement imposed upon him, the pressure and coercion inevitably intensified. Incidents of intimidation and forcible recruitment multiplied. For the government's part, its policy ensured a clean record. It was suggested that 'Civil officers should not actually take part in recruiting except by seeing that zaildars [local administrative officials] etc. understand what is expected of them and keep up to the mark. The zaildars, etc. would have their own methods of inducing recruits to come forward but the civil authorities could not be accused of bringing undue pressure to bear on anyone'.[7] The natives were to bear the brunt of recruiting their kind.

The constant demand for manpower was also dealt out to a host of private contractors who were appointed or recognized by official recruiting agents as a source for men. The precise nature of the methods employed by these men is difficult to determine, but intimidation, bribery and virtual kidnapping were certainly integral to their schemes. Thus the official history of the war effort in one district recorded that 'Perhaps in no district of the Punjab were so many private recruiters going about at all hours of the day or night in search of young men "spoiling for a fight" ... They moved freely among the people unsuspected and were past masters of the game of spiriting away youngsters from every village. They were disliked for a time, but the experience of their activities became so common with the lapse of time that they came to be regarded as an inevitable concomitant of the war'.[8] When all else failed, recruits were sometimes simply bought. The Deputy Commissioner of Ferozepur reported in 1918 that 'in some places as much as Rs500 per recruit is now being paid for men'.[9] The benefits of conspicuous collaboration were obviously substantial.

A similar policy of systematic pressure was pursued in the raising of war loans. Deputy commissioners were informed that, to ensure that assessments of war-loan subscriptions by the government were met, 'it should be made clear to wealthy citizens that failure to do their duty in this matter will be taken into

account in nominations to municipal and notified area committees, in appointments of honorary magistrates, and in any other
forms of Government recognition, on the ground that such
honours are reserved for those who have shown in a practical
form their desire to assist the administration'.[10] The concerted
efforts of individuals eager for reward and the intimidation
exercised by rural officials for fear of default was also occasionally
punctuated by swift coercive action by the government in the
form of punitive measures against reluctant villagers.

Whatever individual motivations, on the surface Sikh loyalty
was intensely expressed during the war. Punjabi peasants might
resent the unwarranted rise in the price of foodstuffs and feel
aggrieved at the high-handedness of rural officials; the price-tag
imposed on government patronage might rancour among the
urban middle classes, but on the whole Punjabis did not express
their disaffection violently. However, exceptions did exist. The
outbreak of hostilities between England and Germany evoked
great excitement among Indian immigrants in America. For
disgruntled immigrant revolutionaries the moment for action had
arrived. Early in August 1914 a series of public meetings were held
at various centres in California and Oregon and revolutionary
leaders exhorted their countrymen to return to India and foment a
revolution. Describing one such meeting in Fresno, California,
the *Fresno Republican* commented in September 1914, 'Three
hundred and fifty Hindus gathered in a mass meeting ... and for
six hours listened to speeches by lecturers favouring a revolution
in India against England. A subscription of more than 2,000
dollars was taken up, and will be used in sending literature to
Hindus throughout the country urging them to return to their
native land and be ready to take up arms against England'.[11] The
events of that summer concerning the voyage of the *Komagata
Maru* had brought anti-British sentiment to the forefront of
immigrant concerns; news of the Budge-Budge riot that followed
in September 1914 convinced many of the injustice of British rule.
Revolutionary leaders exploited immigrant disaffection with
vigour. The Punjab was seething with discontent, the immigrants
were informed, and the British government was preoccupied. The
moment was portrayed as opportune, and in a flurry of excitement large numbers of politicized immigrants began the journey
home. For others, in the face of uncompromising anti-

immigration legislation the prospect of being united with their families abroad was remote, and employment was being curtailed due to the war. They joined the exodus. The *Portland Telegram* reported, 'Every train and boat for the South carries large numbers of Hindus from this city and if the exodus keeps up much longer Astoria will be entirely deserted by the East Indians.'[12] By the end of 1914 some 1,000 immigrants had returned to India. Nor was this movement restricted to Indians resident in America. In 1917 the Punjab government reported that as many as 8,000 Indians resident in the United States, Canada and the Far East had returned to the Punjab.

In India, the government was not unaware of the stated intentions of some of these men, and evoked the Ingress into India Ordinance to screen returning emigrants. In March 1915 the Defence of India Act was passed which authorised the Governor-General to prohibit the entry or residence in any area of a person suspected to be acting in a manner prejudicial to public safety. In an attempt to control the movements of returned emigrants, the Punjab government evoked the act in sixteen of twenty-three districts. By 1917 some 250 emigrants had been interned and another 1,500 restricted to their villages.

Official efforts to deal with disaffected emigrants received assistance from influential Sikh organizations and individuals. A criminal intelligence department report commented in 1915 that

> The example set by Bhai Sahib Arjun Singh of Bagrain, Ludhiana district, in issuing a manifesto disowning the Sikh emigrants, warning his co-religionists against the mischief they have done and are doing, and giving them good advice, has been followed by the Chief Khalsa Diwan of Amritsar ... Both these documents are well worded and ought to do some good. There are indications that in other districts too the example now set will be followed.[13]

The management of the Golden Temple also joined in the chorus of condemnation of the activities of politicized emigrants. In February 1915 a meeting of influential Sikh landed gentry was held at Lahore with the purpose of devising means to check the revolutionary designs of the returned emigrants. Non-official committees of locally powerful Sikhs were formed in various districts to assist the authorities, and in March the Deputy Commissioner of Jullunder reported,

> Sikh Committees have been started in three tahsils, and the remaining Committees will be started on Saturday 27th March. I

anticipate that the members will be very useful, they show great keeness. Considering that we have between 700 and 800 returned emigrants, I consider that this district has behaved very well, also that our zaildars, safedposhes and better class of lambardars [local administrative officials] have done good work in showing that they are opposed to any nonsense, and would not have the peace of the district broken.[14]

In spite of official vigilance, some Ghadr revolutionaries did slip into the Punjab, and others evaded residency restrictions imposed on them. The revolutionary emigrants travelled extensively through Sikh villages, attended religious fairs and public gatherings and exhorted the people to revolt. To their dismay, however, the violent methods they advocated stirred little response among Punjabi peasants who regarded them as dangerous criminals, and the very men they had calculated to enlist in their cause quickly testified against them. Left largely to their own resources they organized gangs and made plans to raid arsenals and treasuries. But their design for a popular revolution rapidly degenerated into a campaign of terrorism and sporadic violence. A series of armed dacoities and murders intimidated the local population in areas where the returned emigrants were active. In March 1915 the Chief Khalsa Diwan decided to abandon the annual Sikh Educational Conference out of fear of violence. However, swift government action resulted in armed clashes with the revolutionaries, the arrest of crucial leaders and the internment of large numbers of Ghadrites.[15]

By the summer of 1915, the Ghadr conspiracy was in shambles. The internment of revolutionaries as they entered the country, the lack of experience and bad leadership, the inability of revolutionaries to get arms and the infiltration of the revolutionary organization by the police took their toll. Above all, the loyalty of influential Sikh leaders and the active co-operation of the bulk of the population with the authorities decided the issue. During the next two years, a few committed Ghadrites who remained at large turned their attention to informers and crown witnesses and dispersed their energy in isolated instances of revenge. Three successive attempts to smuggle arms to the revolutionaries with German assistance proved abortive, and in April 1917, when the United States entered the war, the revolutionaries were deprived of their base and sanctuary. In California, seventeen Indian revolutionaries were arrested and charged with conspiracy to violate the neutrality of the American government. The Ghadr rebellion failed miserably but its ideology of political violence was to surface again in the Punjab a few years later.

The war years were a period of great political change in India. Indian participation in a war characterized as a fight to make the world safe for democracy and to assert the right of self-determination of nations raised nationalist aspirations in the country and intensified the demand for self-government. From 1915 Annie Besant and Bal Gangadhar Tilak mobilized nationalist support through their home-rule leagues and between 1916 and 1917 conducted the first nation-wide agitation for home rule. In August 1917 the Secretary of State for India, Sir Edwin Montagu, announced in the House of Commons that 'The policy of His Majesty's Government ... is that of the increasing association of Indians in every branch of the administration and the gradual development of self-governing institutions with a view to the progressive realization of responsible Government in India as an integral part of the British Empire'.[16] This statement introduced a vital element into Indian political society. In November 1917 the Secretary of State arrived in India with a delegation to consult with the government of India, various provincial governments and representatives of Indian opinion on the nature of forthcoming constitutional reforms. The prospect of constitutional reforms which would extend Indian representation in the government sharpened communal boundaries in India and brought a cascade of conflicting demands of the 'right' to a share in the forthcoming distribution of positions of power and patronage. The *Report on Indian Constitutional Reforms* by the Secretary of State and the Viceroy, Lord Chelmsford, was published in July 1918, but the reform proposals embodied in the Government of India Act of 1919 did not emerge in their final form until June 1920 when the *Further Rules and Regulations under the Government of India Act* were published. In the interlude the response of Indian politicians to the reform proposals varied with differing and changing individual and group perceptions of the advantages to be derived from the new scheme of administration.

Though Sikh political activity had hitherto been marked by a non-participation in nationalist politics, Sikhs were not immune to change in the larger political arena. Political activity generated by the imminent constitutional reforms aggravated tension between the Hindu community and the Tat Khalsa. In contributing to an escalation of communal competition, the impending reforms further provided an impetus to a movement apparent within the Sikh community during the past two decades. The growing educated Sikh elite had provided the sharp edge to Tat Khalsa demands over a variety of issues since the turn of the century. The endemic unrest over the management of Sikh religious institutions and the agitation for Sikh control of the Khalsa College in Amritsar, the campaign against the ill-treatment of Sikh immigrants abroad, the bitter protests generated by the *Komagata Maru* incident and the subsequent riot at Budge-Budge had witnessed the increasing participation of this Sikh elite and endowed them with greater self-assuredness in asserting the 'rights' of their community. The Government of India Act of 1919 was formulated amidst a chorus of communal bickering between Hindus and Sikhs in the Punjab, and in the process the Tat Khalsa elite was moved to militancy in pressing for the fulfilment of the 'legitimate' aspirations of their community. Moreover, recurring conflict between the Sikhs and the government, while imposing a strain on Anglo-Sikh relations, had also made the ineffectiveness of the Chief Khalsa Diwan's leadership apparent to educated Sikhs. The failure of the Chief Khalsa Diwan to secure Sikh demands for political representation under the 1919 Act brought about the establishment of a radical Sikh political organization and paved the way for an alliance between the Sikh community and nationalist politicians.

In December 1916 representatives of the Indian National Congress and the All India Muslim League met jointly for their annual session at Lucknow and resolved: 'the time has come when His Majesty the King Emperor should be pleased to issue a proclamation announcing that it is the aim and intention of British policy to confer self-Government on India at an early date'.[17] The Congress and the Muslim League drafted a scheme of constitutional reform for the future administration of India. At the provincial level, the scheme envisaged that the authority to deal with all matters affecting the internal administration of a province be vested in a legislative council, four-fifths of whose members were to be elected 'on as broad a franchise as possible'. Adequate provision was, however, to be made for the representation by election of important minority communities. In order to safeguard Muslim minority interests, the scheme conceded special representation to the Muslim community on the basis of a set proportion of seats in provincial legislatures being reserved for them, to be elected by exclusively Muslim electorates. In the Punjab, to ensure adequate representation for the numerically significant but educationally backward Muslim community, Muslims were granted 50 per cent of the elected seats in the provincial legislative council.

The adoption of this scheme of constitutional reform in 1916 by the Congress and the Muslim League, in which Sikh representatives had not participated, gave rise to grave apprehensions in Sikh political society. For, while the Congress–League scheme made provision for safeguarding the representation of Muslim interests, no such special representation was conceded to the Sikh community. Sikh politicians had good reason to fear that without separate communal representation Sikh interests would be neglected. The first time the electoral process had been introduced to select representatives for provincial legislative bodies, in 1909, under the constitutional reform scheme devised by the Secretary of State, Lord Morley, and the Viceroy, Lord Minto, the Sikh community had fared badly. Under the Morley–Minto reform scheme the Muslim community had been granted separate electorates and extra weighting in their representation in order to offset the Hindu preponderance in the electorate, but in spite of a demand by the Chief Khalsa Diwan for similar special representation for the Sikhs, they had received no such concessions. Voting in the elections under the new scheme was mainly along communal lines, and consequently the Sikhs had lost to Hindu and Muslim candidates. Sikh representation had to be secured by nomination by the government. In 1909 all three seats open for election went to the Muslim community. In the provincial elections of 1912, of the six candidates to be elected, four Hindu, one Muslim and one Sikh candidate were successful. In the elections of 1916, for the eleven elected seats, five Hindu and five Muslim candidates were elected and a single seat went to a European candidate. No Sikh candidate was elected.

The growth of Sikh communal consciousness and the demarcation of boundaries between the Hindu and Sikh communities by the Tat Khalsa inevitably led to a growing concern among them for their recognition as an independent political entity. For

these Sikhs the Congress–League scheme denied their independent existence, and through the Press they joined in condemning
the Congress for ignoring Sikh representation while safeguarding
Muslim interests. The Secretary of State's declaration of August
1917 intensified Sikh concern for greater forthright in pressing
their demands on the government. Writing in October 1917, the
influential Sikh newspaper the *Khalsa Advocate* expressed the
sentiments of the majority of the Sikh intelligentsia clearly:

> Whereas India is in the throes of a political crisis there is a great hush
> prevailing in the Sikh world. What is the meaning of this great
> silence? Does it mean that the Sikhs have made no sacrifices worth
> the reward? ... Does it mean, then, that the Sikhs are a negligible
> factor – a nation ignorant of politics and militant tactics? No. The
> Sikhs are a definite political entity. Nor are they less political. The
> Sikh nation is a politico-military nation par excellence, silence does
> not imply ... non-existence. The ... Chief Khalsa Diwan has
> pursued a very wise policy so far – viz – that of forbearance from
> taking part in political activity. But Mr. Montagu's decision has
> changed the situation materially. Such extraordinary circumstances
> must be met in an extraordinary manner. We *must* represent our
> needs. We must not lose our opportunity.[18]

Following the adoption of the Congress–League scheme, the
Chief Khalsa Diwan hastened to present the Sikh point of view to
the government. In January 1917 the secretary of the Diwan,
Sunder Singh Majithia, addressed a memorandum to the Punjab
government on the nature of constitutional reforms acceptable to
the Sikh community. Stressing the importance of the Sikh contribution to the war effort and the staunch loyalty of the community
to the British Raj, the memorandum stated that

> hitherto the community has not received that share of encourage-
> ment which is their just due and that in any scheme of further
> progress and development which may be formulated they are likely
> to suffer considerably as against the more vocal sections of their
> countrymen, unless their position and status are distinctly safe-
> guarded by the benign Government. The past history of the
> Councils puts it beyond doubt how any scheme which does not
> specifically provide for the adequate representation of the commu-
> nity is doomed to failure so far as the Sikhs are concerned.[19]

The memorandum demanded that the Sikh community be granted
separate electorates in any future scheme of constitutional reform
and that Sikh representation in the council be based not on their

strength in numbers but 'proportionate to the importance, position and services of the community, with due regard to their status
before the annexation of the Punjab, their present stake in the
country and their past and present services to the Empire'.[20]

While the basis of the Sikh demand for special representation
was the intangible 'importance, position, and services' of the
community, the memorandum interpreted this claim in quite
specific terms. For Sikh leaders, the political arena, dominated by
the Hindu and Muslim communities, was clearly a hostile one.
The Hindu community denied a separate Sikh identity, while the
Muslims were at best unconcerned with Sikh political aspirations.
Isolated as the Sikhs saw themselves, substantial Sikh representation in the legislative bodies was imperative to them. Thus the
Chief Khalsa Diwan insisted that, 'In order that such representation may be adequate and effective and consistent with their
position and importance the Sikhs claim that a one-third share in
all seats and appointments in the Punjab is their just share and
should be secured to them as an absolute minimum. Similarly
their share in the Viceroy's and Secretary of State's Council
should be adequate and fixed on principles of the like nature.'[21]

Not surprisingly, Hindu politicians in the Punjab objected
strongly to Sikh claims to special communal representation. An
acceptance of such independent political representation for the
Sikhs would inevitably reduce Hindu representation in the
Punjab. In November 1917 the Punjab Provincial Congress
Committee, dominated by Hindu politicians, rejected Sikh
demands for separate representation on the ground that the Sikhs
were a part of the larger Hindu community and as such were not
entitled to separate electorates. Earlier, in October 1917, the
Punjabee had expressed Hindu views of Sikh claims and scorned
Sikh demands for a one-third share in all political representation.
Commenting on the Chief Khalsa Diwan's memorandum to the
government on the forthcoming constitutional reforms, it stated

> The most disappointing feature of this memorandum is its constant
> reiteration of communal claims. The movement is thoroughly
> mischievous. It can do no good ... As a matter of fact, the Diwan
> not only insists on communal representation, but asks that the
> community it represents should be granted a share in the represen-
> tation, far in excess of its numerical proportion. We are told that
> nothing less than a third of the seats in the Legislative Council and
> the appointments in the administration can satisfy the community

... We have always regarded the Sikh community as part and parcel of the great Hindu community ... (and) we are constrained to say that in basing the demand for the separate and excessive representation of the Sikhs on the grounds of their historical importance and their present services, the Diwan is betraying a strange ignorance of the essentials of representative Government under modern democratic conditions.[22]

Expressing similar sentiments, the influential Lahore Hindu daily the *Tribune* stated that in fact there was little in the Congress–League scheme of constitutional reform to which the Sikhs could justifiably take objection, since 'The Sikhs know that their case is not on all fours with that of the Muhammadans as, in many respects, if not most, they form an integral portion of the great Hindu family'.[23]

While Sikhs as a whole responded indignantly to such Hindu scorn of their assertion of 'legitimate' Sikh political rights, from the emerging Tat Khalsa elite came the strongest reaction. The comments of a young writer, Sardar Tara Singh, in the Tat Khalsa newspaper the *Khalsa Akhbar* in November 1917 typified their response. Tara Singh, born in 1885, the son of a minor village official, had been educated at the Mission High School, Rawalpindi, and received the BA degree from the Khalsa College, Amritsar. At college he had been deeply imbued with Singh Sabha propaganda and had been prominent among student leaders who organized hostile demonstrations to coincide with the visit of Sir Charles Rivaz in 1907. Following his graduation, Tara Singh attended a teacher training college at Lahore and subsequently helped establish the Khalsa High School, Lyallpur. He served as headmaster of the school at Lyallpur and continued to play a prominent role in the activities of the local Singh Sabha. In 1913 he was notable for mobilizing support in Lyallpur for a visiting delegation of Indian emigrants from Canada who had come to protest to the government of India at their harsh treatment.[24] The *Khalsa Akhbar* in its issue of 9 November 1917 published a communication from Tara Singh warning his co-religionists that the Hindu and Muslim communities had organized a 'conspiracy' to 'trample down the smaller nations'. Further, the writer went on to suggest that if Sikh claims to political representation were not met, Sikhs should oppose any further constitutional reform, since 'They do not wish to replace the Anglo-Indian bureaucracy by a Hindu and Muslim bureaucracy'.[25]

Tat Khalsa's insistence on a separate Sikh communal identity and the Hindu community's denial of it intensified public debate and brought an added emphasis to Sikh militants' assertion of their existence as an independent social and political entity. Incidents of strife between Tat Khalsa and militant Arya Samajists multiplied. A radical Tat Khalsa leader suggested the Sikhs should not inter-dine with Hindus since the latter did not observe Khalsa prohibitions on smoking, and the *Khalsa Samachar* wrote: 'certain Hindus offend the feelings of Sikhs by parading figures of Sikh Gurus on the occasion of the Holi festival ... Is it not surprising that the Hindus should bend to Sikh Gurus when they have 33 crore [330 million] Gods and Goddesses of their own'?[26] Tat Khalsa concern with the recognition of the Sikh communities' aspirations was reflected in their renewed preoccupation with the question of *gurdwara* management and control. In August 1917 the *Punjab Darpan*, a weekly *gurumukhi* newspaper published in Amritsar, reported with some consternation that the *pujaris* of the Golden Temple instructed devotees to seek purification by bathing in the river Ganges according to Hindu custom. The paper deeply resented the fact that the care of this premier Sikh shrine should be in the hands of men who held the views of 'Hindu Brahmins' and warned that this state of affairs was 'weakening' the Sikh community.[27]

Controversy over the management of Sikh *gurdwaras* being in the hands of 'Hinduized' men and outside the control of local congregations reached new heights with a dispute regarding the management of the Babe-de-Ber shrine at Sialkot in 1918. In September 1918, on the death of the *mahant* of the *gurdwara*, the *pujari* of the shrine wrote to the Deputy Commissioner of Sialkot informing him that in keeping with the deceased *mahant*'s wishes, they had appointed his grandson to succeed him as *mahant*. The local Singh Sabha protested vehemently against the right of the *pujari* to make such an appointment and contended that since the previous *mahant* had died, the management of the shrine should be entrusted to a representative committee of local Sikhs. While the controversy persisted, the widow of the deceased *mahant* moved to forestall any attempt to deprive her grandson of his claim to the guardianship of the *gurdwara* by appointing Ganda Singh, an honorary magistrate, the legal guardian of her grandson and manager of the shrine in his minority. The Deputy

Commissioner sanctioned the transfer of property associated with the shrine to the new appointee. This move was strongly resented by the reformers. Resolutions were passed condemning the action, and petitions appealing for justice sent to the Punjab government. The only recourse left to the reformers was to seek redress through litigation, and a civil suit was instituted against the appointment of the new *mahant* in the district court. However, such litigation was a lengthy and expensive matter, and meanwhile the impotence of the reformers in securing their demands continued to rankle.

The development of greater assertiveness by the Tat Khalsa in safeguarding their 'rights' from Hindu 'encroachment' was gradual, but it was reflected clearly in the columns of the Sikh Press. Sikh newspapers and journals repeatedly decried the under-representation of the community in the civil administration of the province and urged the appointment of more Sikhs to public office. They demanded that Sikh be entitled to wear *kirpans* without the necessity of an arms licence and appealed for Sikh religious festivals to be made public holidays in the Punjab. To the dispassionate observer such demands might have appeared trivial in contrast with the greater issues of the day, but to educated Tat Khalsa they were crucial for the recognition and preservation of a distinct Sikh identity in a hostile world.

The Montagu–Chelmsford *Report on Indian Constitutional Reforms* was published in July 1918. The authors of the report rejected the Congress–League scheme as premature, and suggested instead an interim scheme of administration to acclimatize India to responsible government. The two basic principles laid down in the report were the devolution of authority to provincial governments and the introduction of partial responsible government in the provinces. The scheme of provincial administration suggested was based on a principal of dual government, or dyarchy, as it came to be called. Provincial legislative councils were to be expanded in size, with a substantial majority elected by direct franchise. Certain subjects of administration would be transferred to popular control through ministers chosen from and responsible to the majority in the legislatures. Such transferred subjects were to include local self-government, education, agriculture, medical administration, sanitation and public works, the development of industries, and excise. Other aspects of administration, such as law and order, land revenue, famine relief, the control of the Press, and labour questions, were reserved for the provincial Governor acting with his executive council. The authors of the report were opposed to communal representation in principle, but they conceded the necessity of special representation for the Muslims on the basis of separate electorates and a set proportion of seats reserved for the community. Further, the report stated, 'The Sikhs in the Punjab are a distinct and important people, they supply a gallant and valuable element to the Indian army, but they are everywhere in a minority and experience has shown that they go virtually unrepresented. To the Sikhs, therefore, and to them alone we propose to extend the system already adopted in the case of the Muhammadans.'[28] The Sikh demand for special representation had been conceded in principle.

The publication of the Montagu–Chelmsford report brought a mixed reaction in India. The main issue at stake, as laid out in the report, was not constitutional reform at the centre, but autonomy at the provincial level, and that attitude of politicians as to the measure of responsible government acceptable varied with the particular circumstances in each province. Provincial politicians, in each case, reacted to the scheme according to their view of the extent of power likely to come their way under the reformed constitution. At a special session of the Indian National Congress called to discuss the Montagu–Chelmsford proposals, the Congress declared that the reform scheme was 'disappointing and unsatisfactory'. More moderate politicans seceded from the Congress and welcomed the reform proposals as a real and substantial step toward self-government. In reaction, the Congress demanded responsible government at the provincial level immediately.

Sikh politicians had scored a significant political victory. In suggesting separate electorates for the Sikh community, the authors of the report had given effective recognition to their independent political identity, and they had also given a promise of measures to safeguard Sikh interests. Sikh spokesmen were unanimous in applauding the reform scheme. The report was cited as a 'valuable document', and the *Khalsa Advocate*, expressing the Sikh point of view, stated, 'The reforms suggested are of a substantial and liberal nature. On perusal of the scheme one can easily say that at any rate, as far as the provincial administration is concerned, the step is towards a substantial improvement.'[29] On the vital issue of self-government the *Khalsa Advocate* urged moderation in criticism of the report, stating, 'We Sikhs are for the emancipation of the country from its dependent position. And so is the British Government who have so clearly defined the ideal of British rule in India. But we must resist the temptation to take too much all at once and get "overdosed". The approach to our goal should be gradual and substantial.'[30] Similar views were expressed by other Sikh papers sympathetic to the Tat Khalsa movement. The *Loyal Gazette* stated that since the reform scheme constituted a considerable advance towards self-government, it should be thankfully accepted, and the *Khalsa Samachar*, while expressing the gratitude of the Sikh community, warned that under no circumstances should the Sikhs join the extremist politicians in condemning the reform scheme.[31]

But, given their conflict of interest and belief with the Hindu community and their deep-seated mistrust of Muslim intentions, Tat Khalsa politicians were only too aware that Sikh representation would have to be substantial for it to be effective. Thus the *Khalsa Advocate* noted,

> We are glad to note that the draughtsmen of the scheme have been prudent enough, unlike Lords Morley and Minto, to recognize the claim of the important and loyal Sikh community to a separate electorate...But...this recognition, to be of any value, must be very substantial in its practical handling. If the representation to be granted is nominal or small or falls short of what has been stated in the Sikh representation ... the effect of the recognition to the separate electorates would be gone or infinitesimally reduced. The representation of the important Sikh community should be commensurate with its importance, loyalty, service and devotion to the Empire.[32]

The *Punjab Darpan* and the *Loyal Gazette* also reiterated Sikh claims to substantial representation.[33]

Sikh apprehensions regarding the proportion of their representation in the provincial legislature were reinforced in the debate on the reform scheme in the Punjab Legislative Council. Mian Fazl-i-Hussain, a prominent Muslim member of the council, suggested that Muslim representation in the Punjab Legislative Council under the reformed constitution be based on the proportion conceded to the community in the Congress–League scheme. Since the Congress–League scheme had made no mention of separate Sikh representation, Sardar Gajjan Singh, representing the Sikh community, suggested that this resolution be amended by adding the clause, 'subject to the just claims of the Sikhs'.[34] The proposed amendment was vehemently opposed by both Hindu and Muslim members of the council and lost. Gajjan Singh then proposed a resolution articulating Sikh claims to one-third of the seats in the reformed provincial legislature, and once again the two Sikh representatives were swamped by the combined strength of the Hindu and Muslim representatives.[35] Educated and literate Sikhs waited anxiously for the formulation of the detailed structure of the reformed provincial legislative council.

The Montagu–Chelmsford report had enunciated the basic principles upon which the constitutional reforms under the Government of India Act of 1919 were to be based, but a committee led by Lord Southborough was left to formulate the details. The committee visited India and consulted with the various provincial governments. At every stage a multitude of communities and interests lobbied for recognition of their claims to representation. As far as the Sikh community was concerned, the Punjab government endorsed the Montagu–Chelmsford report's recommendation of separate electorates for the Sikhs in its memorandum to the Southborough committee. On the practical working of the system of separate electorates the Punjab government noted,

> It would of course be necessary to maintain three separate electoral rolls ... where Muhammadans, Hindus and Sikhs have separate representation. Anyone claiming to be a Sikh, a Hindu or a Muhammadan, and being prima facie what he represents himself to be, would if possessed of the other qualifications be entered in the appropriate roll and would thereby be debarred from voting in a constituency allotted to either of the other two communities. It is not proposed that there should be any official inquisition into a candidate's claim to belong to a particular religion. As between Hindus and Muhammandans there could never be any reason for doubt. In the case of Sikhs such an inquisition might be a difficult matter, as the line of discrimination between Sikhs and non-Sikhs is often the subject of acute controversy. Some regulation may, however, be necessary.[36]

The report of the Southborough committee was presented in February 1919. The report suggested that the legislative council in the Punjab consist of eighty-five members, including both elected and nominated members, official and non-official. Sixty-one members of the council were to be elected by general and special constituencies, twenty were to be nominated by the government, and there were to be four ex-officio members. The Sikhs were assigned eight seats to be elected by an exclusively Sikh electorate, and one seat was reserved for the community out of four to be elected by a special constituency of landholders. In all, the Sikhs were to receive some 15 per cent of the elected seats in the legislative council.

Since the Sikh community constituted only about 12 per cent of the population of the Punjab, the Southborough committee had in fact recognized the necessity of representation for the Sikhs in excess of their numerical proportion. But constituting a small block in a legislative council dominated by Muslim and Hindu members was a far cry from Sikh demands for representation, and the predominant feeling in Sikh educated circles was one of betrayal. To add insult to injury, the committee had suggested that since 'There is some difficulty in defining with accuracy the distinction between some classes of Sikhs and Hindus, our suggestion for meeting this difficulty is to require that the officer responsible for preparing the electoral roll shall accept the declaration of an elector that he is a Sikh, unless he is satisfied that the declaration is not made in good faith'.[37] Both Kesdhari and Sahajdhari Sikhs were to qualify to vote in the special Sikh constituencies. In the eyes of the Tat Khalsa, this definition of the term 'Sikh' to be applied undermined the very basis of their demand for special representation.

The failure of the Southborough committee to propose representation in keeping with what Sikhs regarded as their 'just' and necessary share came as a great blow to Sikh political society. For educated Sikhs there was a direct link between the Indian war effort and future constitutional reforms. In November 1917 the *Khalsa Advocate* had written, 'The reforms are demanded on the grounds of India's share in the war, and on account of that Sikhs, surely, deserve to receive the Lion's share',[38] and they felt that they had been cheated of the rewards of their loyalty and collaboration. The *Loyal Gazette* expressed these feelings succinctly. 'There can be no doubt', it stated in May 1919,

> that in the reformed councils our condition will be better than what it is at present. But our grievance is that justice has not been done to

us ... We appeal to the British Government and nation to enable the loyal Sikh community to stand on its own legs and not to leave it to the mercy of other communities. The Sikhs have always been and will ever remain, loyal to the British nation. It is now time for the latter to prove loyalty to the former.[39]

The Chief Khalsa Diwn also expressed feelings of 'grave and serious apprehension' at the Southborough committee's proposals.[40]

Tat Khalsa bitterness at this lack of recognition of what they regarded as their right was inevitably expressed in greater militancy in asserting their various demands. The educated Sikh elite took the lead in pressing with greater vehemence for Sikh control over the Khalsa College and the Golden Temple. In February 1919, the *Panth Sewak*, a *gurumukhi* weekly newspaper owned by Chanda Singh, a former school-teacher, reasserted the Sikh demand for control over the management of the Golden Temple:

> The shrine is no longer the charge of the Khalsa, the offerings are not for the Panth, the management is not by the Sikhs ... if the inhabitants of Palestine and the German Colonies are considered fit for the principle of self-determination in the sphere of the Government of their lands, are the Sikhs not even fit to look after their own shrine?[41]

The *Loyal Gazette* published a spate of charges alleging the misappropriation of *gurdwara* funds by the manager of the Golden Temple, and as an example of its debased management elaborated on the now familiar theme of the deferential treatment accorded to low-caste Sikhs regarding their admission to the *gurdwara*.[42]

The continued mismanagement of Sikh *gurdwaras* was linked directly to government policy with the announcement in June 1919 of the judgement in the case concerning the appointment of the new *mahant* of *gurdwara* Babe-de-Ber in Sialkot district. The decision to uphold the right of the Udasi *mahant* to nominate a successor stirred deep indignation in Tat Khalsa circles. The *Sikh Sepoy*, an organ of the Sikh recruiting committee of Ferozepur, wrote that in confirming the appointment of an 'apostate' manager the district court had not acted in conformity with British policy of non-interference in religious affairs, and the *Punjab Darpan* stated that British courts had no jurisdiction in 'deciding who was a Sikh'.[43]

The militant assertion of Sikh demands was not of course limited to issues such as Sikh control of the Khalsa College and the Golden Temple. With the disclosure of the Southborough committee's recommendations, the Sikh community's failure to secure their demands for substantial Sikh political representation had become apparent. The publication of the committee's proposals provided the basis for a demand for the establishment of a representative Sikh political organization. In February 1919 the *Loyal Gazette* noted that if the Sikhs had had a political organization through which they had presented their claims to the Indian National Congress, like the Muslims, they too would have been 'accepted' and 'respected' by their fellow countrymen, and the *Punjab Darpan* stated that the Sikh community had not secured their 'rights' due to their lack of participation in politics.[44] The prevalent sentiments of the educated Sikh elite were represented succinctly by the Lahore *Tribune* in an editorial in March 1919. It stated,

> For sometime past new life has been stirring in the Sikh community, and the feeling has been abroad that without a political organization of their own, their interests run the risk of being neglected altogether or at any rate not adequately safeguarded ... Political self-immolation or a self-denying ordinance to abstain from taking part in politics over an extended period, cannot fail to serve as a handicap for the time being and produce a feeling of groping in the dark as it were, even when the awakening has come and there is a desire to gradually accommodate the eyes to the light before coming into the full blaze of the sun. Some such process is going on among the Sikhs.[45]

On 30 March 1919 a meeting of members of the Sikh intelligentsia was convened at Lahore with the purpose of founding a political organization to represent the community. The meeting, presided over by Sardar Gajjan Singh, the prominent lawyer from Ludhiana and one of the two Sikh representatives on the Punjab Legislative Council, was attended by the educated Sikh elite from various parts of the province.[46] It was decided that the new political organization would be known as the Sikh League, and a sub-committee was formed to prepare a draft constitution to be submitted to a general meeting of the league before the end of June. Before the sub-committee could present its proposals, however, the Punjab exploded in violent political agitation over the passing of the Rowlatt Act.

During the war, the government of India had invested itself

with extraordinary powers under the Defence of India Act of 1915 in an attempt to control political terrorism in India, which was centred around Punjab and Bengal. However, the law did not provide for such authority in peace time and the government feared that 'the persons interned under the Defence of India Act will be due for release and the terms of imprisonment of many dangerous criminals will be coming to an end ... [and] there will be, especially in the Punjab, a large number of disbanded soldiers among whom it may be possible to stir up discontent'.[47] Consequently, in 1917 the government of India appointed a committee headed by Justice S. A. T. Rowlatt to investigate revolutionary violence in India and suggest measures necessary to combat it. The Rowlatt committee suggested a number of changes in the law, and on the basis of its proposals the government of India drafted two bills, the Indian Criminal Law (Amendment) Bill No. 1 of 1919 and the Criminal Law (Emergency Powers) Bill No. 2 of 1919, which were introduced in the Imperial Legislative Council in January 1919. The first of these two bills aimed at investing executive authority with powers to deal effectively with activities regarded as 'prejudicial to the security of the state' by an appropriate amendment of the Indian Penal Code. The second bill vested in the government of India discretionary powers to circumvent cumbersome legal procedure in instances of political crime. In the Imperial Legislative Council the bills were vigorously condemned by Indian members as reactionary, but despite their protest, the legislation was rapidly pushed through the council.

The Rowlatt bills became a highly volatile political issue when Gandhi inaugurated a campaign of passive resistance to protest against them in February 1919. 'To me', Gandhi wrote,

the Bills are the regulated symptoms of the deep-seated disease. They are the striking demonstration of the determination of the Civil Service to retain its grip on our necks ... I consider the Bills to be an open challenge to us. If we succumb we are done for. If we may prove our word that the Government will see an agitation such that they have never witnessed before, we shall have proved our capacity for resistance to arbitrary or tyrannical rule.[48]

Opponents of the bills were invited to pledge themselves to a campaign of non-violent civil disobedience, and a *satyagrah sabha* was formed to give publicity to the campaign.

In the Punjab, protest against the bills was vigorous. From the outset the Punjabi urban-educated elite took the lead in condemning the bills as reactionary. In March 1919 the Lahore *Tribune* commented,

> No civilised Government would adopt a policy of repression in the teeth of opposition from the public. There are now two ways open to us. One is that we should, like the dead, put the noose of this law round our necks, bury in oblivion for ever our fair name, as also that of our great men, and sound the death-knell of the so-called liberty of India. The other is that we should afford proof of our life by refusing to accept the law in question.[49]

At mass protest meetings held throughout the province politicians were less restrained in their exhortations to the people to oppose the legislation. Thus at a meeting in Multan one politician urged the people, 'You die of cholera, plague, influenza, and other diseases, but would it not be better to die nobly the death of a hero and lion than as a dog?'[50] Inflammatory speeches inciting the people to oppose the Rowlatt bills were not, however, limited to Hindu and Muslim nationalist politicians. In the urban areas the Sikh educated elite was pulled into the protests. Prominent among those who mobilized support in favour of the agitation in Lahore was Amar Singh, pleader of Kasur and editor of the *Lyall Gazette*. At Ambala, Jhanda Singh, pleader, was notable in the agitation.[51]

Economic distress heightened the tension generated by the vigorous publicity campaign against the bills. The prices of food grains in the Punjab during the war had increased significantly and had outstripped rises in wages. Between 1912 and December 1917, with the exception of weavers, wages of every class of labourer in the towns rose less than the 43 per cent increase in the price of food grains. In the case of rural wages too, the wages of carpenters alone rose more than 43 per cent and then in only one out of twenty-eight districts.[52] In 1918 the monsoons failed and consequently the winter harvest was disastrous. By the spring of 1919 the price of food grains had reached a record level, an increase of 100 per cent between 1917 and 1919.[53] The urban population was also hit by the imposition of a special income tax, with increases in tax paid in some cases ranging between 100 and 200 per cent. An epidemic of influenza, which had by the end of 1918 claimed some 100,000 Punjabi lives, added to the turmoil. The return and demobilization of large numbers of Punjabi troops only increased the distress. Returning troops heard of the forced recruitment under the quota system, the fines imposed on reluctant villages and the pressures brought to raise war funds. To many, this reward for their sacrifices was a bitter pill to swallow. In May 1919 a senior British administrator in the Punjab wrote,

> During the last month I have been a good deal in touch with public opinion ... and have talked with heaps of village lambardars, etc. and heard also from soldiers of the feeling in the Punjab. The one idea among the masses is that we have been grossly ungrateful. Our praise of their help in war time has occasionally perhaps, been immoderate, but it has got home, and the general feeling everywhere was that Government was about to give some just reward. The present feeling among the people is of resentment and disappointment.[54]

The protest against the Rowlatt bills became the focus for widespread disaffection. In March 1919 the situation in the Punjab was extremely volatile.

The Rowlatt Act became law and Gandhi called for a nationwide hartal, a suspension of all economic activity, in protest. The response surpassed the most optimistic of expectations. In Lahore and Amritsar the hartal was a complete success. However, the arrest of Gandhi for breaking restrictions prohibiting him from entering Delhi precipitated matters. In Amritsar protest demonstrations took a violent turn following news of Gandhi's arrest and of the deportation of two prominent provincial leaders, and infuriated mobs sacked two banks and burnt the town hall and other public buildings. Martial law was declared in the city. Two days later, on 13 April, a protest meeting was summoned at the Jallianwallah Bagh in Amritsar in contravention of an ordinance prohibiting all public gatherings. The martial-law administrator, General R. E. H. Dyer, responded harshly. Troops were ordered to open fire without warning on the unarmed crowd, killing 379 and wounding more than 2,000 others. General Dyer's action in Amritsar set the tone for bitter agitation and equally brutal repression throughout the province. The *satyagrah* had got out of control.

In seven weeks the military authorities had brought the Punjab to its knees but they left behind a legacy of bitter resentment and racial strife. In Amritsar the city's water and electricity supply were discontinued, public floggings were conducted, and, in a street where a missionary had been assaulted, Indian passers-by were made to crawl on their bellies as a penance. In Lahore tradesmen were ordered to resume their businesses on pain of death and students at the university, who had been particularly conspicuous in the disturbances, were singled out for a unique penance. All students were ordered to report to their colleges, in some cases miles from the city centre, four times a day. In Kasur, where two Englishmen had been murdered, the population was punished with collective fines and public floggings, and an order that all Indians must salaam every white man on sight was introduced and enforced by making defaulters rub their nose on the ground. Gujranwala and its neighbourhood were subjected to bombing and machine-gunning from the air. The local Khalsa high school was among the buildings hit.

While the Punjab seethed under martial law, the Chief Khalsa Diwan's spokesmen and traditional Sikh religious leaders like Bhai Sahib Arjun Singh of Bagrian were vocal in publicizing their unflinching loyalty to the government and in appealing to their co-religionists to 'beware of the attempts of agitators to seduce them from their loyalty'.[55] The schism between members of the young Sikh educated elite and their traditional leaders could not have been more marked. Furthermore, from the Golden Temple, a stone's throw from the Jallianwallah Bagh, that emotive memorial to Indian martyrdom in the cause of liberty, came a declaration which astonished the entire Sikh community. The manager of the Golden Temple, Arur Singh, invited General Dyer to the shrine and, as a token of Sikh appreciation of his services, invested him with the five symbols of the Khalsa.[56]

The agitation against the Rowlatt Act had a dramatic effect on Indian politics. For the first time nationalist agitation had percolated beyond the politically conscious elite to the masses, and the campaign had witnessed an unprecedented scale of co-operation between Hindus, Sikhs and Muslims. In the Punjab, as elsewhere, the events of 1919 gave an enormous boost to Indian nationalism. Thus in October 1919 the Punjab government reported, 'Life for a well wisher of Government is becoming increasingly difficult; open boycott in the bar and recreation room, open and veiled insults, eviction from houses, stoppage of trade and refusal to social intercourse are on the increase'.[57] The Sikh community did not remain unaffected by this new nationalist consciousness. Participation in the Rowlatt *satyagrah* had imbued young edu-

cated Sikhs with a vital nationalism which was reflected clearly in
the large numbers of Sikhs from this section of the community
who presented themselves as delegates for the forthcoming
session of the Indian National Congress.[58]

In an attempt to placate Indian opinion the Secretary of State
announced in October 1919 the appointment of an official
committee of inquiry into the Punjab disturbances. The committee, presided over by Lord Hunter, examined a large number of
witnesses, but the Indian National Congress boycotted its proceedings. The Congress demanded the release of imprisoned
Punjab political leaders to depose before the committee, and on
the government's refusal to do so appointed its own inquiry into
the events of 1919. In December 1919 the annual session of the
Congress was held at Amritsar. The Congress reiterated its earlier
declaration that the constitutional reforms were inadequate, and
urged the early establishment of full responsible government in
India. It agreed, however, to participate in working the Government of India Act of 1919.

The inaugural session of the Central Sikh League was also held
at Amritsar on 30 December 1919. Participation in the league's
proceedings required payment of a subscription of Rs6 in addition to an admission fee of Rs5, and the new organization
therefore represented well-to-do educated Sikh opinion. From
the outset the league reflected a concern for greater Sikh participation in nationalist politics, and the first session of the organization
was deliberately fixed to coincide with the annual session of the
Congress and the Muslim League. The provisional secretary of
the Central Sikh League, Gurbux Singh Gyani, barrister-at-law,
declared, 'We have purposely fixed the first session at Amritsar so
as to learn something from the other communities who are in their
full youth and vigour.'[59] Prominent nationalist politicians such as
Gandhi and Madan Mohan Malviya were invited to attend the
league's session. However, the new organization, proceeded
cautiously. Gajjan Singh, the reputable lawyer from Ludhiana and
member of the provincial legislative council, was elected to
preside over the new body. Further, though the Sikh League
passed a resolution demanding that the 'country should be placed
on a footing of equality with the self-governing members of the
Empire', it welcomed the Government of India Act of 1919 as a
'substantial instalment of reform' and assured the government of

its 'hearty co-operation' for its successful working.[60] On the emotive issue of the recent agitation in the Punjab, too, the Sikh League proceeded with moderation. It deferred comment on the conduct of the martial-law administration in anticipation of the publication of the report of the official committee of inquiry and the report of the committee appointed by the Indian National Congress. On the specific demands of the Sikh community, however, the league was more forceful. It declared its regret that 'both in the Provincial and the Indian Legislatures the Sikh community has been denied that adequate and substantial repre-sentation to which it is justly entitled by reason alike of its political status and importance of its military achievements, its services and sacrifices for the King Emperor'.[61] Further, it passed resolutions demanding Sikh control of the management of the Golden Temple, and resolved that in consideration for the 'religious requirements of the Sikhs the sword and other non-firing arms should be exempted from the operations of the Arms Act'.[62]

By May 1920 relations between the nationalists and the govern-ment had begun to deteriorate rapidly. Public opinion in India was deeply stirred at the hesitation with which the government was taking action against officials guilty of brutal suppression of the disturbances in the Punjab in 1919. In March 1920 the report of the commissioners appointed by the Indian National Congress to investigate the Punjab disturbances was published. The report refuted allegations that there had been a widespread conspiracy in the Punjab in 1919 to overthrow the government and questioned the necessity for the introduction of martial law. The commis-sioners charged that the Lieutenant-Governor of the Punjab, Michael O'Dwyer, had by 'his studied contempt and distrust of the educated classes, and ... the cruel and compulsory methods, adopted during the war, for obtaining recruits and monetary contributions, and his suppression of public opinion' incensed the people against the government.[63] 'We feel tempted to say', they wrote, 'that he invited violence from the people, so that he could crush them. The evidence shows that he subjected the Punjabis to the gravest provocation under which they momentarily lost self-control.'[64] They further charged that 'Most of the measures taken under Martial Law ... were unnecessary, cruel, oppressive and in utter disregard of the feeling of the people ...' and cited the

Jallianwallah Bagh massacre as a 'calculated piece of inhumanity towards utterly innocent and unarmed men'.[65] The report demanded the dismissal of O'Dwyer, General Dyer and other officials connected with the martial-law administration and asserted that the Viceroy should be recalled. It also demanded that fines imposed on individuals and indemnities imposed on cities be remitted.

The publication of the report stirred deep feelings in India and the demand for the dismissal of guilty officer was echoed throughout the country. Popular apprehensions regarding official action were compounded by the publication shortly thereafter of the official report on the conduct of the martial law administration. The report of the official inquiry led by Lord Hunter was divided in its verdict. The majority report, representing the views of the British members of the committee of inquiry, criticized the action of General Dyer at Jallianwallah Bagh as a mistaken conception of duty, but stated that there was a danger of widespread rebellion in the Punjab and under the circumstances the proclamation of martial law was justified. The Indian members of the committee, however, disagreed with its findings and condemned the measures adopted by the martial law administration. The case of General Dyer became the focus of public debate. The government of India considered the Hunter committee's report, and concluded that General Dyer's action was indefensible and it was thus unwise to let him continue in office. General Dyer was prematurely retired in March 1920, but official action against him became the subject of a debate in Westminster. Sir Winston Churchill supported the government of India's action and described the Jallianwallah Bagh massacre as a 'monstrous event', but the House of Commons passed a motion against Dyer with only a small majority. The House of Lords, on the other hand, vindicated Dyer with a majority vote. Though the government of India stuck by its decision, public support for Dyer in England was viewed by Indians with grave misgivings. For Indians, the raising of a large fund for General Dyer by his supporters in England undermined the credibility of British justice.

Since the end of the war, Indian Muslims had been becoming increasingly distressed at the treatment accorded to the Sultan of Turkey, the Khalifa or spiritual head of the Muslims, by the

Allies. The publication of reports regarding the proposed Turkish peace terms towards the end of 1919, which threatened the dismemberment of the Turkish empire, had been the subject of considerable consternation in Muslim circles. In November 1919 the All India Khilafat Conference was held at Delhi and it was resolved to begin non-co-operation with the government unless the Khilafat question was satisfactorily settled. The Khilafatists demanded the maintenance of the temporal authority and religious prestige of the Khalifa, which implied the unrestricted jurisdiction of the Sultan of Turkey over Muslim holy places, including Palestine, Mesopotamia and Arabia, and the continued sovereignty of Muslim states. In January 1920 a Muslim deputation presented an address to the Viceroy on their demands, and subsequently a deputation proceeded to Europe to present the views of Indian Muslims to the British government. The deputation was informed that Turkey could not be accorded deferential treatment or be permitted to maintain its control over lands which were not Turkish. Their failure in receiving sympathetic consideration for their demands had a significant impact on Khilafatists in India. A British intelligence report noted, 'The receipt of the news in India of the lack of success of this delegation, coupled with numerous press telegrams which appeared at about the same time foretelling drastic treatment for Turkey, greatly strengthened the position of Khilafat propagandists in India, and the effect of their agitation became more and more extensive.'[66] The publication of the Turkish peace terms in May 1920 became the subject of bitter agitation among Muslims and the British government was attacked for being a party to such harsh terms. The Central Khilafat Committee issued a manifesto announcing that it proposed to begin non-violent non-co-operation with the government of India which included the return of honorary titles and posts, the resignation of posts in the civil service, police and army, and a refusal to pay taxes until the 'wrong was redressed'. Under the direction of Gandhi, the agitation over the Khilafat question was coupled with Indian resentment over government action in the Punjab and provided the basis of a new phase of Indian nationalism and intense anti-government propaganda.

In 1920 the *rabi* or spring harvest was fair, but the failure of the monsoons had disastrous consequences for the *kharif* or autumn crop. The total area sown was reduced by some 16 per cent on that cultivated the previous year. The prices of wheat, barley and grain rose rapidly, until they were some 30 per cent higher than their already high level in 1919, and provided a further impetus to disaffection with the Government.[67] Hindu, Muslim and Sikh politicians, each group motivated by their own particular aspirations and grudges, joined forces in a campaign against the government. Describing this movement, Jawaharlal Nehru later wrote, 'this nationalism was itself a composite force and behind it could be distinguished a Hindu nationalism, a Muslim nationalism party looking beyond the frontiers of India, and, what was more in consonance with the spirit of the time, an Indian nationalism. For the time being they overlapped and all pulled together.'[68]

For the Tat Khalsa elite the formation of the Central Sikh League marked the beginning of an active involvement in politics. Educated Sikhs, spurred by their particular grievances and by the contagion of the prevalent spirit of nationalism, participated with increasing enthusiasm in the mounting campaign of anti-government agitation. At the individual level they collaborated with Hindu and Muslim nationalist politicians in organizing protest meetings and demanding redress for the martial-law excesses in the Punjab, in addition to voicing their own demands, and promised moral support for the Khilafat agitation.[69] The new Central Sikh League also asserted itself on issues of national importance. The publication of the Hunter committee report brought a prompt response from the league, which charged that the report had 'attempted to whitewash the officials of the Indian and the Punjab Governments connected with the introduction, continuation and administration of the Martial Law in the Punjab, even against the weight of published evidence'.[70] The league expressed its regret that 'no adequate punishment has yet been meted out to the several officers who were guilty of unpardonable excesses and gross abuse of power and strongly urges upon the Government the necessity of doing so immediately in order to vindicate the National self-respect of India'.[71]

By the summer of 1920 a number of district Sikh Leagues had been set up. Organization at the local level pulled into the political arena a variety of politically conscious and disaffected Sikhs. Returned emigrants, released Ghadrites and demobilized soldiers swelled the ranks of politically active Sikhs, and the local Sikh Leagues became forums for nationalist propaganda. Though neither the Central Sikh League nor any of its local branches officially endorsed the adoption of non-violent non-co-operation with the government, the move towards militancy was apparent in the proceedings of some local Sikh Leagues. At public meetings held that under the auspices of local Sikh Leagues, it was reported,

> Harrowing accounts were given of such matters as the treatment accorded to the Komagatamaru Sikhs, and to the returned emigrants who were depicted as worthy Sikhs and innocent victims of the brutality of Government. What hope, it was asked, could there lie in approaching such a Government by constitutional means; the Sikhs had made great sacrifices in the war and received nothing in return; they had now become tired of submitting petitions and should assert themselves and take up a stronger attitude.[72]

The evolution of Sikh communal consciousness had led to political organization. The political expression of communal aspirations and grievances bred militancy and saw the emergence of a Khalsa nationalism.

This spirit of an essentially communal Khalsa nationalism was manifest in the growing numbers of Sikhs who attended the Sikh League's proceedings at the local level, and in the widespread adoption of Khalsa symbols denoting solidarity and militancy in the name of the faith. Sikhs began in increasing numbers to wear black turbans (a symbol of militancy) and *kirpans*. The wearing of *kirpans* by Sikh soldiers in the army provided a further point of conflict with the government. In May 1920 the Punjab government reported, 'A young sepoy of the Depot of the 34th Pioneers at Sialkot appeared on parade with a large kirpan, which he refused on religious grounds to give up. He was sentenced by court martial to one year imprisonment for insubordination ... The Sikh League are interesting themselves in the case.'[73] Khalsa nationalism was vividly expressed in the revival of the Akali cult. The Akalis, a militant order of ascetics, were *nihang* or reckless soldiers of the *akal*, or immortal, and had played a significant role in Sikh history. They ascribed their origin to the martial guru, Gobind Singh, and served as self-appointed guardians of the faith. They adhered rigidly to Khalsa precepts and rejected Hindu rites completely. Under Phula Singh Akali, one of Maharaja Ranjit Singh's great commanders, they rose to a position of considerable prominence and were feared and respected. However, following the death of Phula Singh, Ranjit Singh did much to reduce their authority, and subsequently the order lost importance and its numbers dwindled and virtually disappeared. The few Akalis who remained were regarded as harmless cranks. In the summer of 1920 Akalis carrying large *kirpans* began to appear at public gatherings. Though their appearance was not taken seriously by the government, it was indicative of the new spirit permeating the Khalsa.

Khalsa nationalism was rapidly translated into militant action with the revival of agitation regarding the Rikabganj *gurdwara* in Delhi. Towards the end of 1912 the government had, in the course of construction of the new capital at Delhi, acquired property attached to the *gurdwara* and demolished an old boundary wall on it. This action elicited sharp condemnation from Tat Khalsa militants and, at the annual Sikh Educational Conference organized by the Chief Khalsa Diwan in 1914, militants attempted to introduce a resolution severely criticizing the government for this sacrilege. Leaders of the Chief Khalsa Diwan, however, were not anxious to provoke a conflict with the government and the resolution was disallowed and the dissenters forced to leave. The agitation persisted and gathered extensive support, and eventually the Chief Khalsa Diwan was compelled to request the government to restore the wall to its original condition. However, with the outbreak of the war, the controversy subsided and no action was taken. In July 1920 the question of the dismantled wall of the Rikabganj *gurdwara* was revived. At a meeting held at Tarn Taran under the auspices of the local Sikh League, the Sikhs were reminded that the Rikabganj *gurdwara* marked the martyrdom of the ninth guru, Tegh Bhadaur, and an appeal was made for the formation of a *shahidi dal*, a band of martyrs willing to sacrifice their lives, if necessary, for the purpose of forcibly rebuilding the demolished wall. The campaign was initiated largely under the direction of Teja Singh Samundri, born in 1881, who had served as an instructor in the army and subsequently resigned to farm family land at Lyallpur. He had been prominent in earlier protests regarding the Rikabganj *gurdwara*. Some eighty Sikhs immediately volunteered their names and recruitment for the programme continued briskly. Meanwhile, the government attempted to forestall militant action by reaching a settlement of the controversy with a local Sikh organization in Delhi. However, Tat Khalsa politicians refused to recognize the authority of this organization to negotiate a settlement and plans for the dispatch of the *shahidi dal* to Delhi were stepped up. Faced with the possibility of a confrontation with Sikh militants over an issue of religious significance, the government gave in. In January 1920 the wall was rebuilt at the expense of the maharaja of the Sikh princely state of Nabha.

Both sides saved face, but the campaign had caught the imagination of the Tat Khalsa, and militant action with the support of religious volunteers was a tactic employed again in October 1920 over the controversy regarding the management of the Babe-de-Ber shrine in Sialkot District. Following the judgement of the district court upholding the appointment of the *mahant*'s grandson as manager of the shrine in June 1919, the reformers instituted another suit to eject the *mahant*. The second attempt at litigation bogged down over a demand for high court fees, and local reformers resolved to resort to direct action. A Khalsa *sewak jatha*, a group of men pledged to the services of the Khalsa *panth*, was formed to remove the *mahant*. In October the *sewak jatha* forcibly occupied the *gurdwara*, ejected the *mahant*, and a committee of local Sikhs was appointed to administer the shrine. The local authorities agreed to leave the reformers in control of the shrine pending a final settlement.[74]

Meanwhile, in September 1920 a special session of the Indian National Congress had been held at Calcutta. The Congress condemned the attitude of the government on the Khilafat question and its inaction with respect to repeated demands for the redress of excesses committed in the Punjab, and initiated a campaign of progressive non-violent non-co-operation with the government. With the publication of the *Further Rules and Regulations under the Government of India Act* in June 1920, the exact political representation accorded to various communities and details of the franchise to be employed had been delineated. The boycott of the reformed councils became an issue in practical politics. Largely through the initiative of Gandhi, the Congress resolved not to participate in the coming elections in protest.

For Sikh politicians the final form of political representation accorded to them under the reforms came as a great blow. From the outset they had viewed the formulation of details of political representation in the Punjab with increasing anxiety. In May 1920 they had reiterated their demands for substantial Sikh political representation in the provincial legislature in an address to the government of India. The proceedings of the Reforms Advisory Committee of the Punjab government in June 1920 had further given cause for alarm. The government consulted Gurbux Singh Bedi and Arur Singh, manager of the Golden Temple, as representatives of Sikh religious opinion on the subject of the definition of the term 'Sikh' to be employed for elections to the legislative councils. They recommended that the government refrain from placing any definite interpretation on the term and, as suggested by the Southborough committee, accept the declaration of any person that he was a Sikh in the compilation of electoral rolls.[75] The testimony of Arur Singh and Gurbux Singh Bedi created a furore in Tat Khalsa circles. Protest meetings were held throughout the province condemning the proposal, and resolutions were passed insisting that only Kesdhari Sikhs could justifiably be considered Sikhs. The audacity of Arur Singh, as a government-appointed manager of the Golden Temple, in endorsing the Southborough committee's proposal in particular provoked a violent reaction. In July 1920 the newspaper the *Sikh* commented:

> our impression hitherto was that being a happy go lucky Sardar, a member or representative of a family of note, the authorities had selected [Arur Singh] in connection with the management of the Darbar Sahib, which they could ill afford to entrust to a bona fide representative body of the Panth ... we thought ... that he was concerned with the administrative affairs of the Sikh Holiest of the Holy, and was as aloof from the religious side as the Deputy Commissioner of Amritsar himself. But now, to our utter amazement ... we learn that he is our religious guide too! ... while the selection or election of a religious guide in case of all other communities rests entirely with the people concerned, in case of the poor helpless Sikhs the task of selecting a religious guide ... is reserved to a Christian Government.[76]

In a desperate attempt to secure their demands for political representation, in July 1920 a Sikh deputation had proceeded to London and addressed the Secretary of State for India on the subject of Sikh demands. The deputation failed to achieve its objective and its only consolation was that the joint parliamentary committee considering the reforms had on its own initiative increased Sikh representation in the provincial legislative council by two seats. Sikh militants realized that the small proportion of seats allocated to the community would prove ineffectual for pressing Sikh communal demands in the face of opposition from the other communities, and they therefore resolved to adhere to the Congress resolution and withdrew from the elections.

Only 26 per cent of Sikhs entitled to vote for candidates for the provincial legislature exercised their vote. The majority of Sikhs who stood for election to the Punjab Legislative Council were independents and not noted for their political affiliation to any group, and, with the exception of Mahtab Singh, a public prosecutor of the Punjab High Court, and one other candidate, the majority of Sikh candidates did not command any degree of mass support.[77] Under the terms of the franchise, Sahajdhari Sikhs were entitled to vote in the special Sikh constituencies if they so desired. However, Sahajdhari Sikhs did not register themselves in the Sikh electoral rolls in significant numbers. Faced with a choice of entering themselves either as Sikhs or as Hindus, Sahajdhari Sikhs who considered Sikhism to be but a part of the Hindu faith registered themselves as Hindus. The vast majority of Sikh members of the provincial legislative council were thus Khalsa Sikhs sympathetic to the Tat Khalsa.

In October 1920 the second session of the Central Sikh League was held in Lahore. The league's proceedings were profoundly marked by the prevalent spirit of Khalsa nationalism and anti-government feeling. The first session of the league had been notable for its deliberate moderation. Sikh politicians, new to the political arena, had understandably proceeded with caution. Moreover, with the final form of the reformed legislative councils still unclear and the nature and extent of Sikh representation still in the balance, Sikh politicians had been anxious not to precipitate matters. Developments since the inaugural session of the Sikh League removed the basis of earlier moderation. From the Sikhs' point of view, they had been treated with gross injustice in the matter of political representation and the government continued to regard other legitimate Sikh demands with an insensitivity which amounted to disdain for deep-felt popular grievances. The league's proceedings, attended by a large number of Sikh delegates from the local Sikh Leagues, proved a forum for an outburst of popular bitterness. Under the influence of Gandhi, who also attended the session, the league passed a resolution initiating a programme of non-violent non-co-operation with the government on lines similar to those endorsed by the Congress. Gajjan Singh, the league's president, and Captain Gopal Singh, its vice-president, both of whom had come under severe criticism from various district leagues during the previous few months for their support of a fund being collected for the outgoing Lieutenant-Governor, Michael O'Dwyer, were ousted from their offices and militant politicians elected in their stead.

Kharak Singh, born in 1867, the son of an army contractor, was elected to preside over the Central Sikh League. Though Kharak Singh had not hitherto played a leading role in Sikh politics, his career reflected the movements towards identity and militancy apparent within the Sikh community during the previous few decades. Among one of the earliest graduates of Punjab University, Kharak Singh had been intimately associated with the Tat Khalsa movement. He had served as chairman of the reception committee of the fifth Sikh Educational Conference, held at Sialkot in 1912, and subsequently presided over the same body. Recently he had been associated with the Khalsa *sewak jatha* and the efforts of militant reformers at Sialkot.

The impact of the adoption of a policy of progressive non-co-operation by the Central Sikh League was immediate. Sikh militants joined in the propaganda campaign with vigour. Sikh grievances were added to the list of Indian demands, and government was soundly condemned. The effect of the agitation was rapidly felt at the Khalsa College, Amritsar, where the faculty presented an ultimatum to the government to remove official control over the college council or accept their immediate resignations, and Sikh students went on strike in a similar protest.[78] However, for the Sikh community the advent of non-co-operation with government was quickly surpassed by the initiation of a militant campaign for *gurdwara* reform by an organisation which styled itself as the central committee for the management of Sikh shrines.

For the previous few years demands for control by the Sikh community of the management of the Golden Temple had been increasing in intensity. Reformers pointed with growing bitterness to the 'non-Sikh' customs prevalent in Sikh ceremony at the premier Sikh shrine and to the practice of discrimination against low-caste Sikhs by the Temple's *pujaris* (priests). The emergence of a Khalsa nationalism provided additional fervour to accusations of misconduct directed at the manager of the Golden Temple. Arur Singh's generous treatment of General Dyer and his recent testimony before the Reforms Advisory Committee of the Punjab government only heightened the urgency for reform. In July 1920 the Punjab government issued a communiqué proclaiming its intention to withdraw its association with the management of the Golden Temple and stated: 'It has been decided to defer the action until the Reform scheme has been brought into operation. The elected representatives of Sikh constituencies will then be consulted as to any changes which may be contemplated.'[79] This announcement failed to appease the Tat Khalsa reformers, who demanded the immediate resignation of the government-appointed manager. Arur Singh was himself perturbed at the wave of resentment directed at him, and the government moved to quell dissension by instructing him to proceed immediately on leave. Sunder Singh Ramgarhia, a honorary magistrate, was appointed temporary manager of the shrine pending formulation of a new scheme for its administration.

Early in October 1920 an otherwise routine dispute brought matters dramatically to a head. The Khalsa *biradri* held its annual meeting at Amritsar, which was accompanied by the public baptism of low-caste men into the Khalsa in a manner similar to the *shuddhi* ceremonies of the Arya Samaj. The low-caste and outcaste converts had been promised an end to discrimination against them within the Khalsa brotherhood, but the matter had to be put to the test. The administrators of the Golden Temple had repeatedly made it clear that such converts would not be permitted within the precincts of the shrine, but members of the Khalsa *biradri* accompanied the proselytes in procession to the shrine and demanded entry. A theological dispute followed, the Granth Sahib was consulted, and the *pujaris* were forced to withdraw. The reformers occupied the Akal Takht and charged the *pujaris* with sacrilege for leaving the Granth Sahib unattended. Shortly thereafter a provisional committee was appointed to manage the shrine. The committee consisted of nine members, including Professor Teja Singh of the Khalsa College at Amritsar, who had been prominent among recent disturbances at the college, Teja Singh Bhuchar, a fanatical Sikh reformer who had been active in the recruitment of the *shahidi dal* at Tarn Taran that summer, and Kartar Singh Jhabbar, a zealous Tat Khalsa reformer who had been sentenced to death for his activities during the Rowlatt *satyagrah* but subsequently released under the royal amnesty.[80]

In the second week of November 1920 the Punjab government, perturbed by recent events and anxious that government indifference should not imply a 'surrender to the advocates of ultra-Sikhism', consulted with the Maharaja of Patiala and announced the appointment of a provisional advisory committee of thirty-six members to propose rules regarding the management of the Golden Temple, and, pending the formulation of definite proposals, to supervise its management. The committee was composed entirely of Khalsa Sikhs, and was drawn from members of reputable Sikh landed and aristocratic families. It also included Sunder Singh Ramgarhia, the recently appointed manager of the Golden Temple. In response Sikh militants immediately announced a public meeting of Sikhs to elect a committee to manage the Golden Temple. Invitations to attend the gathering were sent to various Singh Sabhas, Sikh schools, Sikh regiments in the army, and to other Sikh religious organizations. On 16 November 1920 a large gathering was held at the Golden Temple and a committee of 175 members was elected. The gathering expressed its disapproval of the official provisional advisory committee on the ground that it had been appointed without consultation with the Sikh community, but in an effort to avoid further controversy the members of the committee appointed by the government were included in the new committee. Further, moderate Chief Khalsa Diwan leaders were elected as leading office-holders of the committee. Sunder Singh Majithia was elected president and Harbans Singh of Attari appointed vice-president. The election of this new management committee was based on the allocation of a definite number of seats to each district of the Punjab and to each Sikh princely state. The Punjab government noted with relief that the formation of the committee had proceeded along 'constitutional lines' and did not interfere further in its proceedings.[81]

Spurred by their success in gaining control of the Golden Temple, Sikh reformers rapidly moved towards greater militancy. Groups of reformers who called themselves Akalis were formed in various parts of the province. The Akali *jatha*s, as the groups were known, were of 'mushroom growth and did not contain any element of stability', noted an official intelligence report.[82] They were independent units and adopted the name of the area to which they belonged. Most of their members adopted Akali symbols and carried large *kirpan*s and hatchets and pledged themselves to the service of the Sikh *panth*. In December 1920 militant members of the new *gurdwara* committee met, renamed the committee the Shiromani Gurdwara Prabhandak Committee (SGPC) and resolved to 'reform' forcibly mismanaged *gurdwara*s and eject corrupt *mahant*s. Though the original committee comprised 179 members, including thirty-six appointed by the government, the SGPC was in fact dominated by a small caucus of militant individuals. Its president elect, Sunder Singh Majithia, for example, had virtually no contact with the committee itself.

The SGPC instituted an organization known as the Shiromani Akali Dal, a centralized body to direct the activities of Akali *jatha*s, subordinate to the SGPC. A vigorous campaign of publicity to encourage the recruitment of Akalis was instituted. With the failure of September rains, drought conditions persisted in the Punjab and the disaffected Sikh peasantry proved a fertile ground for the recruitment of Akalis, as did the large number of returned emigrants.[83]

The next few weeks witnessed a flurry of activity by the Akali *jatha*s. In December 1920 a *gurdwara* in Sheikhupura was seized, and within a few days two other *gurdwara*s were occupied. In each instance the pattern followed was the same. Akalis brandishing *kirpan*s and axes arrived at the shrine, occupied it and ejected the *mahant* in charge, and appointed a local committee of Tat Khalsa for its management. Only strict Khalsa Sikhs were to be permitted to serve in the shrine and 'non-Sikh' elements prevalent in the mode of worship were purged.

Notes to Chapter 3

1 M. S. Leigh, *The Punjab and the War* (Lahore, 1922), pp. 41, 44–5.
2 Leigh, *Punjab and War*, pp. 37–8.
3 Leigh, *Punjab and War*, pp. 54, 140–74, 184–95, 196–7.
4 Leigh, *Punjab and War*, pp. 140–74.

5 Fortnightly Report, 15 Dec. 1915, GOI, Home (Political), Deposit, no. 35 of Jan. 1916.

6 Quoted in *The Congress Punjab Enquiry, 1919–1920*, Report of the Commissioners appointed by the Punjab Sub-Committee of the Indian National Congress (Lahore, 1920), vol. 1, p. 16.

7 David Brief, 'Recruitment and the Punjab, 1914–1918', unpublished paper presented to the South Asia History Seminar, Oxford University, 1977.

8 Brief, 'Recruitment'.

9 Fortnightly Report, 31 Jan. 1918, GOI, Home (Political), Deposit, no. 39 of Mar. 1918.

10 *Congress Punjab Enquiry, 1919–1920*, vol. 1, p. 17.

11 Quoted in Ker, *Political Trouble*, pp. 224–5. Hindu was the general term used by the American Press for all Indians.

12 Ker, *Political Trouble*, p. 224.

13 Weekly Report, DCI, 27 Apr. 1915, GOI, Home (Political) proceedings B, nos 416–19 of Apr. 1915.

14 Fortnightly Report, 31 Mar. 1915, GOI, Home (Political), Deposit, no. 39 of Apr. 1915. See also Fortnightly Report, 15 Jan. 1915, GOI, Home (Political), Deposit, no. 54 of Mar. 1915; Fortnightly Report, 31 July 1915, GOI, Home (Political), Deposit, no. 28 of Aug. 1915.

15 Isemonger and Slattery, *Ghadr Conspiracy*, p. 87. See also Fortnightly Report, 31 Mar. 1915, GOI, Home (Political), Deposit, no. 39 of Apr. 1915; Fortnightly Report, 15 Apr. 1915, GOI, Home (Political), Deposit, no. 48 of May 1915.

16 *Report on Indian Constitutional Reforms, 1918* (London, 1918), p. 1.

17 *Indian National Congress, 1917*, G. A. Nateson & Co (Madras, 1917), vol. 2, p. 180.

18 *Khalsa Advocate* (6 Oct. 1917).

19 Memo from Sunder Singh Majithia, Hon. Sec., Chief Khalsa Diwan, to Chief Sec., Punjab Govt, 3 Jan. 1917, GOI, Home (Political) proceedings B, nos 44–5 of Mar. 1917.

20 Memo from Sunder Singh Majithia.

21 Memo from Sunder Singh Majithia.

22 *The Punjabee* (20 Oct. 1917), Punjab Government, *Selections from the Indian Newspapers Published in the Punjab*, vol. 30, no. 43.

23 *Tribune* (7 Oct. 1917). For similar views see also *Desh* (1 Nov. 1917), *Urdu Bulletin* (2 Nov. 1917), Punjab Govt., *Selections*, vol. 30, no. 45.

24 S. P. Sen (ed.), *Dictionary of National Biography* (Calcutta, 1974), vol. 4, pp. 323–5.

25 *Khalsa Akhbar* (9 Nov. 1917), Punjab Govt, *Selections*, vol. 30, no. 46.

26 *Khalsa Samachar* (5 Apr. 1917), Punjab Govt, *Selections*, vol. 30, no. 16. See also *Loyal Gazette* (1 July 1917), Punjab Govt, *Selections*,

vol. 30, no. 28; *Loyal Gazette* (15 July 1917), *Selections*, vol. 30, no. 31.

27 *Punjab Darpan* (15 Aug. 1917), Punjab Govt, *Selections*, vol. 30, no. 35.

28 *Report on Indian Constitutional Reforms, 1918*, p. 150.

29 *Khalsa Advocate* (13 July 1918).

30 *Khalsa Advocate* (13 July 1918).

31 *Loyal Gazette* (14 July 1918), Punjab Govt, *Selections*, vol. 31, no. 29; *Khalsa Samachar* (18 July 1918), Punjab Govt, *Selections*, vol. 31, no. 31.

32 *Khalsa Advocate* (13 July 1918).

33 *Punjab Darpan* (10 July 1918, 24 July 1918), Punjab Govt, *Selections*, vol. 31, no. 31; *Loyal Gazette* (14 July 1918), Punjab Govt, *Selections*, vol. 31, no. 29.

34 Statement of Gajjan Singh in *Punjab Legislative Council Debates, 1918* (Lahore, 1919), p. 528.

35 *Punjab Debates, 1918*, p. 528.

36 Letter from the Offg Additional Sec., Punjab Govt, to GOI, Home Dept, 23 Nov. 1918, in the *Report of the Committee Appointed by the Secretary of State for India to Inquire into Questions Connected with the Franchise and Other Matters Relating to Constitutional Reforms* (London, 1919), vol. 1, pp. 206–7, 211.

37 *Report of Committee on Franchise*, p. 7.

38 *Khalsa Advocate* (17 Nov. 1917).

39 *Loyal Gazette* (25 May 1919), Punjab Govt, *Selections*, vol. 32, no. 22.

40 *Khalsa Advocate* (3 June 1919).

41 *Panth Sewak* (26 Feb. 1919), Punjab Govt, *Selections*, vol. 32, no. 10. See also *Khalsa Advocate* (14 Feb. 1919).

42 *Loyal Gazette* (9 Feb. 1919), Punjab Govt, *Selections*, vol. 32, no. 7; *Loyal Gazette* (28 Sept. 1919), Punjab Govt, *Selections*, vol. 32 no. 41.

43 *Sikh Sepoy* (20 June 1919), Punjab Govt, *Selections*, vol. 32 no. 26; *Punjab Darpan* (25 June 1919), Punjab Govt, *Selections*, vol. 32 no. 28.

44 *Loyal Gazette* (26 Jan. 1919), Punjab Govt, *Selections*, vol. 32 no. 5); *Punjab Darpan* (19 Feb. 1919), Punjab Govt, *Selections*, no. 8.

45 *Tribune* (18 Mar. 1919).

46 *Tribune* (30 Dec. 1919).

47 *Report of the Committee Appointed by the Government of India to Investigate Revolutionary Conspiracies in India* (Calcutta, 1918), p. 180.

48 Mahatma Gandhi to V. S. Srinivas Shastri, 9 Feb. 1919, Mahatma Gandhi, *Collected Works* (Ahmedabad, 1963), vol. 15, pp. 87–8.

49 *Tribune* (11 Mar. 1919).

50 Quoted in P. C. Bamford, *Histories of the Non-Cooperation and Khilafat Movements* (Delhi, 1925), p. 9.
51 *Tribune* (16 Feb. 1919, 11 Mar. 1919).
52 Professor Brij Narain, 'Unrest in the Punjab, its economic causes', *Tribune* (3 Aug. 1919).
53 GOI, *1921 Census Report*, Punjab, vol. 1, p. 69.
54 Fortnightly Report, 31 May 1919, GOI, Home (Political), Deposit, no. 37 of July 1919.
55 Fortnightly Report, 30 Apr. 1919, GOI, Home (Political), Deposit, no. 47 of July 1919.
56 Ian Colvin, *The Life of General Dyer* (London, 1929), pp. 201–2; *Civil and Military Gazette* (20 Jan. 1920).
57 Fortnightly Report, 15 Oct. 1919, GOI, Home (Political), Deposit, no. 14 of Nov. 1919.
58 See *Tribune* (13 Dec. 1919, 16 Dec. 1919, 17 Dec. 1919, 18 Dec. 1919, 23 Dec. 1919, 25 Dec. 1919).
59 *Tribune* (5 Dec. 1919, 10 Dec. 1919).
60 *Tribune* (24 Jan. 1920).
61 *Tribune* (24 Jan. 1920).
62 *Tribune* (24 Jan. 1920).
63 *Congress Punjab Enquiry, 1919–1920*, vol. 1, p. 157.
64 *Congress Punjab Enquiry, 1919–1920*, p. 23.
65 *Congress Punjab Enquiry, 1919–1920*, p. 158.
66 Bamford, *Non-Cooperation*, p. 149.
67 *Punjab Administration Report, 1920–1921* (Lahore, 1922), pp. 5–6.
68 Jawaharlal Nehru, *An Autobiography* (London, 1936), p. 75.
69 Fortnightly report, 15 July 1920, GOI, Home (Political), Deposit, no. 105 of July 1920.
70 *Tribune* (22 July 1920).
71 *Tribune* (22 July 1920).
72 C. M. King, Offg Chief Sec., Punjab Govt, to Sec., Home Dept, GOI, 26 Mar. 1921, GOI, Home (Political) proceedings A, nos 282–315 of May 1921. See also 'Extract from Punjab Police secret abstract of intelligence', no. 27, 10 July 1920, GOI, Home (Political) proceedings, A, nos 71–2 of Aug. 1920.
73 Fortnightly Report, 31 May 1920, GOI, Home (Political), Deposit, no. 95 of July 1920; Fortnightly Report, 15 July 1920, GOI, Home (Political), Deposit, no. 105 of July 1920.
74 'The Akali Dal and the Shiromani Gurdwara Prabhandak Committee, 1921–1922', confidential memo by V. W. Smith, Supt of Police (Political), Criminal Intelligence Dept, Punjab Govt, GOI, Home (Political) proceedings, no. 459/II of 1922.
75 *Tribune* (16 July 1920, 30 July 1920).

76 *Sikh* (4 July 1920), Punjab Govt, *Selections*, vol. 33, no. 28.
77 Return showing the results of elections in India, 1921, Parliamentary Papers, Cmd 1261, 26:11 (26).
78 Fortnightly Report, 31 Oct. 1920, GOI, Home (Political), Deposit, no. 66 of Dec. 1920; Fortnightly Report, 15 Nov. 1920, GOI, Home (Political), Deposit, no. 74 of Dec. 1920.
79 *Tribune* (16 July 1920).
80 Teja Singh, *Essays in Sikhism* (Lahore, 1944), pp. 168–9, *Gurdwara Reform Movement*, pp. 163–4.
81 'The Akali Dal and SGPC'.
82 'Akali Dal and SGPC'.
83 Fortnightly Report, 15 Feb. 1921, GOI, Home (Political), Deposit, no. 12 of June 1921.

4

Solidarity and Agitation

In the face of rapidly escalating Tat Khalsa militancy the Punjab government maintained a policy of inaction. The local government was in a difficult position. While it was greatly alarmed at the spread of Khalsa fanaticism and acutely concerned with Akali disregard for the rule of law, it was anxious not to provoke a conflict between the Akalis and government which might consolidate the alliance between the nationalists and extremist Sikh reformers. On the highly volatile issue of *gurdwara* management the Punjab government's concern was primarily with being seen to pursue a policy of neutrality and non-interference pending the adoption of suitable legislation by the newly formed provincial legislative council. For the moment, the Punjab government reported to the government of India, official policy was conducted with 'a view to avoiding anything which might drive the Sikhs ... into anything like opposition to Government'.[1] Thus, *mahants* and *pujaris* apprehensive of being ousted by Akali reformers were informed that executive government had no direct role to play in the maintenance of the status quo, and that their appeals for protection could only be entertained by the civil courts. While government would not of its own accord take action to prevent a conflict, the incumbent managers of any shrine were free to apply for police protection on the basis of a private contract, or else institute judicial proceedings against specified reformers. As testimony of its good faith in seeking a settlement of the dispute over *gurdwara* management, the Punjab government announced its intention to move the provincial legislative council at the earliest opportunity to appoint a committee to investigate the controversy over *gurdwara* reform and to propose suitable legislation. The government communiqué did little to still Akali fanaticism, and three days later a group of reformers armed with axes and *kirpans* forcibly occupied the Khadaur Sahib *gurdwara* in Amritsar district and expelled the *mahant*. The seizure of yet another shrine by the Akalis accentuated tension between the *mahants* and *pujaris* and the reformers. At Khadaur Sahib there were bitter allegations of the destruction by the Akalis of Hindu idols within the *gurdwara* precincts and equally vehement denials.

Clearly more decisive official action was called for, and in another communiqué, the Punjab government announced that at the first meeting of the legislative council, Mahtab Singh, deputy-president of the council, would introduce a resolution recommending that the local government appoint a committee of inquiry to 'consider the existing management of Sikh *gurdwaras* shrines etc. and the efforts being made to alter such management and to report on the best method of settling disputes and of regulating future control of the institutions'.[2] The committee was to be constituted so as to give adequate representation to all parties concerned in the controversy. Moreover, the government announced that in order that the forthcoming resolution be implemented as rapidly as possible, a conference was to be arranged at Lahore to determine the precise questions in dispute with regard to the management of Sikh religious institutions, and where a compromise between contenders appeared possible to bring about an amicable settlement. The conference was to be attended by forty representatives of the SGPC and a similar number of delegates of the *mahants* and *pujaris*, presided over by an official nominee. The conference never met. The Tat Khalsa reformers continued to organize for the further seizure of shrines and ignored the proposal. The *mahants* and *pujaris* for their part announced a conference of their own. Their conference met and passed a resolution condemning the 'interference' of Singh Sabha reformers in the management of the Golden Temple and other *gurdwaras* and petitioned government to 'remove the Singh Sabha control and restore peace'.[3] The conflict over *gurdwara management* was leading rapidly to a polarization of opinion and organization on both sides of the dispute. Before further official initiative could be formulated, rising tension between Akali reformers and Sahajdhari Sikh *mahants* exploded violently at Nankana Sahib in the Lahore district.

Nankana Sahib occupied a premier position among Sikh places

of religious worship and pilgrimage. In addition to being the site of the Janam Asthan *gurdwara*, built to commemorate the birthplace of Guru Nanak, it had associated with it more than half a dozen shrines marking various events in the guru's childhood. The management of the Janam Asthan *gurdwara* had been the subject of considerable controversy for some years. The *mahant* of the *gurdwara*, Narain Das, had a reputation for immorality and licentiousness, and in 1918 his conduct had elicited sharp condemnation from the local congregation. Narain Das was accused of scandalous behaviour, of sacrilege and of the misuse of *gurdwara* funds with little effect. The considerable revenue derived from estates associated with the *gurdwara*, amounting to some Rs500,000 annually, made the *mahant* relatively immune from censure. Following the seizure of the Golden Temple by Akali reformers in October 1920, attention once again focused on the management of the *gurdwara* at Nankana. Public meetings were held by the reformers and resolutions were passed condemning the conduct of Narain Das. The Akali movement for the 'reform' of Sikh religious institutions by force was gaining momentum rapidly and an attack on the Janam Asthan *gurdwara* seemed imminent. Narain Das moved to safeguard his position. A conference of *mahant*s and *pujari*s was called at Nankana to formulate means to counter the Akali threat. The conference, attended by some sixty *mahant*s, resolved not to recognize the authority of the SGPC and established an organization to be known as the Udasi Mahamandal to represent their interests. Narain Das was elected to preside over the new organization, and the association instituted a newspaper known as the *Sant Sewak* in Lahore to counter Akali propaganda.[4] Narain Das had good reason to be afraid. A tirade of attacks on his conduct by the Sikh Press and a vociferous campaign of appeals to the religious fervour of the devout to end this sacrilege had created an atmosphere of growing resentment towards the management of the Janam Asthan *gurdwara*. The *mahant*'s refusal to submit to the reformers and his disdain for popular opinion intensified demands for militant action. The approaching annual religious fair to be held at Nankana seemed an appropriate moment for such action, and for Narain Das rumours of an impending attack on the shrine persisted alarmingly.

In December 1920 the Udasi Mahamandal, with the assistance

of Kartar Singh Bedi, an influential member of the Sikh landed
gentry and a religious leader of some standing, represented the
mahants' and *pujaris'* case to the government. Though not
directly concerned with the Udasi Mahamandal, Kartar Singh
Bedi had a large following among Sahajdhari Sikhs, particularly in
the Rawalpindi district, and as such his interests were in conflict
with those of the Akali reformers. The son of Sir Khem Singh
Bedi, a one-time nominated member of the Punjab Legislative
Council, Kartar Singh Bedi himself had a record of conspicuous
service to government and had been the recipient of considerable
official patronage. He had been appointed an honorary lieutenant
in the army in addition to being a civil judge and an honorary
magistrate. Kartar Singh Bedi led a deputation of the Udasi
Mahamandal to petition the Commissioner of Lahore Division.
C. M. King, for official protection of the 'right' of *mahants* and
pujaris to continue peacefully to hold offices they had held for
generations as a matter of established custom. The Commissioner
agreed that any attempt to evict a *mahant* forcibly from his office
constituted a breach of the law, but insisted that the initiative for
suitable preventive action must come from the *mahants* themselves. A *mahant* in duress, the Commissioner informed the
petitioners, might 'apply to the District Magistrate for protection
provided he pays the cost of such protection. He may also, if he
wishes ... ask for security to be taken from persons likely to use
force to him. If in spite of precautions he is ejected from his shrine
he can sue for recovery of his rights and also bring criminal
proceedings'.[5]

Repeated appeals to the Punjab government for protection
against attack brought a similar response. Meanwhile, the SGPC
considered the management of the Janam Asthan shrine and
resolved that a big *diwan* would be held at Nankana to consider
means to end its corrupt management. The committee's resolution brought a desperate appeal for official protection from the
mahant of the Janam Asthan shrine. Narain Das telegraphed the
Punjab government, 'Sikhs announced to seize Durbar Janam
Asthan forcibly, leaders have gathered ten thousand men for the
purpose, mercifully save, I am ready to bear the expenses of police
guard etc.; I will not hold myself responsible if any death
occurred on the spot, at the time of fear the gate of Durbar Sahib
will be closed, kindly send police guard immediately'.[6] The

mahant's report was considered unduly alarmist by the Punjab government and no action was taken.

The *mahant*s were in a quandry. The civil law to which they were repeatedly referred did not in fact provide effective protection in the existing situation. Action under section 107 of the criminal procedure code could only be taken with due cause against specific persons deemed as likely to cause a breach of the law, and it was impossible under the circumstances to specify which Akali *jatha* might take the initiative. Even if particular individuals or a particular group of individuals were singled out as likely to attempt the forcible expulsion of the *mahant*, and a plea made for security in lieu of good behaviour to be taken from them, another group of reformers could easily take their place. Indeed, even requests for the supply of police guards were not always complied with, for the Punjab government was not anxious to provide sanctuary to men of dubious reputation. Thus, in spite of repeated appeals by Narain Das, the nearest police post to Nankana remained eleven miles away.[7]

Narain Das took matters into his own hands. An elaborate plan for the defence of the Janam Asthan *gurdwara* was instituted. The *gurdwara* was surrounded by a high wall and its gate was fortified. In addition the *mahant* hired some eighty mercenaries to defend the shrine, and commenced stockpiling arms and ammunition. The *mahant*'s preparations gave rise to alarmist rumours, and were discussed repeatedly by the Sikh Press, which only aggravated the tension. The Udasi Mahamandal's attempts to mobilize public sympathy by publicizing a letter from the Commissioner of Lahore Division to Baba Kartar Singh Bedi which emphasized the illegality of any attempt to evict any *mahant* forcibly from his office only led to a greater polarization of both camps. By February 1921 the situation had become highly volatile. The explosion came early on the morning of 20 February. An Akali *jatha* made an unscheduled trip to Nankana and precipitated the conflict. Moments after the *jatha* entered the precincts of the *gurdwara*, the *mahant*'s men opened fire upon them without warning. Those who attempted to seek refuge within the shrine were hunted down and hacked to pieces. The dead and the dying were then collected in heaps and burnt, in an attempt to obliterate traces of the massacre. Informed by a local official of the occurrence, the Deputy Commissioner of Lahore arrived at Nankana at noon to find the remains of some 130 men still smouldering. But he could do little without the assistance of the police. On his request a contingent of troops was dispatched to Nankana, but they did not arrive until late that evening. Narain Das and twenty-six of his henchmen were arrested. The Janam Asthan *gurdwara* was placed under military guard.

News of the Nankana massacre spread like a bush fire across the countryside and aroused intense passions. Within a few hours large numbers of Akalis, embittered by reports of the barbarous slaughter of their brethren and deeply stirred by this affront to their religion, were hastening towards Nankana. They were joined by others of the faithful who journeyed to pay homage to the remains of the martyrs. The local authorities made a desperate bid to halt this influx. Access roads to Nankana Sahib were blocked, trains re-routed so as to bypass the station, and a cordon of troops deployed to isolate the area. Nevertheless, by the afternoon of the following day a thousand Akalis, including several members of the SGPC had gathered in the vicinity of the Janam Asthan shrine. They were confronted by the Deputy Commissioner of Lahore and informed that access to the shrine was temporarily barred. But the Akalis were in no mood to be dictated to and 'were apparently resolved to advance on the troops and be shot down'.[8] Government was forced to concede, and the management of the shrine was handed over to a temporary committee of Akalis of which Harbans Singh of Attari was to be president and Sunder Singh Ramgarhia vice-president. The committee was declared to be in possession of the shrine and its property pending a settlement of the matter in a court of law. The troops and police contingents sent to the area were withdrawn.

The hideous massacre at Nankana compelled the Punjab government to reassess its stance of non-involvement in potentially explosive disputes over *gurdwara* management. The government instructed all district magistrates to take temporary charge of any shrine where a controversy over its management was likely to lead to violence. Their jurisdiction in such cases was to remain in force pending a final settlement in a court of law, though provision was to be made for the proper continuance of customary worship. The government's intention was to 'enable District Magistrates to remove such shrines from the field of dispute and to enable peace to be kept without committing Government either to the reforming party or to the status quo'.[9]

Though government alacrity in making over charge of the Janam Asthan *gurdwara* to a representative committee of the SGPC served to prevent an immediate conflict with the Akalis, it did little to temper the feverish excitement generated by the massacre. Thousand of Sikhs continued to flock to Nankana to do pilgrimage and groups of armed Akalis took up residence in the neighbourhood of the shrine. The Nankana massacre was widely discussed and inevitably gave rise to a spate of rumours. It was alleged that not only had Narain Das butchered a defenceless party of religious men who had arrived at the shrine simply to perform their devotions, but that local officials were fully cognisant of the *mahant*'s designs and had in fact abetted him in his preparations. The Sikh Press voiced similar allegations. The *Sikh* in its issue of 27 February, for example, commented,

> The butcherly Narain Das maintained a regular workshop for the manufacture of chavis (billhooks) and other arms for use against the Sikhs ... four thousand chavis ... are reported to have been found in his possession, besides sixty rifles and a large quantity of ammunition ... only the other day he received a full wagon of kerosine oil. And as is well known, his preparations and movements were not secret ... But it is nothing short of a miracle, if not a mystery, that all this escaped the notice of the police, the magistrate of the station, the Deputy Commissioner and the Commissioner ... Those who know ... that the mahant and his protegés have very often been going ... to see the officials, cannot be led but to only one conclusion that all the preparations went on progressing under official connivance.[10]

A tirade of such allegations, noted the Director of the intelligence bureau of the Government of India, rapidly created 'an environment full of suspicions against the Government'.[11]

The Punjab government unequivocally expressed its abhorrence at the occurrence and the Governor, Sir Edward Maclagan, immediately promised an impartial inquiry, but, in an atmosphere thick with prejudice, official assurances of a thorough investigation quickly wore thin. A committee to investigate the incident was set up and, as a concession to Sikh opinion, Sardar Mehtab Singh was requested to make the preliminary investigations. The pro-Akali press and SGPC spokesmen were, however, quick to undermine the credibility of the inquiry committee by pointing to the association with it of several local police and Criminal Investigation Department officials alleged to have connived with the *mahant*. The Punjab government responded sharply to such persistent unsubstantiated criticism of members of the investigating body and by so doing further compounded popular suspicions. A government communiqué warned that legal proceedings would be instituted against persons challenging the credentials of investigating officials without good cause or making unfounded allegations of partisanship. Moreover, while the Sikh Press voiced demands for the censure of the Commissioner of Lahore Division, C. M. King, that arch villain, in popular belief, was promoted to joint chief secretary to the Punjab government and instructed to proceed immediately to his new appointment. For the sceptical, the scenario for a cover-up of official complicity was complete.

The massacre at Nankana brought several prominent nationalist politicians to the site, and they exploited prevalent anti-government sentiment and attempted to give it direction. At a *shahidi diwan*, a public meeting to honour the martyrs held at Nankana, Gandhi addressed the gathering and stated,

> you ... naturally suspect that high officials contemplated with equanimity if they did not encourage, the preparations of a heinous deed ... A moment's reflection must convince you that even if it is found that some Government officials were guilty of such complicity, the discovery takes you and India no further than where we stand today. You and practically the whole of India want to sweep the whole of the Government out of existence unless the system under which it is being carried on is radically altered. It would be wrong to divert the attention of any section of the nation from the main or the only issue which is before the country.[12]

Since the issue of *gurdwara* management was a subject of great controversy among the Sikh community, Gandhi suggested that the question be either resolved peacefully through the appointment of arbitration boards or else postponed until the attainment of self-government by India. Meanwhile, the Sikhs were exhorted to join in the movement of non-co-operation with the government and urged to demonstrate their discontent by boycotting the official inquiry into the Nankana massacre. The presence of prominent nationalist politicians at Nankana and their exhortations certainly served to perpetuate the intensity of anti-government feeling but their appeals for non-co-operation with the government with respect to the Nankana inquiry brought little immediate response. In expecting members of the SGPC to be guided in this instance by a concern for practical politics, these nationalists completely misjudged their deep sense of outrage. For a majority of Akali reformers the crying need for an end to irreligious practices in their religious institutions could hardly be shelved in the name of *realpolitik*. The conduct of the official inquiry might be very questionable, but to see justice go by default was totally unpalatable; they resolved to continue, though grudgingly, to assist with the investigation.

Intense resentment among the Tat Kalsa was not of course directed solely at the government. Passions evoked by the Nankana massacre found expression in greater militancy among Akali reformers, and their success in gaining control of the Janam Asthan *gurdwara* added confidence to their reinforced zeal for *gurdwara* reform. A group of Akalis visited a small shrine in Lahore city known as Sadhu Ram's *dharamsala* and subjected the *mahant* to a penance for alleged moral lapses. The following day at a large public meeting held at the shrine the reformers further attempted to intimidate the *mahant* into relinquishing all claims to the *dharamsala*. The *mahant* resisted and sought assistance from the civil court. In the absence of the local district magistrate, the superintendent of police visited the *dharamsala* and found 'the door locked, the mahant in possession and a party making preparations to assault the shrine by ladders'.[13] He ordered a police guard to be placed on the shrine. Shortly thereafter the district magistrate directed the police guard to be removed and in accordance with the Punjab government's instructions took temporary charge of the shrine. The moment the shrine was deprived of its police protection, however, the reformers disregarded this order and forcibly took possession. The local authorities had no alternative but to enforce the district magistrate's instructions; the shrine was occupied by the police and those found in unlawful possession were arrested. Government strategy to temper excitement over *gurdwara* reform with minimal official involvement was beginning to go wrong.

Meanwhile at Nankana the presence of large numbers of embittered Akalis inevitably led to periodic attacks on any legacy of the Udasi *mahant*'s authority. There were reports of the desecration of graves (*smadhs*) and religious symbols associated with the *mahant* and his predecessors and of reprisals against persons believed to have been in sympathy with Narain Das. Akali *jathas* brandishing *kirpans* roamed the countryside demonstrating their authority. Perturbed at this growing campaign of intimidation and endemic lawlessness, the Punjab government consulted with several prominent members of the SGPC. It was agreed that government would not step in to curb popular excitement provided that 'jathas ... in Nankana and its neighbourhood ... be removed within five days (and) the Committee and all other persons concerned ... (use) their influence to prevent any other ... armed bodies from coming to Nankana or to any of the villages in which the property of the shrine is situated'.[14] The SGPC did not, however, exercise the measure of control over its supporters that the agreement implied. This understanding had hardly been reached when an armed band of several hundred Akalis took forcible possession of two shrines at Nankana. The Punjab government responded by placing the shrines under the authority of the district magistrate and arresting the Akalis found in possession. The government also dispatched troops to Nankana in an attempt to control a clearly deteriorating situation and instructed all deputy commissioners that the leaders of armed *jathas* were to be identified and prosecuted under the Arms Act. The advent of official repression increased Sikh cries of injustice. The president of the SGPC, Harbans Singh of Attari, accused the government of breaking the agreement with the committee.

Meanwhile, a delegation of twelve Sikh members of the Punjab Legislative Council had visited Nankana to investigate allegations of Akali high-handedness and of police brutality. The delegation noted in a widely publicized report that several of the charges registered by the police against the Sikhs were baseless and that police action had instilled deep panic among the local population.[15] Sikh suspicions regarding government sincerity in conducting an impartial inquiry were confirmed. The Punjab government noted,

> Although some of the leading Sikh gentleman have given valuable help in the investigation, others have not worked as well as was expected with the officers conducting the enquiry. They are freely alleging incompetence and want of sympathy on the part of the investigating staff and they have resented deeply the many complaints of misbehaviour that have been made against the Sikh jathas at Nankana ... the recovery of various Gurdwaras from the Akali party [has] added to the tale of Sikh grievances.[16]

Encouraged by popular sympathy for its cause, the SGPC moved towards greater militancy. In March 1921 it decided to issue an ultimatum to the government. As the self-proclaimed representative of the *panth*, the community of the devout made supreme in temporal matters by the tenth guru, the committee demanded the right to manage *all* Sikh shrines and all property associated with them, and declared that the government must reject the claim to hereditary succession by *mahants* of any shrine.[17] It also announced that it would resort to passive resistance unless all Sikhs arrested in connection with *gurdwara* reform were released and legislation for the satisfactory management of Sikh shrines adopted within four weeks.

In the newly formed provincial legislative council, the Punjab government attempted to diffuse the situation. The education minister, Fazl-i-Hussain, conceded that, under the provisions of the existing law regarding the management of religious institutions, the judical process for preventing the mismanagement of such institutions was cumbersome and ineffective and in fact worked in favour of its incumbent manager and to the detriment of those who would reform its management. Matters relating to charitable and religious endowments were a subject transferred to the jurisdiction of provincial legislatures under the reformed constitution, and the education minister introduced a resolution in the council recommending that the Punjab government take steps to introduce a bill overhauling the law relating to charitable and religious endowments in the province. Pending the formulation of such legislation, the resolution suggested that the Governor-General of India be asked to issue an ordinance establishing a special commission to deal immediately with the conflict over *gurdwara* management. The commission to be established would consist of three members, two of whom would be non-official 'Sikh gentlemen' and its jurisdiction would extend temporarily over all disputed *gurdwara*s. The commissioners were to conduct an inquiry into disputes concerning *gurdwara* mismanagement, and, where they could effect a compromise between reformers and the *mahant* in possession of the shrine in question, their jurisdiction was to be final. Contentious cases, however, could be appealed by either party under legislation shortly to be passed by the council. Pending the settlement of disputes, the commissioners would exercise full authority over the administration and financial management of disputed shrines but would have no authority to alter the mode of worship current in the shrine in any way.[18]

The resolution was adopted the same day, but discussion in the council revealed fundamental differences between Khalsa Sikhs and representatives of Sahajdhari Sikhs and *mahant*s and *pujari*s. Speaking in support of the Akali movement for *gurdwara* reform, Dasaundha Singh, supported by Mahtab Singh, emphasized a point of crucial significance. In the matter of Sikh *gurdwara*s, he noted, the notion of 'possession' of *gurdwara* property did not apply as it might in the case of possession of secular property. Sikh *gurdwara*s and shrines were in fact the sole property of the Sikh *panth*, and not of any particular *mahant*. The *mahant* of a religious institution was only attached to it in the service of the *panth* and as such had no claim to ownership of any of the shrine's property. It was this British notion of 'possession' of property, he argued, which had wrongly been applied to Sikh religious institutions and created the problem. Further, he insisted, in so far as *mahant*s and *pujari*s laid claim to possession of Sikh *gurdwara*s or their property, all such Sikh religious institutions were in dispute. Baba Hardit Singh Bedi, brother of Kartar Singh Bedi, represented the Sahajdhari Sikh point of view. Since the controversy over *gurdwara* management was between the Tat Khalsa and Udasi Sikhs, Baba Hardit Singh Bedi urged that while corrupt *mahant*s should be removed, they must be replaced by an appointment from the same sect of Sikh. He was supported by the Hindu members of the legislative council. Ganpat Rai, who styled himself as a Sahajdhari Sikh, alleged that in the name of *gurdwara* reform one sect of Sikhs was trying to force its mode of worship on others. Since Sikhism was in fact represented by a total of five sects, Ganpat Rai insisted that the commission to be established must be representative of each sect.[19] Not surprisingly this notion of different 'sects' within the Sikh faith provoked a strong response from the Khalsa Sikhs in the council. The resolution was carried by the council, but the Sikh members with the exception of Baba Hardit Singh Bedi and Sunder Singh Majithia, the official nominee, abstained from voting. At a subsequent meeting between these Sikh members of the council and the government, the Sikh members explained that, though they supported the resolution in principle, they were not willing to endorse it until details of the legislation were formulated.

The proposal for issuing an ordinance was dropped, but a *gurdwara* bill was drafted by the Punjab government with the assistance of the Sikh members of the council and introduced in the provincial legislature. The proposed Sikh Gurdwaras and Shrines Act of 1921 empowered the establishment of a temporary board of commissioners to be appointed by the Punjab government, provided that at least two-thirds of its members be non-official Sikhs. The term 'Sikh' to be applied was not, however, defined in the bill. The board would be presided over by an official nominee and hold office for a period of three years. Its jurisdiction would extend over all disputed *gurdwaras*. The board was empowered to conduct the daily management and administration of such disputed shrines through, if necessary, a manager or managing committee appointed by it. Customary worship, however, was to remain unaltered. The board was further to conduct an inquiry into the 'origin, nature and objects of the foundation of the shrine; the value, title, conditions, management of all its estates and property; the law or custom regulating the succession to any office connected with the shrine; the nature and character of any religious or charitable duty, ceremony or observance connected therewith'.[20] The board's jurisdiction under the bill was for the duration of its tenure to be absolute and no civil suit could be entertained in connection with a shrine under its authority except with the consent of the Punjab government. Further, the board was empowered to consider proposals for the settlement of any dispute, and any solution arrived at was to be regarded as final and above contention in a court of law.[21] The objects of the bill were clear. The inquiry to be conducted by the board of commissioners was to provide the basis for subsequent permanent legislation regulating the future control of these institutions. In the interim the immediate problem regarding the management of disputed shrines could be dealt with. Thus the Punjab government noted, 'As soon as this machinery is created, this Government feels that one great incentive to violence will be removed, and that if violence is still resorted to, Government will command the fuller support of public opinion in suppressing it.'[22]

The publication of the Sikh Gurdwaras and Shrines Bill brought a cascade of protests from a variety of sources. A memorandum was presented to the Governor of the Punjab on behalf of the Punchaiti societies, or *akharas*, of Hardwar, representing the ascetic orders of Nirmalas and Udasis. These societies exercised supervision and control over *mahant*s belonging to their respective ascetic orders and had been incorporated under the Societies Registration Act XXI of 1860. The memorandum expressed apprehension at the 'movement of a certain body of men unreasonably hostile and antagonistic to all *mahant*s in general and at the certainty of this agitation developing into a very serious turn' and appealed for measures by the government to protect the interests of Udasi and Nirmala *mahant*s.[23] It rejected allegations of unchecked corrupt conduct directed at various *mahant*s and warned that 'certain religious people in the Punjab are trying to change the established and ancient order of things handed down from generations and sanctified by religious tenets and respected by a large body of disciples and followers all over India'.[24] The proper procedure for reform of religious institutions, the *mahant*s stated, was to appeal to the *akhara*s, and failing that to seek redress through the civil law. A similar protest was voiced in a resolution adopted by the *mahant*s of Kankhal, representative of various Udasi *akhara*s. The council of the Hindu Sabha, Lahore, adopted a resolution urging that any *gurdwara* commission must give adequate representation to the Hindus who also revered Sikh Gurus and the Granth Sahib.[25] Similarly, the executive committee of the Hindu Sabha, Peshawar described the proposed act as a 'hasty and extra-ordinary measure . . . absolutely uncalled for and appears as a mere concession to the opinion of the Sikh community known as Akali Sikhs or Tat Khalsas'.[26]

If opposition to the Sikh Gurdwaras and Shrines Bill from Sahajdhari Sikhs and the Hindu community was vigorous, Tat Khalsa Sikhs were equally vehement in their criticism of the proposed legislation. In fact even before the bill had been published, Professor Teja Singh had expressed the SGPC's views on any legislation based on the resolution adopted by the provincial legislative council. In a letter to the editor of the *Tribune* on 26 March 1921, he stated that any 'intervention by Government or any non-Sikhs in the management or administration of Gurdwaras will be considered as an encroachment on the religious liberty of the Sikhs'.[27] He further stated that any proposals to appoint a board of commissioners to conduct an inquiry into disputed *gurdwara*s was unacceptable, since it would in fact amount to only a veiled extension of the present defective law under which Gurdwaras are being attached and which treated the whole Sikh Panth, the rightful owners as a mere party against its servants, the mahants. The effect of such legislation will be that instead of one Sarbrah [manager], whom the Sikhs have with great difficulty ousted, there will be many Sarbrahs, and instead of one Golden Temple, the Government will be controlling all Sikh temples.[28]

At a large public meeting attended by some 7,000 Sikhs at Nankana Sahib, the SGPC announced its response to the *gurdwara* bill. It asserted that, for the proposed legislation to be acceptable to the Sikh *panth*, all members of the proposed board of commissioners must be Khalsa Sikhs, and two-thirds of these must be appointed by the SGPC. However, it refused to participate in the formulation of any legislation until all persons arrested in connection with *gurdwara* reform were released. The SGPC's stance towards the bill was supported by a series of resolutions passed by the Tat Khalsa in various parts of the province. The Singh Sabhas of Sialkot, Rawalpindi, and Peshawar City, the students and staff of the Khalsa College, Lyallpur, and public meetings of Sikhs at Ferozepur and Jhelum passed resolutions in support of the SGPC.[29]

The debate in the provincial legislative council reflected a similar division of opinion between Khalsa Sikhs and those sympathetic to Sahajdhari Sikhs. Representing the Sahajdhari Sikh point of view, Raja Narendra Nath, president of the Punjab Hindu Sabha, opposed the bill on the ground that it lent state support to religious reform and was thus in contravention of British policy of non-interference in religious affairs. He further insisted that the board of commissioners to be formed must represent each sect within the Sikh faith. The Khalsa viewpoint was predictably the contrary. Since Nirmalas, Udasis and Sahajdhari Sikhs in general were on their own admission Hindus, Mahtab Singh asserted that the Sikhs were 'not prepared to admit that Sadhus [ascetics] belonging to the Nirmala or Udasi sects possess a right of interfering in our religious affairs and wounding our sensibilities'.[30]

The bill was referred to a select committee of thirteen members, including four members sympathetic to the Tat Khalsa and three who represented the Sahajdhari Sikh case to the council. With the representatives of Sahajdhari Sikhs in a minority and the government anxious to adopt the bill as rapidly as possible, the outcome of the select committee's deliberations was predictable. The select committee's report made only two major changes to the draft bill. The composition of the board of commissioners to be appointed under the bill was laid down as (i) a non-Sikh to be appointed by the local government as president, (ii) a Sikh to be appointed by the local government, and (iii) two Sikhs to be selected by the local government from a panel of eight to be proposed by a majority of the Sikh members of the legislative council. It also suggested that the president of the board should exercise a second, or casting, vote in case of a deadlock between the Commissioners.[31] Though the select committee steered clear of attempting any definition of the term 'Sikh' to be applied, the composition of the board of commissioners to be appointed as laid out in its report was in fact a veiled concession to Tat Khalsa opinion. By drawing two of the three Sikh members of the proposed commission from a panel suggested by a majority of Sikh members of the legislative council, the government had placed the credibility of the board of commissioners above reproach. Yet, since the majority of Sikh members of the provincial legislative council were Khalsa Sikhs in sympathy with the Tat Khalsa movement, the *gurdwara* commission was bound to strongly represent their interests.

The draft *gurdwara* bill was rapidly pushed through the select committee under official pressure, but it failed to satisfy either of the two parties in conflict. Four Sikh members of the provincial legislative council, Kartar Singh, Mahtab Singh, Harnam Singh and Dasaundha Singh, appended a minute of dissent to the select committee's report. They stated,

> The feelings of the Sikhs, which we ourselves fully share, are very keen, that all members of the board should be of the Sikh faith elected or selected by the Sikh members of the Legislative Council. But we have agreed as a last resort to the constitution of the Board as given in the Bill as amended, in the hope, that the Sikh member to be nominated by the Government ... will not be one whose views may be antagonistic to the spirit of religious reform among the Sikhs. We feel bound to express our opinion on this point because the success or failure of the proposed legislation depends entirely upon the constitution of the Board.[32]

The two Hindu members of the select committee also disagreed with its report. In another minute of dissent, Raja Narendra Nath stated, the Board of Commissioners ... has been formed in such a way as to give distinct advantage and a disproportionate representation to the advanced section of the Sikhs. The presence of one Hindu and non-Sikh member on the Board will be as ineffectual as the presence of this class of member on the Select Committee has been. Whilst two members of the advanced section have to be selected from a panel to be furnished by the elected members of the Legislative Council, the orthodox section is to be represented by one member only who is to be nominated by Government.[33]

Ganpat Rai, the other Hindu member on the select committee, agreed with him.

While the division of opinion on the select committee focused on the vital question of the composition of the board of commissioners, its proceedings inevitably witnessed sharp disagreement over what was a Sikh. Members sympathetic to the Tat Khalsa insisted that since Sikhism was a separate faith, only Sikhs could be entitled to exercise control over shrines erected in memory of their gurus. While denying the existence of any sect within the Sikh faith besides the Tat Khalsa, they argued that such other persons who might revere Sikh gurus were by their own admission Hindus, did not observe the tenets of the Khalsa, and thus had no role to play in the administration of Sikh shrines. Hindu members of the committee, however, insisted that followers of the Sikh gurus included others besides the Tat Khalsa and pointed to historical tradition for support. Sahajdhari Sikhs, though they regarded themselves as Hindus and the Sikh Gurus as Hindu religious reformers, were certainly entitled to exercise a voice in the administration of shrines sacred to them. The select committee's proceedings also witnessed sharp disagreement between members over the definition of the term *gurdwara* to be adopted. With official support, the definition approved by the select committee stated that a 'Gurdwara means a Sikh place of public worship erected by or in memory of or in commemoration of any incident in the life of any of the ten Sikh Gurus'.[34] In an editorial on the select committee's proceedings, the Lahore *Tribune* summed up the controversy succinctly. In its issue of 10 April 1921 it stated,

the Sikh members begin by accepting the definition (of the term gurdwara) and proceed to argue on the basis of this definition they are entitled to complete and unreserved control of the gurdwaras and shrines included in it, and that this Bill does not give them. But the shield has another side. The other party starting from the last point, namely the failure of the Bill to give complete control to the Sikhs, proceed to argue that the definition itself is not acceptable. The very fact they say that the Government is not in a position to give the Sikhs complete control of all the gurdwaras and shrines included in the definition and admit both the necessity of having a non-Sikh president with a casting vote and a Sikh member of the board, who shall be a nominee of the Government, pure and simple, shows that the definition does not really define, that the words, however simple looking, do not convey the same meaning to all ears.[35]

In view of the failure of the legislative council to reach agreement over the *gurdwara* bill, the government had no alternative but to postpone the legislation. A resolution elucidating the government's stand on the controversy over *gurdwara* reform was adopted by the Governor of the Punjab's executive council and subsequently published in the form of an official communique'. The resolution stressed the good will demonstrated by the government towards the Sikh community and stated,

> Government desire to make clear their attitude towards the Gurdwara Prabhandak Committee as their attitude has at times been misrepresented. The Committee . . . states that it has been formed to look after all the Panthic gurdwaras within the Province and outside, and that it is entitled to make such changes as it thinks fit in the management of such shrines . . . but these claims have neither been acknowledged nor denied by Government, as such claims do not in themselves affect the relations of Government to the people. If the Committee or its agents are able, without using any intimidation or violence, and without sending organized parties of persons whose appearance at a shrine has the practical effect of intimidating the occupant, to persuade the existing incumbents to modify in a lawful manner the existing arrangements of gurdwaras and shrines, the Government has no desire whatever to interfere, and so far as such modifications may tend to secure real reform they have the sympathy and approval of the Government.[36]

Following the postponement of the *gurdwara* bill several attempts to effect a compromise between the two parties were made by the Punjab government. Once more the composition of the board of commissioners remained a stumbling block to any settlement, and consideration of the *gurdwara* bill had to be postponed indefinitely. However, the government made clear its sympathetic attitude to the settlement of *gurdwara* disputes by legal means, and instructions were issued to all civil courts in the province to give priority to litigation involving disputes over *gurdwara* management. If the number of such cases pending before the civil courts so required, the government also indicated its willingness to establish special procedures to expedite matters. Finally, the government stated, 'if further legislation is thought necessary for securing these objects, it will be open to any Sikh member of the Legislative Council to put forward a private Bill, and if the provisions of such a Bill can be shown to be of a kind likely to meet with substantial approval of the Council, the Bill will receive the sympathetic attention of Government.'[37]

However, the Punjab government's gestures of good will and its assertions of sympathy with the desire for *gurdwara* reform had little impact on the SGPC. A meeting of the SGPC held at Amritsar to discuss plans for future action was attended by only forty of the 175 members and dominated by members in favour of militant action. Despite opposition from some members, the committee resolved that in view of the government's failure to adopt suitable legislation regarding the management of Sikh *gurdwara*s, it would proceed immediately with a policy of non-co-operation with the government and resort to passive resistance against any executive opposition encountered in the pursuit of *gurdwara* reform. It was also decided that, in keeping with the non-co-operation campaign of the Indian National Congress, the SGPC would advocate the boycott of British goods. This decision was vigorously opposed by Harbans Singh of Attari, vice-president of the SGPC, who argued that such political action by the committee would detract from the religious cause of *gurdwara* reform. Following the decision on passive resistance and non-co-operation, Harbans Singh of Attari resigned his office and membership of the working committee of the SGPC in protest. Jodh Singh, another prominent member, was only induced to withdraw his resignation with some difficulty. Division within the SGPC over tactics spilled into dissension among its supporters, and at least one Singh Sabha passed a resolution in support of Harbans Singh of Attari.[38]

The split in the ranks of the SGPC resulted in the body remaining in a state of indecision as to future tactics regarding *gurdwara* reform for some months. Though the SGPC had declared its resolve to resort to passive resistance, its control over the various Akali *jatha*s was weak, and there was a danger of the *jatha*s degenerating into an indisciplined mob when meeting official opposition. Moreover, the Sikh peasantry, which had hitherto played a vital role in the composition of Akali *jatha*s was preoccupied with the commencement of the harvesting and sowing of crops. At a meeting of the SGPC on 26 June 1921, it was decided, therefore, to concentrate for the moment on seeking a fresh mandate for the committee through elections, establishing an efficient Akali organization, and increasing the strength of Akali numbers.[39]

Elections for the new SGPC, consisting of 175 members, had been completed by August 1921. The elections were conducted on a district basis and all Khalsa Sikhs were entitled to vote. Membership of the SGPC was also restricted to Sikhs who adhered strictly to the teachings of the Granth Sahib and observed the five symbols of the Khalsa. The new committee returned in the elections was dominated by members in favour of militant action. On 28 August 1921 a general meeting of the newly formed SGPC was called and a resolution reiterating the policy of non-co-operation and passive resistance adopted by the previous committee was passed with only one dissenting vote. The committee also decided that Sikh members of the legislative council should resign their seats in protest at the government's inability to pass suitable *gurdwara* legislation. Mahtab Singh, a sponsor of this resolution, shortly thereafter resigned his seat and his post of deputy-president of the Punjab Legislative Council. Kharak Singh was elected to preside over the new SGPC, Captain Ram Singh was elected vice-president, and Mahtab Singh was declared secretary. The SGPC established an executive committee of 35 members of whom 19 would form a quorum. In addition a working committee of seven members was set up. The executive committee of the new SGPC reflected the predominance of politically oriented militants in its membership.

Following the election of its office-holders, the SGPC turned its attention to the establishment of a regular Akali organization. District *gurdwara* committees, subordinate to the central committee, were set up in virtually all districts representing a substantial Khalsa Sikh population, with the object of dealing with the daily problems of *gurdwara* management in their respective districts. These district *gurdwara* committees usually consisted of seven members. Local *gurdwara* committees were also established for the management of important Sikh shrines such as the Golden Temple, the Tarn Taran *gurdwara*, and the Janam Asthan *gurdwara* at Nankana. The manager of the Nankana shrine appointed by the local managing committee and the secretaries of the Golden Temple and Tarn Taran *gurdwara* committees were appointed to serve as ex-officio joint secretaries of the SGPC.

The establishment of a regular organization provided the SGPC access to substantial funds. In addition to the monthly subscription from its members, the committee was provided with a reported sum of Rs7,000 per annum from the income of the Tarn Taran *gurdwara*, and a sum of some Rs150,000 from the funds of the Golden Temple. The committee also controlled the substantial income of the Nankana *gurdwara*s, amounting to more than Rs500,000 annually, and was able to raise significant resources by levying a charge of 10 per cent on the income of all *gurdwara*s under its charge. Access to staggering financial resources enabled the SGPC to expand its activities rapidly. To begin with, a publicity bureau was established. The primary objective of this bureau was to issue the SGPC's Press communiqués and to refute official charges whenever necessary. A publicity staff for the preparation and dispatch of such material was designated. The SGPC began publication of large numbers of religious tracts, which contained extracts from the scriptures appealing to Sikh religious fervour along with a call for support in its crusade for *gurdwara* reform, and distributed them in the rural areas.[40]

The new SGPC concentrated on marshalling its forces through a vigorous campaign of recruitment for the Akali Dal. A deputation of prominent members of the committee, including its president, Kharak Singh, and its secretary, toured the province urging Sikhs to join the movement to free their sacred *gurdwara*s from abuse. Under the auspices of the district *gurdwara* committees and such Akali organization as existed, a series of religious *diwan*s were held in the rural areas to boost Akali recruitment. The Central Akali Dal was reorganized and a working committee of eleven members set up to conduct routine business. Subordinate to the Central Akali Dal were a variety of Akali *jatha*s, though their strength and internal organization varied considerably. The Punjab government reported,

In districts in which the organization of the Akalis is well advanced it is customary to allocate a definite area to a *jatha*, individual villages or groups of villages forming distinct sub-jathas, each in charge of a jathedar who works under the instructions of the head jathedar. Elsewhere the inter-relationship of the village sub-jathas is loose and they are subordinate to a jathedar who exercises a general undefined authority over a whole district or even a larger area.[41]

Most of the *jathas* had their own rules of membership and every Akali recruit was required upon enlistment to take a sacred oath to observe the regulations of the *jatha*. Akali recruits were also required to observe the strict tenants of the Khalsa, and some *jathas* performed baptismal rites for recruits and administered a sacred oath over the Granth Sahib in addition to requiring a signature on an admission form.

In theory there were no restrictions of caste in the enlistment of Akalis, but in practice some *jathas* were exclusive to one or more castes while others did not encourage the recruitment of menials. Women, too, were enlisted to join the Akali *jathas* and become Akalans. Each *jatha* possessed its own *granthi* (scripture reader), *ragis* (singing bards) and *updeshaks* (preachers), who toured the area under its jurisdiction, encouraged recruitment and disemi-nated Akali propaganda. The *jathas* were financial independent of the SGPC, each having its own *jatha* fund. The *jathas* were expected to meet all expenses relating to enlistment and local propaganda and maintained paid agents. The *jathas* also main-tained a number of special messengers for communications with other *jathas* and with the SGPC, and in general refrained from using the state telegraph and postal networks.[42]

Recruitment for the Akali Dal proceeded rapidly. The primary factor contributing to the substantial increase in Akali numbers was the intense pride of the Sikh peasant and his deep commit-ment to his faith and religious identity inculcated by years of exposure to Singh Sabha propaganda. The success of Akali recruitment was proportionate to the success of the SGPC in convincing the illiterate Sikh peasant that his religion was in danger. Continued high prices of food grains added to popular dissent against the government and provided an impetus to Akali recruitment. Akali recruits, with the exception of the small number of paid employees, were not, however, occupied full-time in the service of the *panth*. The bulk of Akalis pursued their normal vocations and only temporarily pledged their services to a particular *jatha* when called upon.

The Akalis enlisted in the various *jatha*s reflected the occupations of the local Sikh population, much as the efficiency of their organization was related to local Sikh literacy. Since the Sikh community was dominantly an agricultural one, the composition of the Akali Dal was also overwhelmingly agriculturalist. In the predominant *jat* districts of the central Punjab, *jat* Sikhs contributed some 70 per cent of the total number of Akalis enlisted. In the Rawalpindi District, however, where the Sikh community was largely occupied in trade, traders provided the major source for Akali enlistment. In Jullunder District, where the returned emigrants were most numerous, emigrants provided the basis for the Akali movement. The Doab Akali *jatha*, encompassing the districts of Jullunder, Hoshiarpur and Kapurthala State, was led by Piara Singh, a returned emigrant. In areas where the local Sikh population was well-to-do and literate, Akali organization was superior. Thus an official report commented,

> The Jathas in the Bar ilaqa, where the colonists are in affluent circumstances and the proportion of literates is considerable, show signs of careful organization. Their respective spheres of activity are clearly defined, their directing committees are regularly appointed and know their work, and each Akali understands to whom he is subordinate. In the Rawalpindi district, where the vast majority of the Akalis consist of educated Khatri Sikhs, a similar state of affairs exists.[43]

In districts such as Gujranwala on the other hand where the standard of literacy was comparatively low, it was noted, 'the relationship[s] of the small village sub-jathas are loosely defined, the registers are not properly maintained and the district jathedar in the absence of a competent working committee exercises a vague authority over his followers'.[44] The appeal of Akali propaganda cut across caste and class boundaries and affected varied sections of the community. But the Punjab government noted, 'The brains behind the Akali movement are supplied neither by the Jats nor the menials, but by the educated Sikh townsmen of the professional trading and shopkeeper classes. Their environment, their upbringing and the superior educational facilities which they enjoy have combined to secure for them the political leadership of the Sikh community.'[45]

In September 1921 in an attempt to stimulate Akali recruitment and inject greater enthusiasm into the movement for *gurdwara* reform, the SGPC called for the establishment of a *shahidi dal*, a band of martyrs who were prepared to sacrifice everything for the *panth*. The *shahidi dal* was to have a strength of 5,000 men, and a quota of volunteers for each district was fixed. This body was to be used on occasions when there was a danger of conflict with the government, and its members were pledged to passive resistance. The response to this new demand for volunteers varied considerably, but in the districts of Lahore and Amritsar, in particular, it was reported that Akalis joined in large numbers.

Though the enormous success of Akali recruitment was not immediately apparent to the government, the development of a regular Akali organization caused considerable alarm among district officers. In August 1921 the Deputy Commissioner of Lahore reported to the local government, 'I am convinced that 95 per cent or more of the Akalis I have seen ... are out and out enemies of Government', and warned that the present lull in Akali activity was only temporary.[46] Other district officers also expressed their apprehensions and urged that the entire Akali organization be declared illegal at the first signs of trouble. Their apprehensions proved well founded and in September 1921 the movement for *gurdwara* reform escalated rapidly with a series of forcible seizures of shrines by the Akalis. This new phase of Akali activity provided a vivid demonstration of the effectiveness of the Akali organization built up during the previous few months.

On 23 September an Akali *jatha* led by Bhag Singh, pleader of Gurdaspur, attempted to evict the *mahant* of Baba Budha Shrine at Teja in Gurdaspur District for allegedly breaking conditions of righteous conduct imposed upon him by the Akalis in February. The attack was resisted by the *mahant*'s supporters, but within hours bands of armed Akalis numbering some 1,000 men were congregating at Teja village. The Akalis occupied the *gurdwara*, and the local district magistrates instituted proceedings against them. Within a few days, however, a neighbouring *gurdwara* at Hothian had been seized by the Akalis in the absence of the *mahant*. Subsequently the *mahant* applied to the district authorities for help and the Akalis were asked to leave. The Akalis disregarded the eviction order and the local *tehsildar* [the official in charge of a *tahsil*, a sub-division of a district] was instructed to forcibly expel them. Before such action could be taken a large Akali *jatha* led by Mahtab Singh joined the Akalis in possession at Hothian, and the Punjab government was forced to conclude that it would be 'impolitic to evict them forcibly'.[47] The efficiency of Akali communications in the seizure of these two shrines non-plussed the Punjab government. An official report later noted, 'At Teja and Hothian in the Gurdaspur district, summoned by orders of the Gurdwara Prabhandak Committee through the Central Akali Dal, large numbers of Akalis appeared as if by magic'.[48]

Notes to Chapter 4

1 C. M. King, Offg Chief Sec., Punjab Govt, to Sec., Home Dept, GOI, 26 Mar. 1921, GOI, Home (Political) proceedings, A, nos 282–315 of May 1921. See also Fortnightly Report, 15 Oct. 1920, GOI, Home (Political), Deposit, no. 59, of Dec. 1920; Fortnightly Report, 31 Oct. 1920, GOI, Home (Political), Deposit, no. 66 of Dec. 1920; Fortnightly Report, 15 Nov. 1920, GOI, Home (Political), Deposit, no. 74 of Dec. 1920; Fortnightly Report, 15 Jan. 1921, GOI, Home (Political), Deposit, no. 41 of Apr. 1921.

2 Punjab Govt Press communiqué, *Tribune* (10 Feb. 1921, 19 Feb. 1921).

3 *Tribune* (20 Feb. 1921).

4 Based on statement of Gomi Das, Nankana Sahib legal case, *Tribune* (12 Apr. 1921); evidence of Patwari Amar Singh, Nankana Sahib legal case, *Civil and Military Gazette* (10 Apr. 1921); Teja Singh, *Gurdwara Reform Movement*, p. 221; Gurbux Singh Jhabalia, *Shahidi Jiwan* (Nankana, 1938), p. 74.

5 Undated letter (c. 28 Dec. 1920) from C. M. King, Commissioner, Lahore Division, to Baba Kartar Singh Bedi, GOI, Home (Political) proceedings no. 179/II of 1922. See also Ruchi Ram Sahni, *Struggle for Reform in Sikh Shrines* (Amritsar, undated), pp. 243–4.

6 C. M. King, Offg Chief Sec. Punjab Govt, to Sec., Home Dept, GOI, 26 Mar. 1921, GOI, Home (Political) proceedings no. 179/II of 1922.

7 Statement of Mahant Narain Das, Nankana Sahib legal case, GOI, Home (Political) proceedings no. 179/II of 1922; Sahni, *Struggle*, p. 74.

8 C. M. King, Offg Chief Sec., Punjab Govt, to Sec., Home Dept, GOI, 26 Mar. 1921. See also Punjab Govt Press communiqué, *Tribune* (1 Mar. 1921, 12 Mar. 1921).

9 C. M. King, Offg Chief Sec., Punjab Govt, to Sec., Home Dept, GOI, 26 Mar. 1921.

10 *Sikh* (27 Feb. 1921), Punjab Govt, *Selections*, vol. 34, no. 10. See also *Panch* (2 Mar. 1921), Punjab Govt, *Selections*, vol. 34, no. 10.

11 Note by C. Kaye, 2 Sept. 1921, GOI, Home (Political) proceedings, A, no. 282–315 of May 1921.

12 *Tribune* (6 Mar. 1921).

13 Punjab Govt Press communiqué, *Tribune* (16 Mar. 1921).

14 C. M. King, Offg Chief Sec., Punjab Govt, to Sec., Home Dept, GOI, 26 Mar. 1921.

15 *Tribune* (13 Mar. 1921, 15 Mar. 1921, 16 Mar. 1921).

16 C. M. King, Offg Chief Sec., Punjab Govt, to Sec., Home Dept, GOI, 26 Mar. 1921.

17 SGPC Press communiqué, *Tribune* (25 Mar. 1921).

18 Fazl-i-Husain, statement in *Punjab Legislative Council Debates*, vol. 1, no. 8.

19 Dasaundha Singh, Baba Hardit Singh Bedi and Ganpat Raj, statements in *Punjab Legislative Council Debates*, vol. 1, no. 8.

20 Sikh Gurdwaras and Shrines Act of 1921, GOI, Home (Political) proceedings A, nos 276–81 of May 1921 and K.W. (keep with).

21 Sikh Gurdwaras and Shrines Act of 1921.

22 E. Joseph, Sec., Transferred Dept, Punjab Govt, to Sec., Home Dept, GOI, 24 Mar. 1921; GOI, Home (Political) proceedings, A, nos 276–81 of May 1921 and K.W.

23 *Tribune* (25 Mar. 1921).

24 *Tribune* (6 Apr. 1921).

25 *Tribune* (6 Apr. 1921).

26 *Tribune* (6 Apr. 1921).

27 *Tribune* (26 Mar. 1921).

28 *Tribune* (26 Mar. 1921).

29 *Tribune* (7 Apr. 1921, 17 Apr. 1921).

30 Raja Narendra Nath and Mahtab Singh, statements in *Punjab Legislative Council Debates*, vol. 1, no. 10.

31 'Report of the Select Committee, Sikh Gurdwaras and Shrines Act, 1921', *Tribune* (9 Apr. 1921, 12 Apr. 1921).

32 'Report of Select Committee'.

33 'Report of Select Committee'.

34 'Report of Select Committee'.

35 *Tribune* (10 Apr. 1921).

36 Punjab Govt Press communiqué, *Tribune* (21 Apr. 1921).

37 Punjab Govt Press communiqué, *Tribune* (30 May 1921).

38 Based on Fortnightly Report, 15 May 1921, GOI, Home (Political), Deposit, no. 63 of June 1921; Weekly Report, DCI, 20 May 1921, GOI, Home (Political) proceedings, B, no. 55 of June 1921; *Tribune* (9 June 1921, 11 June 1921).

39 'Akali Dal and SGPC'.

40 Details of the composition and organization of the SGPC and the
   Akali Dal based on 'Akali Dal and SGPC'; Sahni, *Struggle*, pp. 85–6;
   Ruchi Ram Sahni, 'History of my own times' and special volumes on
   the Akali movement, unpublished MSS, private papers.
41 'Akali Dal and SGPC'.
42 'Akali Dal and SGPC'.
43 'Akali Dal and SGPC'.
44 'Akali Dal and SGPC'.
45 'Akali Dal and SGPC'.
46 'Akali Dal and SGPC'.
47 'Akali Dal and SGPC'.
48 'Akali Dal and SGPC'.

5

Agitation Extended

In November 1921 relations between Sikh activists and the local authorities deteriorated further, and firm official action precipitated a large-scale conflict between the SGPC and the Punjab government. In October the executive committee of the SGPC passed a resolution demanding that the manager of the Golden Temple, Sunder Singh Ramgarhia, hand over the keys to the *toshakhana* (treasury) of the shrine in his possession to the committee. The resolution paid tribute to the efficiency with which the manager had conducted affairs but insisted that since Sunder Singh Ramgarhia was an official nominee, the SGPC could no longer tolerate government control over the sacred treasures of the Golden Temple through its representative. Sunder Singh Ramgarhia, being both a member of the SGPC's Golden Temple managing committee and the official manager of the temple appointed by government, was placed in a difficult position, and he consulted the Deputy Commissioner of Amritsar. Informed of this development, the Punjab government moved swiftly. The government feared that 'the extremist Sikhs were possibly aiming at possession of the considerable treasure stored away in the Darbar Sahib, and that it was possibly the intention of the Committee to utilise these resources for the financing of a political movement'.[1] It thus pre-empted the SGPC's action by taking possession of the keys to the *toshakhana*. In a communiqué explaining its position regarding this new development, the Punjab government stated that since the SGPC had neither been appointed by government nor received any lawful authority to control the affairs of the Golden Temple, it was temporarily taking charge of the keys pending a final settlement. To this end it was announced that the government intended to institute a 'friendly civil suit' to determine where authority to manage the

Golden Temple lay and to divest itself finally of all responsibility for the administration of the shrine. The keys were surrendered to the custody of an Indian magistrate.

The Punjab government's action brought a violent reaction from the SGPC. The committee charged the government with interfering in the religious affairs of the Sikh community, and immediately issued a rejoinder to the official communiqué. The SGPC argued that the original committee to manage the affairs of the Golden Temple, consisting of thirty-six members, had been appointed by the government, and thus official involvement in the administration of the shrine had been severed. Further, it stated, this original body had been amalgamated without protest into the SGPC and the latter thus carried a degree of official recognition. Finally, the committee argued that the Punjab government had by its subsequent actions made it abundantly clear that it no longer wished to be involved with the management of the Golden Temple. The radical Sikh Press was equally vocal in condemning the government's action and issued appeals to the Sikh community to rally in support of the SGPC in this 'moment of crisis'. The *Akali* declared, 'O Khalsas! Awake and rub your eyes ... Be prepared to become martyrs ... The bureaucracy interfered with your religion and is always ready to crush you. You should always be ready to go gladly to jails and accept the sweet offer of bullets, because religion is in danger and it is proper for the Sikhs to protect their religion'.[2] The *Loyal Gazette* and the *Panth Sewak* complained bitterly of government repression of the religious liberty of the Sikh community and urged the Sikhs to be prepared to make sacrifices.[3] In response to an appeal from the SGPC, Akali *jathas* began congregating at Amritsar from various parts of the province. By early November thousands of Akalis were in the city. The SGPC organized large public meetings to protest the 'seizure' of the keys to the *toshakhana* and Akali bands marched through the city demonstrating their support for the committee. On the SGPC's instruction, Akalis, picketed the Golden Temple and, in a gesture of defiance for the Punjab government's authority in this matter, affixed their own locks to the *toshakhana*. The SGPC also appealed to Sikh members of the Punjab Legislative Council to resign their seats in protest, and Sikh soldiers were asked to withdraw from service in the army. Within days the atmosphere in Amritsar had grown highly volatile.

By the middle of November the approaching annual religious fair at Nankana brought a large-scale movement of Akalis to the village and the scene of popular protest shifted temporarily from Amritsar. However, the religious fair at Nankana provided an unprecedented demonstration of Akali solidarity and organization. The Punjab government reported that some 50,000 Sikhs attended the fair of whom 20,000 professed to be Akalis, and 12 or 15 thousand belonged to recognised Jathas'.[4] Moreover, Akali activity at the fair was marked by the thoroughness of their organization. The SGPC had appointed a special sub-committee of ten persons to arrange accommodation for the Akali *jathas*, and the efficiency with which they had performed their task immediately became apparent. Akali *jathas* were housed in a special camp laid out in military fashion. The camp was guarded by Akalis armed with swords. Members of the Akali *jathas* also performed duties of a semi-military nature. Akali guards displaying unsheathed swords patrolled the Janam Asthan shrine, the sentries were relieved at fixed intervals, and registers were maintained to ensure the smooth functioning of the operation. A body of some 400 Akalis was directed to conduct security duties, and the local police authorities reported that the lower than usual incidence of crime at the fair was a tribute to their efficiency. The SGPC had also organized a body of 5,000 Akalis containing a large number of ex-soldiers for any emergency that might arise. An intelligence bureau had been created, staffed by students from the Khalsa College under the supervision of the SGPC, which kept a watch on government officials attending the fair. The Punjab government later noted, 'It is reported that the work of this staff was most efficient, that every person with pro-Government sympathies was marked down, and that no body could move in the direction of the Janam Asthan without being shadowed'.[5]

The high point of the fair was the sensational appearance of Gurdit Singh of the *Komagata Maru* who had been absconding since the Budge-Budge riot and was officially believed dead. In a carefully organized scheme, Gurdit Singh appeared at the Nankana fair and delivered a violently anti-government speech. He was arrested by the local police amidst a demonstration of strength by Akalis marching in military formation. Equally dramatic was the appearance of Mota Singh and several other Sikh revolutionaries absconding in the face of criminal conspiracy charges. The revolutionaries appeared unannounced at the fair along with an armed escort, delivered speeches and immediately disappeared, despite the presence of large numbers of police.

The thoroughness of Akali oganization at the Nankana fair had an enormous impact on the SGPC's prestige and greatly enhanced the Akalis' solidarity and belief in their own strength. By the end of November anti-government agitation among Sikhs was spreading rapidly. Sikh unrest, coupled with prevalent nationalist activities of non-co-operation with government, presented a picture of rapidly escalating disaffection among Punjabis. The Punjab government felt compelled to enforce the Seditious Meetings Act, forbidding all political meetings, in the districts of Lahore, Amritsar and Sheikhupura. The government of India was in favour of more stringent measures and advised the Punjab government that the only way to deal with the Sikh agitation was to 'successfully prosecute five or six leading men'.[6] Accordingly the local government adopted a tough stance towards agitators and prohibited protest meetings at the first signs of trouble. At a public meeting held at Ajnala in November 1921, speeches were made urging the Sikhs to withdraw their co-operation with government. The Punjab government declared the meeting illegal and arrested several prominent speakers. The arrest of leading Sikh militants brought a deluge of protests. The pro-Akali Press charged that in fact the arrested leaders were only commenting on a matter of religious concern. For its part, the SGPC responded promptly to official repression. When news of the arrests at Ajnala reached Amritsar, the committee, then in session, immediately adjourned its meeting to Ajnala and continued the protest. Faced with this challenge to its authority, the Punjab government arrested all the members attending the meeting. Among those taken into custody were Kharak Singh, president of the SGPC and Mahtab Singh, its secretary. The arrest of the committee's leading office-holders did not, however, impede its functioning. The SGPC elected new office-holders to take temporary charge of the campaign and intensified the protest. These leaders continued to be arrested, they refused any defence on the ground that they were not willing to co-operate with government and were awarded rigorous terms of imprisonment. Their arrests only added to popular conviction that government was determined to destroy the Sikh religion.

Meanwhile, the Punjab government attempted to negotiate with the SGPC over the institution of a civil suit to settle the controversy over the administration of the Golden Temple. But the SGPC refused to participate in any legal proceedings until all persons arrested in connection with the recent agitation were released unconditionally. The government was compelled to institute legal proceedings *suo loco*. While the hearing of the civil suit was pending, the Punjab government made a gesture of conciliation towards enraged Sikh opinion and announced that, pending the decision of the civil court, it had had no objection to the keys of the *toshakhana* being handed over to the SGPC to enable it to proceed with celebrations for the forthcoming birth-day of Guru Gobind Singh. The SGPC scornfully rejected the offer and reiterated its demand that all Sikh prisoners be released. Two days later when devout Sikhs paid homage to the memory of their warrior guru, they were reminded of their present 'humili-ation' in not being permitted to manage their own affairs.

On 7 January 1922 the government civil suit in connection with the keys to the *toshakhana* came before the district court of Amritsar. To counter the SGPC's claims to represent the entire Sikh community, the Punjab government had arranged that representatives of the Sikh princely states of Faridkot, Kalsia, and Kapurthala and Sikh members of the Punjab Legislative Council also be consulted on the question of the future management of the Golden Temple. However, the SGPC had gathered a formidable following over this religious issue, and it was impolitic for any Sikh individual or organization to oppose it. Thus these indi-viduals did not publicly oppose the SGPC's claim to manage the shrine. The proceedings of the civil suit undermined the basis for government action.

Bitterness among Sikhs at the attitude of government towards the SGPC was escalating, and it had become apparent that the majority of Sikhs deeply resented what they saw as official interference in the religious affairs of their community. In January 1922 the Punjab government noted,

> The Akali movement is gaining ground in the villages, and by an organized system of propaganda the Shiromani Gurdwara Prabhan-dah Committee has succeeded in persuading the ordinary Sikh zamindar that it is really representative of the Panth generally and that the actions of Government are both dubious and harsh . . . at the

present rate of conversion of the average villager to this state of mind, the entire rural Sikh population is within measurable distance of turning against Government and joining the propagandists in active denunciation of Government. Should this come to pass, (the Deputy Commissioner of Lahore) believes that words will soon give way to deeds and open rebellion will begin.[7]

There were indications that Akali propaganda had permeated among Sikh troops in the army, and recruiting officers were indicating difficulties in obtaining recruits among *jat* Sikhs.[8] The loyalty of the two staunch bastions of British administration in the Punjab, Sikh troops and the simple Sikh peasantry, had begun to be undermined, and, what was perhaps even worse, the Sikh community had begun to play an active role in the prevalent nationalist campaign of non-co-operation with government. The Punjab government relented. 'It has become imperative', it noted, 'to bring back the simple minded non-political majority of the Panth to reason'.[9] A campaign of conciliation towards popular Sikh opinion was initiated. In view of the fact that no Sikh body had declared its opposition to the management of the Golden Temple being entrusted to the SGPC during the hearing of the official civil suit in the matter, the government decided to withdraw from any connection with the management of the shrine and 'to leave any further proceedings that may be thought necessary to the Sikh community itself'.[10] It was also announced that all Sikhs arrested in connection with the recent agitation would be released.

The return of the keys of the *toshakhana* to the SGPC and the release of all Sikh prisoners arrested in connection with the affair was hailed as a great victory in militant Sikh circles. The *Akali*'s comments typified the jubilation expressed by the radical Sikh Press: It declared, 'In the short time of two months the Sikhs have broken the pride and humbled the Government given to forcibly interfering with their religion. The bureaucracy which held its head high up till only yesterday is today standing amid the shoes [sic] of the Khalsa with the bunch of Keys in its hands. Brave, O heroes! You have vindicated your honour'.[11] The Commissioners of Jullunder and Lahore Divisions reported that official action in the keys affair was being regarded as an 'unqualified triumph' by the Sikh community.[12] The Punjab government had hoped that its conciliatory attitude would 'reconcile moderate Sikh opinion' and reduce the appeal of extremist Sikhs and the nationalists for the majority of the Sikh community, but the immediate impact of the affair of the keys was to provide an enormous boost to the prestige of the SGPC and the Akalis and to the confidence of Sikh militants in their ability to agitate successfully against government. Vigorous Tat Khalsa propaganda quickly translated this mystique of the Akalis into an avalance of recruits for their cause, while greater Akali self-assuredness was expressed in vivid demonstration of contempt for official authority. In 1921 the Punjab government had commissioned the criminal investigation department to conduct a thorough investigation into the SGPC and the Akali Dal. Its enumeration of the strength and the composition of various Akali *jathas*, carried out between November 1921 and early February 1922, revealed more than 15,000 active Akalis, over sixty per cent of whom were *jats*, and reflected the great success of the Akali movement in enlisting the support of the common Sikh peasant.[13] By early March 1922 the Punjab government reported to the government of India that the numbers reported by this investigation were now 'considerably below the true figure and may be doubled'.[14]

Since the summer of 1921 militant Tat Khalsa Sikhs had devoted their energies to the establishment of an Akali *jatha* organization and towards speeding up Akali recruitment. Consequently Sikh militants had paid little attention, beyond verbal support, to the campaign of non-co-operation with government being conducted by the Indian National Congress. In April 1921 the Central Sikh League had met at Lahore and amended its constitution on lines similar to those adopted by the Congress at its session at Nagpur in 1920. It had been resolved that henceforth the objective of the league was the 'attainment of Swarajya [self-government] by the people of India by all legitimate, peaceful and constitutional means' and 'the promotion of Panthic unity, fostering of patriotism and public spirit among the Sikhs and development and organization of their political, moral, economic resources'.[15] However, the working element of the Central Sikh League was constituted of largely the same men who directed the affairs of the SGPC, and though the league appeared to fall in line with the Congress programme it remained mainly inactive. Sikh unrest over the keys affair witnessed active co-operation between Sikh militants and nationalist politicians, and Sikh communal concerns were linked to wider Indian demands. Government action in settling the controversy over the management of the Golden Temple to the advantage of the SGPC, far from discouraging further agitation by Sikh militants, added vigour to their co-operation with the nationalists. Prominent nationalist politicians also encouraged such political activity among Sikhs. Gandhi, for example, telegraphed the SGPC on their success over the keys affair, 'Congratulations, First decisive battle for India's freedom won'.[16] In January 1922 the Central Sikh League resolved to increase its participation in the non-co-operation campaign and issued an appeal to the Sikh community to commence civil disobedience with the government in collaboration with the Congress and Khilafat organizations. The formation of an Akali *fauj* (army) similar to the National Volunteers organized by the Congress and Khilafat committee was also announced. At the same time the SGPC declared its intention to limit itself solely to religious concerns and to leave the political arena to the Sikh League. However, this division of functions was purely a theoretical one. Not only were the activities of the SGPC and those of the Central Sikh League directed by the same men, but the enunciation of Sikh political demands, indeed, the very demarcation of the Sikh community as a separate political entity, was based on religious considerations.

The increasing participation of Sikhs in political affairs of national importance, together with the agitation of local Congress and Khilafat volunteers, brought an outburst of political activity in the province at every level. Sikh militants, responding to Sikh League propaganda, swelled the number of active political agitators, and local nationalist politicians strove to enlist Sikhs in their activities. By the end of January 1922 the Punjab government reported that the number of political meetings held in the province during the previous two weeks had increased to 250, from the hundred odd political gatherings held during the previous fortnight. By the second half of February the number of political gatherings held in the Punjab had increased to 350, the majority of which were held in Sikh villages.[17] In Jullunder District, heartland of the Sikhs, an enormous spurt in political organization and agitation was noted. By February 1922 the Jullunder district Congress committee had 8,023 members, with ninety-eight Congress sub-committees under its jurisdiction; the

Jullunder City Congress Committee had 842 members. In all cases the office-holders were largely Sikhs.[18] A report produced by the army general staff also noted that the Akali *fauj* had enlisted some 10,000 Sikh volunteers and that its leaders had declared that they now aimed at a strength of 30,000 men.[19] Sikh militants in the guise of members of the Akali *fauj* and the Akali Dal organized public *diwans* in rural areas at which Akalis stood guard with drawn swords. Exuberant Akalis further demonstrated their contempt for authority by marching through the countryside in military formation and urging civil disobedience against the government. Regarding the Akali *fauj*, the army general staff noted with grave concern that 'Detachments of the Fauj have been seen marching in fours, flags are carried, camps have been organized on military lines, and badges and numbers given'.[20] Such open defiance of authority by the Akalis was contagious, and their political propaganda and contemptuous attitude towards the government spread quickly among the rural Sikh community. In February the Punjab government reported an instance of contempt for authority which provided a good indication of the confidence with which a large number of Sikhs viewed their own power. The government noted,

> A bad case of contempt for authority is reported from the Hoshiarpur district where a Sikh, who was wanted in connection with a political case, came garlanded on horseback with a following of a couple of thousand men to give himself up. He made terms about the time of his arrest and only yielded his Kirpan after praying aloud with his companions in the gate of the police station, where the magistrate had decided to hold his court, for the speedy destruction of the British Government. Throughout the proceedings he sat with his back to the Magistrate.[21]

Further, the government commented, 'Akalis are regarded by the Sikh villagers as a privileged class, owing to the manner in which they move about in armed bodies, travel in trains without tickets and display contempt for Government and its servants at their many meetings. For this reason the Akalis have things almost entirely their own way in rural areas'.[22] Such Akali self-confidence was not limited to the political arena, and towards the end of February an Akali group took forcible possession of a *gurdwara* at Hafizabad and another at Heran.

The Punjab government viewed the rapid escalation of political activity in the province and the attitude of Sikh extremists with grave concern. It noted, 'it has become abundantly evident that the Akali Movement is in the main a political one, aiming at the subversion of the present Government, and claiming succession for the Sikhs'.[23] Yet the government was reluctant to take drastic action against the Akalis for a number of reasons. It considered the possibility of calling in the army to deal with militant Sikhs, and reported to the government of India,

> The possibility that military action on an extended scale may be necessary in the Sikh districts must now be faced but a meeting of officers recently held to discuss this possibility did not disclose a general conviction that the time for it has arrived. Steps are being taken by Government to impress upon officers the importance of the steady enforcement of the law even if this should involve the use of fire arms, to prevent intimidation and violence, and it is not impossible that the danger may be tided over till the time arrives for harvesting operations.[24]

Besides the recent experience of confrontation with Sikh agitators gave cause for hesitation. The enormous success with which the SGPC had been able to represent government action as interference in Sikh religious affairs made the Punjab government wary of pursuing any policy which might be portrayed as repression of the Sikh religion and community. Moreover, the authorities believed that the SGPC was itself alarmed at the growing indiscipline of its supporters and they therefore wished to encourage the development of 'moderate counsels' among its ranks.

The Punjab government decided to proceed cautiously, aiming to separate its stance towards Sikh political activities from consideration of essentially religious grievances. In dealing with the political activities of Sikh militants the government's policy was one of gradual suppression rather than immediate action on a large scale. Orders were issued to district officers to begin the disarming of Akali bands 'on an experimental scale', but it was decided not to prohibit the carrying of *kirpans* for the moment to avoid the risk of allegations of religious interference. The Punjab government reported to the government of India that it was thus hoped that 'the disarming of bands would be successfully carried out and no serious out-breaks would occur before the harvest operations commenced ... There was, contrary to expectation, some cessation of activity last year, and this experience might be repeated this year'.[25] Regarding the SGPC's religious demands, the Punjab government issued a communiqué which stated,

> Government desire[s] to explain in deciding in January last to leave the administration of the Golden Temple in the hands of the Committee, it was guided by the consideration that no opposition was made by any Sikh body to the adoption of this course and that accordingly the Committee might be looked on as representing a large section of Sikh religious opinion on the subject of Sikh gurdwaras. In dealing with questions connected with Sikh shrines the Government is prepared to take a similar attitude so long as the Committee confines itself to religious matters and does not adopt undesirable political activities. In cases where offences are committed in respect of shrines, local officers will of course be guided by the requirements of order and of the law, but in dealing with such offences and in discussing possible arrangements in connection with shrines for the prevention of the breach of the peace ... the local officers are at liberty ... to consult the Shiromani Gurdwara Prabhandak Committee or its local representatives, and to give to their views on gurdwara questions the attention due to the representatives of a large section of Sikh religious sentiment on the subject.[26]

To achieve a settlement of the problem of *gurdwara* management the government announced that Sikh members of the provincial legislative council had been invited to draft suitable *gurdwara* legislation. The government also consulted the SGPC on the adoption of suitable measures to curb increasing instances of intimidation and lawlessness by Akalis brandishing large *kirpan*s. The SGPC was strongly against any move to restrict the length of a *kirpan*. Such a restriction on a Sikh religious symbol would, they insisted, be an infringement of Sikh religious liberty since Sikh tenets did not themselves prescribe any limitation to the size of a *kirpan*. However, a compromise was reached with the SGPC by which government would take action to prevent the misuse of the *kirpan* rather than issue any ordinance restricting its size.[27]

The Punjab government's policy of conciliation towards Sikh religious concerns initially met with success. Anxious to reassert its authority over zealous Akalis, the SGPC co-operated with the government in evicting a group of Akalis who had forcibly occupied the Heran *gurdwara* without prior instruction from the committee. Further, the committee issued a communiqué stating that it viewed with deep concern and condemnation that some Sikhs have insulted and boycotted some very respectable Sikhs for difference of views ... that Jathas sometimes take possession of Gurdwaras without permission of this Committee ... such incidents are signs of grave defects in our organization and prove the utter necessity of securing good discipline among workers. The work of reform will suffer a serious setback if the spirit of indiscipline is not curbed at once.'[28]

In addition, the SGPC called upon Sikhs in the army to observe army regulations regarding the wearing of *kirpans* and black turbans and also announced the formation of a sub-committee to enter into detailed negotiations with the government on proposed *gurdwara* legislation. Accordingly, representatives of the SGPC and the Punjab government met, and it was agreed that while negotiations regarding further *gurdwara* legislation were being conducted, 'In order to produce the requisite atmosphere nothing should be done by either party to prejudice the chances of conciliation'.[29]

But the Punjab government's reports on the Sikh situation, and its enunciation of the policy to be pursued in dealing with Sikh political activities, brought strong criticism from the government of India. S. P. O'Donnel, secretary in the government of India's home department, noted,

The Punjab Government hope that the danger may be tided over till the time arrives for harvesting operations, but they seem oblivious to the probability, if not certainty, that the trouble will be all the greater if it comes after these operations are completed. It is said that there is no general conviction among local officers that the time has arrived for military operations in the Sikh districts, but clearly some officers must be of opinion that this time has arrived, and it is a matter for the most serious consideration by the Government of India whether drastic action should not be taken at once against the Akalis ... I ... suggest a definite line of action be settled at once.[30]

The Sikh situation was discussed by members of the Viceroy's council and the general consensus was for immediate severe action against the Akalis. C. A. Innes commented, 'I am in favour of dispersing [Akalis] by force and re-asserting ourselves in the Punjab. The position appears to me to be very serious, and the sooner we explode the mine, the better', and B. N. Sharma noted, 'It is the exhibition of the open contempt for authority that is ominous, and I agree that we cannot allow respect for law to be impaired further ... there is little use in ignoring the fact that disease is widespread, and that our remedial measures must be sought in numerous directions'.[31]

Concurrently with the Punjab government's reports on the Sikh situation in the province, the government of India received a deluge of ominous reports from the army general staff and from the intelligence bureau warning of the dangerous proportions political activity had reached in the province. The intelligence bureau reported in March 1922,

> Sikh agitators have met some success in engineering agitation among Sikhs in the Indian Army, and ... Sikh units ... seek the advice and assistance of the Committee in all matters which arise in the regiments. The Sikh agitators who are in fact working for a revolution, are now active in spreading the idea (which is bound to reach the Sikhs in the army soon) that Government no longer trusts the Sikhs. A rumour in this connection is that all the Sikh regiments are going to be disbanded.[32]

A report on the military aspects of the political situation in the Punjab produced by the army general staff confirmed this view. The report warned of 'sedition' spreading in the army and noted,

> That the Indian Army has so long withstood such a campaign of sedition is a subject for gratification, but doubts have been felt as to how long any Army can remain entirely unaffected, and the time has come when it is no longer possible to say that it is still so ... it is the opinion of your General Staff that the time has now arrived when definite action should be taken ... delay in dealing with the situation will only increase the difficulties of an inevitable conflict and the possibility of considerable bloodshed.[33]

The army general staff further asked that the length of the *kirpan* be immediately restricted to nine inches and appropriate action be taken against offenders. These reports only strengthened the government of India's conviction that the local government was being timid in its assessment of the official action required to deal adequately with the Akalis.

Under pressure from the government of India, the Punjab government issued instructions to district officers to prepare for the immediate forcible disbandment of Akali groups on a large scale. Local officers were informed that, 'The Governor in Council now desires that before the onset of the hot weather systematic and simultaneous measures should be taken in all districts which are affected by the Akali political movement to put an end to the disturbance which it has late been producing'.[34] District officers were warned, however, of the delicate nature of their task. The Punjab government's instructions stated,

As few pretexts as possible should be given for representing the action taken as interference with religion, shrines should not forcibly be entered, meetings at which the Granth Sahib is present should be respected till the members are leaving ... Care should be taken by Deputy Commissioners to explain to Sikhs that the action taken is solely against the political activities of Akali bands and that it is being accompanied by strenuous efforts for the settlement of the gurdwara question on lines which will commend themselves to all reasonable Sikhs. The Government is still, as ever, the defender of religious liberties, but will not tolerate the continuance of what is virtually rebellion against its authority.[35]

The government of India signified its assent to the Punjab government's scheme for widespread repression of Akali political activities, but was vexed by the local government's policy regarding the use of *kirpans*. S. P. O'Donnel wrote to the chief secretary of the Punjab government,

The Government of India have acquiesced in the view of the Punjab Government that the question of limiting the size of Kirpans should be postponed, and they recognise that the developments mentioned ... in particular the more moderate attitude of the Prabhandak Committee and the prospect that a settlement of the Gurdwara question may now be capable of achievement may render it inopportune that limitations on the size of Kirpans should be enforced at the present moment. They are not, however, clear as to the reasons which have led the local Government to authorise the wearing of swords and of kirpans indistinguishable from swords by Sikhs.[36]

The government of India pointed to regulations under the Arms Act limiting the possession of swords to persons who either were entitled to wear them as part of their uniforms or else had been presented with Swords of Honour for services to the government, and insisted that the Punjab government's stance on the permissible uses of *kirpans* had by implication contravened these regulations. Thus S. P. O'Donnel wrote,

it is one thing to refrain from instituting prosecution and another thing explicitly to authorise, even though subject to conditions, the carrying of weapons prohibited by law. Similarly, it is one thing to refrain from imposing by rule limitation on the size of kirpans, and another thing to announce that kirpans of any size, and practically

indistinguishable from swords may ... be worn with impunity ...
The Government of India has previously suggested that the length
of kirpans worn in the Punjab should be restricted, the Punjab
Government has not seen it their way to accepting the suggestion
... but if measures now being taken in regard to the Akalis should
not prove sufficient, it is clear that the question of imposing a
definite limitation on the size of Kirpans may require to be recon-
sidered.[37]

The controversy over the Punjab government's policy
regarding the use of *kirpans* was shelved for the moment, but to
the government of India it was indicative both of the failure of the
local government to appreciate fully the inherent dangers in Sikh
unrest, and of its inability to take concerted action against the
Akali movement. The proceedings of the criminal case against
mahant Narain Das provided an opportunity for the government
of India to review further the Punjab government's policy
towards Sikh demands for *gurdwara* reform. Legal proceedings
regarding the Nankana massacre had been begun in April 1921,
and in October Narain Das and seven of his henchmen were
sentenced to death, eight of his supporters to transportation for
life, and seven others to seven years' imprisonment each. Narain
Das appealed against the verdict in the Punjab High Court, his
appeal was partially accepted and his previous sentence revised to
a verdict of transportation for life. However, the *mahant*'s appeal
for mercy attracted the attention of the government of India. In
his statement before the court, Narain Das contended that in fact
he had been given no alternative but to organize for his own
defence and stated,

> Not only did I attempt in every possible way to appease the Sikhs,
> but being still apprehensive of attack, I approached every quarter for
> help and assistance. I ... made representations to ... the Governor,
> to the Members of the Executive Council, and to the Ministers. I
> laid my case before nearly all high police officials ... [and] pleaded
> for protection against apprehended attack ... Though it was sug-
> gested in the course of these interviews and representation that I
> should take proceedings under Section 107 Criminal Procedure
> Code, it was impossible to follow this advice without knowledge of
> and specifying the persons who intended to join the attack ... In
> fact, I was told by responsible Government officials that this was a
> religious matter, and I was told to make my own arrangements.[38]

On perusal of the judical proceedings in the appeal case, the
Viceroy, Lord Reading, commented,

I am concerned to note the written statement of the Mahant which, if accepted, indicates that he only resorted to the incitement to violence after making representations and appeals to the local authorities for protection, whose answer was to refer him to the civil courts ... The inference to be drawn, namely that had police protection been given this wholesale massacre would not have taken place, requires attention.[39]

Subsequent inquiries revealed that there had been a vital lack of communication between the Punjab government and the government of India on the former's policy towards *gurdwara* reform. On receipt of details of Narain Das's statement before the appeal court, the government of India requested the Punjab government to respond specifically to the *mahant*'s allegations in his petition for mercy. In its reply the Punjab government attempted to justify its response to various appeals made to it by Narain Das. Though the *mahant* was within his right in requesting police protection for his shrine, the local Government wrote, 'it was for the Government to decide whether in all the circumstances of the case it was expedient or possible to comply with such a request'.[40] In this instance the Punjab government believed such assistance was clearly not politic. The local government insisted that the sanction of police protection for the *gurdwara* at Nankana would have savoured of partiality towards a man of ill repute, and had a conflict with the reformers taken place, as was highly probable, government would have been placed in the tragic position of defending such a man against a body of men many of whom were moved by a genuine desire for reform of their sacred shrines. Further, the Punjab government noted, an adequate defence of the Janam Asthan shrine would have required a body of some 500 men, which was larger than the resources available at the time.

The Punjab government's report was discussed at length by the Viceroy's council and by senior government officials in Delhi. S. P. O'Donnel, dismissed the Punjab government's reluctance to protect a man of 'ill repute' as 'one of the most extraordinary arguments ever put forward by a responsible Government', and stated, 'the suggestion that the Government was justified in not sending police to Nankana because the police might have been attacked by the Akalis, can only be described as amazing'.[41] Members of the Viceroy's council were equally unrestrained in their criticism of the Punjab government's reported policy. Sir

Mohammed Shafi commented, 'I am unable to see how any question of "expediency" would possibly arise in a case like this'; and E. M. Cook noted, 'There can be no such thing as "neutrality" when it is a question of preserving order'.[42] In the government of India's view, the local government's policy regarding repeated requests for protection from Narain Das had implications for the larger policy of the Punjab government towards Tat Khalsa agitators. Thus, S. P. O'Donnel wrote, 'The situation was no doubt one of considerable difficulty, though it must be remembered that the difficulty was largely the result of the failure of the Punjab government to deal with the Akali movement firmly and consistently from the beginning'.[43] The cumulative effect of the Punjab government's reports to the government of India on its policy towards Akali political activities and its compromise with the *gurdwara* committee on controlling the use of *kirpans* by Akalis was profound. They revealed to the government of India the extent to which it had remained isolated from the local government's formulation of policies regarding Sikh unrest, and resulted in closer supervision of the Punjab government's response to Akali activity.[44]

Meanwhile, on 20 March 1922 extensive operations aimed at suppressing Sikh political activities were begun simultaneously in the thirteen districts representing the majority of the Sikh population. District authorities were provided with large contingents of police to enable them forcibly to disband Akali groups and to enforce the law, and punitive police posts were imposed upon troublesome villages. The military authorities were allied with these operations, and troops were stationed in districts which did not contain an army cantonment to provide additional support for the civil administration. The government of India monitored this campaign closely and sceptical officials in Delhi insisted upon weekly reports on the progress of the local government's actions.

Initially, large-scale repression increased the tempo of Sikh unrest. Sikh politicians organized *diwan*s and urged their co-religionists not to be browbeaten into submission. As groups of Akalis organized their resistance, there were reports of Akali guards being posted at public meetings to ensure the exclusion of officials and government sympathizers. But concerted official action proved effective. By early April more than 700 Akalis, including Kharak Singh, president of the SGPC, had been arrested, several unlicensed *kirpan* factories raided, and the local authorities reported that Akali bands were dispersing of their own accord. Indeed from the advent of systematic official repression of Akali political activity, the SGPC sensed the futility of resistance. It instructed the Akali Dal,

> It seems the Government has come to the conclusion ... that time has come for them to crush the Akali Movement by force ... It is said that in the past few days a number of Akalis have been arrested for actions which neither formed part of the programme of the Shiromani Gurdwara Prabhandak Committee nor of the Congress. If it is true, it is an undue waste of national energy ... Please ... guide the activities of your Akali Jathas and individual Akalis on such peaceful lines that the Government should find absolutely no occasion for using repressive methods. Please do not grudge time and comfort in carrying out this propaganda and thus save your brethren from fruitless sacrifices and the sacred Gurdwara and Akali movements from mutilation.[45]

As the Punjab government had anticipated, the beginning of harvesting in later March occupied the Sikh peasantry and provided an additional factor in the cessation of militant Akali activity. By 3 April 1922 the government was able to report that troops had been withdrawn from four districts and that the remaining troops might be able to resume their regular duties within a week. Official optimism proved well founded and six days later all troops were in fact withdrawn from their participation in the special operations against Sikh militants. By the end of April 1922 agitation among Sikhs had virtually ceased.[46]

Official repression had an immediate adverse impact on negotiations between the Punjab government and the SGPC over future *gurdwara* legislation. All consultation with the authorities by the SGPC was suspended, and the government noted, 'vigorous action taken by the Government has ... impeded, if not altogether terminated reconciliation between the Prabhandak Committee and Government'.[47] Sikh militants charged the government with duplicity in claiming sympathy with their demand for *gurdwara* reform while unleashing a campaign to crush the Akali movement. They insisted that matters relating to *gurdwara* legislation could not be considered until all persons arrested in connection with the *gurdwara* reform movement were released.

The next few months witnessed an intense propaganda battle

between the SGPC and the Punjab government with familiar allegations of official repression and interference in Sikh religious matters and counter-allegations of Akali lawlessness. Though negotiations between the government and the committee over a suitable *gurdwara* bill came to an abrupt halt, official consultations with Sikh members of the legislative council continued hesitantly, much to the committee's chagrin. It issued repeated communiqués warning that 'in view of the unaminous decision of the Committee to accept no Bill under the present circumstances, it is expected that no Sikh will participate in the drafting or passing of the Bill'.[48] Since the Sikh legislators chose to disregard these instructions, the SGPC retorted by excommunicating them in the name of the *panth*.[49] Reports of consultation between the government and Sikh members of the Punjab Legislative Council also aroused the suspicions of Sahajdhari Sikhs and various Udasi organizations. The All India Udasi Mahamandal petitioned the Viceroy expressing its fears concerning the drafting of *gurdwara* legislation without its participation, and various Sahajdhari Sikh organizations issued a spate of resolutions appealing for due consideration of their rights.[50] In the midst of this chorus of mutual recriminations the Punjab government strove to draft *gurdwara* legislation acceptable to Sikh legislators who themselves repeatedly shifted their stance.

This uneasy calm was not to last. In August 1922 an innocuous incident at Guru-ka-Bagh (the garden of the guru), the site of a small shrine built to mark the visit of Guru Arjun, situated some twelve miles from Amritsar City, sparked off another confrontation between the Tat Khalsa and the government. Controversy over the management of this shrine had come to notice in January 1921, when a meeting was held at the shrine by Akalis in an attempt to press the *mahant* to reform his conduct. A settlement was reached between the reformers and *mahant* Sunder Das under which the *mahant* continued to serve as manager of the shrine under the supervision of a managing committee of which he himself was a member. However, in March 1921 Sunder Das revolted against this agreement, forcibly occupied the office of the managing committee and destroyed its records. Some six months later an Akali *jatha* proceeded to Guru-ka-Bagh and in the absence of the *mahant* took possession of the *gurdwara*. The shrine was the scene of fresh trouble between the Akalis and

Sunder Das a year later. In August 1922 the Akalis at Guru-ka-Bagh cut down a tree on land adjoining the *gurdwara* for use as fuel in the *Guru-ka-langar* (free community kitchen) provided at the shrine. Sunder Das complained to the district authorities of this theft from what he claimed was his property, the local district magistrate ruled that the *mahant* was legally entitled to continue in possession of the property unless evicted through a civil court, and the Akalis concerned were arrested. A few weeks later, a number of Akalis acting under instructions from the SGPC cut down more trees on the land claimed by the *mahant*. Sunder Das again complained to the police and the Akalis concerned were taken into custody. Fearing an escalation of the conflict, the Punjab government sent a detachment of police to Guru-ka-Bagh to safeguard the *mahant*'s 'person and property'. Prompt official action did not, however, deter the Akalis, and despite the presence of police repeated attempts were made to gather wood from the land neighbouring the *gurdwara*. The police responded by making arrests for theft and criminal trespass. By 24 August some 110 Akalis had been arrested at Guru-ka-Bagh.[51]

The arrests at Guru-ka-Bagh rapidly became a subject of bitter controversy. For the Akalis it was a clear and unjustifiable infringement of their religious liberty. The land adjoining the *gurdwara*, they asserted, was in fact attached to the shrine and indeed had habitually been used to provide for it. The *mahant*, a mere custodian of the shrine, could not claim private possession of sacred property which rightfully belonged to the Sikh *panth*. News of the arrests at Guru-ka-Bagh inevitably attracted other zealous Akalis to the spot, and by 26 August the District Commissioner, Amritsar, reported that some 1,200 Akalis had assembled at the shrine. The Akalis continued to enter the disputed land, and the local authorities made arrests daily. In response the SGPC launched an extensive propaganda campaign to enlist support. Public meetings were held at the Golden Temple and Sikhs were warned that the government, by denying them their religious duty of collecting fuel for the *Guru-ka-langar*, was evidently determined to undermine their faith. Such propaganda and the efficient Akali organization were quick to produce results, and the Deputy Commissioner, Amritsar, warned that the strength of Akalis at the shrine would rise to 6,000 within days.[52]

The dispute at Guru-ka-Bagh was rapidly developing into a

major controversy between the Tat Khalsa and the government, but in view of bitter past experience the Punjab government noted,

> The real issue is whether Government is to discharge its primary duty of protecting individuals in the enjoyment of property of which they are in possession or whether it is to abdicate its function in this matter under pressure of force or show of force ... In the circumstances Government has been compelled to perform its elementary duty ... The only alternative would have been to allow the mahant to protect himself, a course which might have resulted in far more violence ... It must be remembered that in this matter Government are dealing with men who have publicly announced that they have a right to seize and administer any Sikh shrine. If Government gives way in the present instance these men will enforce that right, as indeed they have already threatened to do, in the case of other shrines.[53]

The government resolved to remain firm. Additional police were sent to Guru-ka-Bagh and troops at nearby Amritsar were put on alert. Police pickets were placed on all access roads to Guru-ka-Bagh to prevent the further influx of Akalis to the area, and supplies to the Akalis already at the shrine were intercepted. To curtail inflammatory propaganda emanating from the SGPC, its President and eight office-holders were arrested and charged with abetment of theft and criminal trespass. The offices of the SGPC and Akali Dal were raided and searched.

Government efforts to contain the situation proved unsuccessful. As a direct challenge to Government authority, the SGPC dispatched an Akali *jatha* of fifty men to Guru-ka-Bagh. The Akalis were intercepted by the police, declared an illegal assembly on the grounds that they intended the forcible seizure of private property, and asked to disperse. On their refusal to do so they were dispersed by force. The SGPC responded by launching a campaign of non-violent civil disobedience. Daily prayer meetings were held at the Akal Takht and Akali volunteers took a sacred oath to remain non-violent and undeterred in their resolve to fulfil their religious duty. The *jatha* then marched amidst much ceremony towards Guru-ka-Bagh. Daily a *jatha* was thus dispatched from Amritsar and daily it was forcibly dispersed by the police. But the non-violent demeanour of the Akalis confronting severe beatings by the police only added a sharper edge to the SGPC's propaganda and enlisted widespread support and sympathy. A deputation of the Sikh members of the legislative council and another of the Chief Khalsa Diwan visited the scene and passed resolutions condemning official harshness.[54] Members of the All India Congress Committee also visited the scene and the Congress appointed a committee of inquiry to report on allegations of police high-handedness. Even the pro-government newspaper the *Civil and Military Gazette* of Lahore was moved to comment, 'One cannot help being impressed by the accounts of the way in which the Akalis have met the beatings that have been inflicted on them by the police and feeling that they are brave men ... when the irreducible minimum of truth has been reached, it must be admitted that the beatings which these Akali Jathas endured was one which required no small moral courage to face in cold blood'.[55]

The daily attempts to proceed to Guru-ka-Bagh in defiance of the government soon took the form of a holy pilgrimage, a path to martyrdom in the cause of the faith. The religious sanctity and social prestige conferred upon members of these Akali *jathas* became in itself an incentive to the recruitment for the *jatha*s. The intense religious conviction which permeated the campaign is best illustrated by an incident which received much local publicity and credence. Soon after the daily clashes between the Akalis and government en route to Guru-ka-Bagh began, a golden hawk was sighted in the vicinity of the shrine. The arrival of this hawk, a symbol of Guru Gobind Singh, was immediately hailed as a sign that the guru had shown his presence in support of the faithful. Following his visit to the spot, C. F. Andrews described the scene succinctly,

> We saw two Sikhs ... pointing to the sky, where a great bird was circling in its flight towards Amritsar ... [they] eagerly ... told me that every day, as soon as the beatings at Guru-ka-Bagh began, the golden hawk rose from the Guru's garden and took its flight to Amritsar to tell those who were serving at the Golden Temple what was taking place ... There was a light in their eyes as they spoke ... which betokened joy ... The whole scene, the intense faith of my companion, the look of reverence in their faces ... moved me very deeply. It was the first event which really ... put me in touch with the Akali reform movement in its spiritual aspects as perhaps nothing else could have done'.[56]

The Punjab government was in a difficult position. In an attempt to minimize the possibility of a large-scale conflict with the Akalis at Guru-ka-Bagh, the government had restricted access to the area. Yet forcibly restricting access to a place of worship seemed only to stir more Sikhs to militancy and strengthen the hand of the SGPC. The government decided to modify its strategy. It announced that access to Guru-ka-Bagh would be permitted, but trespassing on the disputed land would not be tolerated. H. D. Craik, chief secretary of the Punjab government, explaining this shift in strategy, wrote to the home department secretary in the government of India,

> There is no doubt that the situation has been obscured by the injuries actually caused by the police in repelling the Akalis, and by exaggerated accounts of police excesses ... There is also no doubt that these stories and the sight of these injuries have excited a large measure of sympathy for the Akalis on the part of loyal and moderate Sikhs and other persons not generally in sympathy with the Akali movement. It was for this reason that the change in ... tactics ... was decided on.[57]

The Punjab government also hoped that the excellent rainfall in the central Punjab during the previous few days would compel Sikh peasants to return to their fields for sowing of the crop, and thus deprive the SGPC of volunteers willing to undergo a long period of imprisonment.

The government had, however, underestimated the extent of the Akali Dal's organization, and the decision to permit free access to Guru-ka-Bagh only shifted the scene of conflict to the shrine. The SGPC continued to dispatch daily *jathas* to Guru-ka-Bagh, who attempted to squat on the disputed land in small batches and were arrested. By the end of September the number of Akalis arrested at the shrine amounted to more than 400 men; by the middle of October their number had risen to more than 1,300. Moreover, the SGPC's campaign was now receiving wide support from Sikhs in the army and from military pensioners. The cantonment Singh Sabha, Peshawar, was among several organizations of Sikh soldiers which sent subscriptions to the SGPC expressing their support.[58] The Punjab government also noted that the 'Jathas proceeding to Guru-ka-Bagh contain a fair proportion of ex-soldiers'.[59] To emphasize this point the SGPC announced its intention to dispatch a *jatha* composed exclusively of Sikh army pensioners. The pensioner's *jatha* of some 100 officers and men was duly dispatched from Amritsar amidst much publicity. Two days later the *jatha* was arrested. The SGPC then announced plans for the formation of similar special *jatha*s representing various sections of the community. One such special *jatha* was to consist of Sikh graduates, another of students of the Khalsa College, and a second pensioners' *jatha* was also to be raised. Meanwhile, the strength of *jatha*s sent to Guru-ka-Bagh was raised to 100 men per *jatha*; two weeks later the strength of the daily *jatha*s was further raised to 120 men. As a result, the total number of Akalis arrested at Guru-ka-Bagh multiplied rapidly, and the government strove in vain to limit the numbers of those arrested. District magistrates were instructed to discharge Akali offenders under the age of 18 or over the age of 60, but the released Akalis often simply joined the next *jatha* arriving at Guru-ka-Bagh. By the beginning of November 1922 some 4,000 Akalis had been arrested at the shrine.[60]

Disaffection among Sikhs due to the conflict at Guru-ka-Bagh was spreading rapidly and the local government was understandably keen to find an early solution to the controversy. In October 1922 as report from a commanding officer of a Sikh regiment had suggested ominously that 'if the Prabhandak Committee ordered "down tools" the Sikhs ... in his regiment would do so, not out of hostility to British Officers ... and not violently but quietly and regretfully and merely because the Prabhandak Committee advises this'.[61] The Punjab government took stock of its options. In a desperate bid to seek a settlement, it had repeatedly endeavoured to persuade Sunder Das, the *mahant* at Guru-ka-Bagh, to compromise with the Akalis, with little success. Alternatively concerted repression of the SGPC's activities, beginning with the arrest of the remaining office-holders, was considered. But, the local Government reflected, past experience had demonstrated that the arrest of office-holders of the SGPC made little impact upon its ability to agitate. The committee would simply, as it had done in the past, elect new members to direct its affairs. Under the present circumstances it might also be extremely difficult to prove the complicity of individual members of the committee with the acts of Akalis. Further, considering the acute state of Sikh unrest, the government noted,

> The arrest of the members of the Committee, which is now recognised by practically the whole body of the Sikh community (including even the thoroughly loyal section) as the chief authority

in religious matters, would probably increase Government's difficulties ... it is possible that ultimately Government may be compelled to attempt to crush the Prabhandak Committee ... but the
Governor in Council is of the opinion that at present such a step
would be a mistake.[62]

Moreover, the government was acutely aware that a solution to
the conflict at Guru-ka-Bagh, while removing the immediate
cause of Sikh unrest, would do little to provide a solution to the
fundamental problems presented by Tat Khalsa militancy. The
conflict at Guru-ka-Bagh derived its basis from the larger
problem of *gurdwara* management, and in the absence of legislation governing the management of Sikh shrines acceptable to the
Tat Khalsa, Akali militancy was bound to be endemic.

Negotiations between the Punjab government and Sikh
members of the legislative council relating to such *gurdwara*
legislation had made slow progress, but by July 1922 agreement
had been reached on the basic principles upon which a *gurdwara*
bill would be based. The draft bill was essentially similar to the
Sikh Gurdwaras and Shrines Bill of 1921 as it emerged from the
select committee, but with some crucial modifications. The
principal point on which the Sikh legislators had disagreed with
the provisions of the Sikh Gurdwaras and Shrines Bill of 1921
related to the composition of the board of commissioners to be set
up under the measure. The board of commissioners was to take
temporary charge of all disputed *gurdwaras*, provide for their
daily management, attempt to seek a settlement of disputes
through arbitration and conduct an inquiry into the origin and
history of the shrines upon which future legislation would be
based. This board was originally intended to be composed of
three members. One member representing the reformers, another
nominated by government on the understanding that he would
represent the interests of Sahajdhari Sikhs, and a third, British
officer also to be nominated by government. In the finalization of
the report of the select committee considering the 1921 bill, the
composition of the board had been altered to consist of four
members, providing an additional representative of the Tat
Khalsa. But the Sikh members of the legislative council had refused
to accept this basis for the commission of inquiry and temporary
management of disputed shrines, on the ground that the Sikh
community could not tolerate the interference of 'non-Sikhs' in

Sikh religious affairs. The Sahajdhari Sikh and Hindu members for their part had objected to this composition of the board of commissioners since it would place the Sahajdhari Sikh representative in a hopeless minority. The presence of a British president of the board had been designed specifically to allay their fears. Further, the Sahajdhari Sikhs and Hindus were apprehensive that a measure which provided specifically for temporary control of disputed shrines to be handed over to a body in which the Tat Khalsa Sikhs exercised considerable power would only encourage disputes between Akalis and *mahant*s for partisan reasons.[63]

Under the new draft bill, the Sikh Gurdwaras and Shrines Bill of 1922, the government made vital concessions to Tat Khalsa Sikh opinion. The British president of the board of commissioners was omitted, thereby reducing the strength of the board to three members and ensuring that the Tat Khalsa representatives would exercise an absolute majority. Another important concession aimed specifically at the SGPC concerned the method of appointment of the board. Under the original measure two Sikh members of the board were to have been selected by the Punjab government from a panel of eight members proposed by a majority of Sikh legislators, while the other two were to be appointed directly by the government. Under the new bill, the SGPC was, by public meeting of its members, to elect one of the commissioners, the Sikh members of the legislative council were to elect another, and the Punjab government would nominate the third. The only qualification placed upon these commissioners was that they 'must be a Vakil [lawyer], Advocate or Barrister of not less than five years' standing or a person who has held a civil judicial post for not less than five years'.[64] To meet the apprehensions of Sahajdhari Sikhs and Hindus, the jurisdiction of the board of commissioners was specifically laid down. The board was to exercise authority over *gurdwara*s declared as under 'dispute' by the Punjab government, and a list of such *gurdwara*s or shrines was to be compiled to avoid controversy. Only the government could declare that a shrine was disputed, and it was incumbent upon it to do so after a thorough inquiry.

In other respects the working and objectives of the draft bill were similar to those of the bill of 1921. Like its predecessor, the bill was designed essentially as a temporary measure for a maximum of two years. By placing all disputed shrines under the jurisdiction of the board of commissioners, the government aimed at removing such shrines from the sphere of popular controversy and conflict, and, through the inquiry to be conducted by the board, it aimed at providing the basis for permanent legislation relating to *gurdwara* management. A significant feature of the new bill was that it provided that if the SGPC or the Sikh legislators or both failed to nominate Sikh representatives to the Board of Commissioners, the Punjab government could make the nominations in their stead. The draft Sikh Gurdwaras and Shrines Bill of 1922, did not, like the earlier bill, define the term 'Sikh' to be employed.[65]

The Sikh Gurdwaras and Shrines Bill of 1922 was not the only measure relating to *gurdwara* management under the consideration of the Punjab government. The Chief Khalsa Diwan, anxious to reassert its somewhat eclipsed position in Sikh affairs, was preparing a *gurdwara* bill the principles of which were presented to the government by its secretary Sunder Singh Majithia. Unlike the government bill, the Chief Khalsa Diwan's proposal was a permanent measure. The Diwan claimed that the essential feature of the measure was to maintain the status quo regarding the present management of Sikh shrines while permitting popular control over Sikh religious institutions. The bill envisaged the management of all Sikh shrines as being under local managing committees consisting of three persons, including the *mahant* in question. The other two members of the managing committee were to be elected by the SGPC and by those persons of the area who met the franchise qualifications necessary to vote for elections to the provincial legislative council in the special Sikh constituencies. The *mahant* was to be secretary of the committee and one of the other two members its president. The *mahants* were to be secure in their appointments and could only be removed if found to be of bad character by a special Sikh tribunal to be set up. The *mahants* were entitled to any property registered in their name until the Sikh tribunal decided the status of the property in question, and they were free to decide on their successors according to 'the existing rules of succession among mahants'.[66] All religious ceremony at the shrines was to be conducted in accordance with the Guru Granth Sahib.[67]

The Sikh Gurdwaras and Shrines Bill of 1922 was published by the Punjab government on 15 September with a view to introducing it in the provincial legislative council shortly. But the conflict at Guru-ka-Bagh had dramatically affected the dynamics of power within the Sikh community. While the government had demonstrated its determination to uphold the legal rights of *mahant*s and *pujari*s at Guru-ka-Bagh, the success of the SGPC's campaign had also fortified it with unimpeachable authority. As the local government itself had noted, the success with which the SGPC drew support from varied sections of the community, and the substantial number of Sikhs who had rallied to its cause, lent credence to its claim to represent the majority of the Sikh community on the issue of *gurdwara* management. Thus, shortly after the bill was published, the Sikh members of the legislative council who had been negotiating with the government over the bill in defiance of the SGPC's instructions refused to co-operate any longer. The events at Guru-ka-Bagh, they claimed, had completely altered the circumstances in which the bill would be acceptable to the Sikh community. Nor were the Sikh legislators in favour of the bill being drafted by the Chief Khalsa Diwan, which they insisted made unwarranted concessions to the *mahant*s and *pujari*s. The Hindu and Sahajdhari for their part alleged that both bills, by providing disproportionate influence to the Tat Khalsa, would trespass against their religious rights.[68] The Punjab government's attempts at legislation seemed doomed to failure. Meanwhile, the arrests at Guru-ka-Bagh continued to mount, and the government of India, as well as the Secretary of State for India, in London, pressed the Punjab government to hasten the passage of legislation and put an end to Sikh unrest.

In the absence of a foreseeable solution to the dispute at Guru-ka-Bagh, the Punjab government resolved to expedite the passage of *gurdwara* legislation which would at least serve as a gesture of government earnestness in seeking a settlement of the controversy over *gurdwara* management. The chief secretary of the Punjab government reported to the Government of India,

In the circumstances Government have decided ... that if the Sikh members or the bulk of them show themselves in the course of the next few days ready to accept the second bill [the Chief Khalsa Diwan's proposal], Government will introduce that Bill. If on the other hand the bulk of the Sikh members continue to show hostility to the second Bill, Government would introduce the original Bill on which the Sikh members have already agreed in

writing. Government is anxious to convince the public of its desire
to terminate the dispute ... and it intends therefore to introduce
either one Bill or other.[69]

In the event, the Sikh and Hindu members of the legislative
council remained firm in their opposition to both measures, and
the Punjab government chose to adopt what it considered to be
the path of least resistance. It reported its decision to introduce
the Sikh Gurdwaras and Shrines Bill of 1922 in the provincial
legislative council to the government of India and noted, 'we
consider it practically certain ... that permanent Bill (Chief Khalsa
Diwan's measure) would be opposed by nearly all Sikh and Hindu
members, whereas Hindu opposition to temporary Bill would
probably be less acute, while previous agreements to temporary
Bill by the Sikh members should facilitate its passage'.[70]

Officials in Delhi were, however, in sharp disagreement with
the provincial government over which of the two bills under
consideration might be introduced in the Punjab Legislative
Council. The Sikh Gurdwaras and Shrines Bill of 1922 was, in the
government of India's view, of limited utility, providing only
temporary relief from the controversy over *gurdwara* reform
even if both parties accepted the measure. If the Sikh members of
the legislative council or the SGPC refused to select representatives for the board of commissioners, the bill, while providing for
such representation to be nominated by government, would place
the authorities in an untenable position. Legislation relating to
Sikh religious institutions under the provisions of the bill would
have little meaning if the Sikh legislators themselves found it
unacceptable and refused to co-operate in its functioning. The
Chief Khalsa Diwan's proposal, on the other hand, at least held
out the possibility of a permanent solution to Tat Khalsa unrest.
Since the Chief Khalsa Diwan's bill provided for the establishment of local *gurdwara* committees to be elected by Sikh
electors, the SGPC, the Government of India felt, might lose
much of its power of veto over the functioning of the measure.
While the SGPC was unquestionably in a position to prevent the
nominations of Sikhs from a limited number of candidates of
provincial prominence to the single board of commissioners set
up under the Sikh Gurdwara and Shrines Bill of 1922, it was
unlikely that the committee would be able to exercise such control
over elections to numerous local *gurdwara* committees. Malcolm

Hailey, a member of the Viceroy's council and a primary architect of the Government of India's appraisal of the proposed *gurdwara* legislation at the time, later noted,

> The weak part of the temporary Bill besides the fact that it is temporary is that it constitutes a central body, and in the event of failure by the Prabhandak Committee or members of the local Council to make nominations, Government has to supply the deficiency. The strong point of the second Bill [the Chief Khalsa Diwan's proposal] was that it created tahsil committees, and it is possible that the Prabhandak Committee would not have been strong enough to prevent the creation of a number at least of these committees, which are of course elective. It would, therefore, perhaps have been easier to make the second Bill function than the first.[71]

The government of India intimated its strong preference for the Chief Khalsa Diwan's bill to the Punjab government, but the latter remained firm in its belief that the bill would be staunchly resisted by both parties and that, under the circumstances it had no option but to introduce the Sikh Shrines and Gurdwaras Bill of 1922. The goverment of India decided not to press its views upon the Punjab government.

On 7 November the Sikh Gurdwaras and Shrines Bill of 1922 was introduced by the provincial education minister in the Punjab Legislative Council. The SGPC immediately reiterated its earlier decision that pending the release of all prisoners arrested in the pursuit of *gurdwara* reform, no legislation could be considered, and various Sahajdhari Sikh organizations also proclaimed their opposition to the bill. The Udasi Mahant Mahamandal Punjab passed a resolution stating, 'this Sabha claims that the SGPC is not representative of the Sikhs as apart from the Akalis. None of the various sects of the Nanak Panth are represented by it, that this Sabha believes that the newly framed Gurdwara Bill is against the decision of this Committee'.[72] In the legislative council, the Sikh members refused to support the bill. A motion to refer the bill to a select committee was carried with official support, but the Sikh members would not participate in its proceedings.

The select committee made few changes to the *gurdwara* bill, but at the instigation of official members of the committee a clause limiting the period within which the SGPC and Sikh members of the legislative council were to elect representatives to the board of Commissioners was introduced. The amended bill stated that failing the election of commissioners by the *gurdwara* committee or the Sikh legislators within a period of fifteen days from the declaration by the Punjab government of the first *gurdwara* as disputed, nominations of the commissioners would be made by the government. Another amendment, similarly aimed at countering any blocking tactics by the SGPC, gave the Punjab government authority to fill any vacancy on the board of commissioners caused by the resignation of any of its members. The other amendments of significance adopted by the select committee were clearly designed to reduce Hindu opposition to the measure. The term Sikh *gurdwara* was defined precisely to mean 'a Sikh place of public worship erected by or in memory of, or in commemoration of any incident in the life of any of the Ten Sikh Gurus'.[73] The jurisdiction of the commission was thus to extend over any such Sikh *gurdwara* under dispute rather than over any shrine declared as disputed by the Punjab government as was originally intended. No such precise definition, however, was applied to the term 'Sikh' itself. The select committee further clearly laid down that the Punjab government's nominee to the board of commissioners was to represent the Sahajdhari Sikhs. These amendments to the bill did not prevent the Hindu members of the select committee from adding notes of dissent to the committee's recommendations.

The Punjab government had from the outset intended to introduce the Sikh Gurdwaras and Shrines Bill of 1922 primarily as tactic to demonstrate its desire to seek a settlement of the controversy over *gurdwara* management. With official support, the bill was adopted by the provincial legislative council on 18 November in the face of opposition from both Kesdhari and Sahajdhari Sikhs. With the introduction of the bill the Punjab government, in conjunction with the government of India, moved to maximize its tactical advantage by launching a systematic propaganda campaign to undermine the credibility of the SGPC's allegations. An officer with wide experience in the Punjab was specially deputed to prepare propaganda literature directed at the Sikh peasantry, and meetings were arranged with Sikh troops to elucidate government's position regarding popular Sikh unrest. An interesting feature of the literature subsequently prepared was that it was provided with titles suggesting that it emanated from the SGPC in the hope that it would thus attract greater interest.[74]

Meanwhile, negotiations behind the scenes yielded an unexpected boon for government regarding the dispute at Guru-ka-Bagh. Sir Ganga Ram, a notable Hindu philanthropist, offered to lease the disputed land at Guru-ka-Bagh from the *mahant* and then permit access to the property. With official assistance, the land was accordingly leased to Sir Ganga Ram for one year. The new tenant requested the government to remove the police deployed around the site, and on 17 November the arrest of Akalis at Guru-ka-Bagh ceased.

The Punjab government had provided a viable means of *gurdwara* management, and the immediate cause of Sikh unrest had been removed. The local government was content not to carry matters further. The government of India, however, was inclined to take a very different view of official strategy. In November the Viceroy's council had met to discuss the Punjab government's report on the Sikh situation, and Malcolm Hailey was again a primary influence on the government of India's formulation of official tactics. Hailey noted, 'I think that if the Bill was properly utilised, it affords, some chance of getting rid, not of course of the agitation or the Prabhandak Committee, but of the feature which keeps the latter alive, namely the continual arrests'.[75] Government strategy, Hailey argued, should be to put the bill into operation and to utilize it, not as a solution to the controversy over *gurdwara* management, but as a means to undermine the basis of the SGPC's support. Once the bill was passed, government should press ahead with the formation of the *gurdwara* commission laid out under the measure, which could then take charge of disputed *gurdwara*s, including the one at Guru-ka-Bagh, and allow free access to them. The stoppage of arrests at Guru-ka-Bagh would remove the immediate basis for the SGPC's strength, while the extension of the Board of Commissioners jurisdiction to other disputed shrines would remove them from the sphere of popular unrest. Thus Hailey noted,

I believe that, with proper management, a [commission] could be formed. The Government would not get the best or most representative men; that I admit. But if it appointed men on a temporary basis, making it clear that they would yield their places to the representative of these ... bodies as soon as the latter chose to make nominations the position would be a fairly strong one. What then, in this case would be the course of action of the Prabhandak Committee? They might refuse to recognise the position of the [commission], but if the [commission] merely took possession and then declared the land open to the public the Committee would not have much basis for open action. Later on, the [commission] would no doubt be appointing mahants ... and the Committee might refuse to recognise them and seek to turn them out. But there again I think that the Committee would have an infinitely weaker position than at present, and it would require a great deal of persuasion to whip up the ordinary Sikh into agitation on the subject.[76]

Other members of the Viceroy's council were in agreement with Hailey. The settlement at Guru-ka-Bagh preceded any action by the government of India, but the Punjab government was subsequently urged to proceed with the establishment of the Board of Commissioners under the new bill. S. P. O'Donnel wrote to the chief secretary of the Punjab government, to suggest future tactics discussed by the Viceroy's council and concluded, 'The Government of India, therefore, regard it as of greatest importance that the Act should not be allowed to become a dead letter, and the establishment of the [commission] be secured at the earliest possible date'.[77]

The announcement of the settlement at Guru-ka-Bagh simultaneously with the passage of the *gurdwara* bill, threatened to undermine the basis of the SGPC's authority and predictably brought a sharp reaction from it. The committee condemned the agreement at Guru-ka-Bagh on the ground that 'it gives to the Panth as an act of grace what it claims as a right', and stated that 'Panthic control over the Sikh shrines must be secured by means of Panthic sacrifices and sufferings'.[78] Regarding the bill, it stated that the passage of the legislation in the face of Sikh opposition had made a peaceful solution of the controversy quite impossible, and threatened to renew militant tactics at the site of another disputed shrine. Behind this public stance, however, a divergence of opinion as to future tactics developed among Sikh militants. The leaders of the Akali Dal were in favour of immediate militant activity beginning with the seizure of other *gurdwaras*, but the SGPC urged moderation, preferring to settle disputes through negotiations at this stage. For SGPC leaders, the passage of the bill posed a very real threat to their authority and they were anxious not to push the government into the establishment of the commission provided for in the bill.[79] Momentum generated by recent events certainly seemed to favour the SGPC's tactics. The settlement at Guru-ka-Bagh was seen by many, supporters and adversaries alike, as a significant victory for the SGPC. In the weeks following the cessation of agitation at Guru-ka-Bagh, several *mahants*, sensing the futility of further opposition to the SGPC, voluntarily affiliated themselves to the committee and placed their offices under its jurisdiction. Similarly, the Punjab government reported that several meetings had been held throughout the province to demonstrate support for the SGPC and condemn the bill and noted, 'At one of these meetings in Sialkot City a resolution opposing the Bill was moved by a Sikh Honorary Magistrate whose loyalty has always been above suspicion, and it appears that in the matter of immediate Gurdwara reform the whole orthodox Sikh Community is solidly behind the Akalis'.[80]

However, the Punjab government continued to resist the government of Indian's reccomendation on future tactics. Information reaching the local government regarding the divergence of opinion among militant Sikhs and the relative inaction of Akalis made it hesitant to precipitate matters at this juncture. Instead, it reopened negotiations with the SGPC over *gurdwara* legislation. It reported to the government of India that in view of the 'reasonable' attitude of some members of the SGPC, there was some prospect of agreement being reached on permanent *gurdwara* legislation acceptable to government, and that 'unless things take an unexpected turn, it would be better to await the result of negotiations with the Committee, even though these may be protracted'.[81]

Officials in Delhi reluctantly accepted the Punjab government's assessment of future strategy, but the government of India remained sceptical about the local government's ability to deal firmly with Sikh unrest. S. P. O'Donnel wrote to the chief secretary of the Punjab government, 'The Government of India recognise the necessity of negotiations which are being carried out [but] ... it appears to them that if too much time is allowed to elapse before any steps are taken to make the bill effective, the impression will be created that the Government cannot or dare not set up the [commission] contemplated by the Bill ... if such an impression should be created, the whole position would be worse than ever'.[82] In anticipation of the failure of present negotiations and the resurgence of militant activity, the Viceroy's council considered future strategy. For the moment, it was decided, the government of India would not interfere in the Punjab government's policy, but should militant seizures of shrines begin, it would impress firmly upon the local Government the necessity of pursuing the establishment of a commission under the *gurdwara* bill.

Negotiations between the Punjab government and the SGPC continued sporadically for several months but yielded no conclusive results. The government, in private consultations with the committee, offered to release all prisoners arrested in connection with *gurdwara* reform except those convicted for crimes of violence, provided the committee publicly announced its disapproval of any illegal seizures of shrines. The SGPC was not prepared to make such a declaration, but offered instead that if the prisoners were released, it would refrain from militant action for a period of time provided that suitable *gurdwara* legislation was passed in the meantime. The government for its part was unwilling to accept such a vague undertaking, and the negotiations bogged down.

In the interim, both sides resorted to a variety of devices to rally public sympathy. The SGPC focused its energies on demanding the release of all Akali prisoners and in a campaign alleging the ill-treatment of these prisoners. Militant members of the Akali Dal continued to press for aggressive tactics, but the SGPC managed to keep them in check. In February 1923 the committee successfully redirected its energies into building up Akali organization at the *tahsil* level. By the end of March 1923 the beginning of harvesting operation once again served to lull Akali activity.[83] For its part, in April 1923, the Punjab government attempted to provide an impetus to the negotiation by releasing Akali prisoners in small batches on the ground of 'good conduct'. It reported to the government of India, 'It is hoped that this release may do something though possibly not a great deal – towards establishing better relations between Government and the Sikhs and it will at any rate get rid of a troublesome class of prisoners ... at as opportune a moment as is likely to occur'.[84] This strategy failed to bring any flexibility to the SGPC's familiar stand on any *gurdwara* legislation. However, the Punjab government was not unduly perturbed at this lack of progress. It noted, 'The lull in the activities of the Akalis is ... all to the good ... the longer the lull continues the more difficult it will be for the Shiromani Gurdwara Prabhandak Committee to resusitate excitement'.[85]

Notes to Chapter 5

1 'Akali Dal and SGPC'.

2 *Akali* (15 Nov. 1921), Punjab Govt, *Selections*, vol. 34, no. 48. The *Akali*, a *gurumukhi* newspaper published from Lahore was begun in May 1920. The newspaper reflected the new spirit of Khalsa nationalism manifest among Sikhs. The objective of the paper, as stated by its editor, Mangal Singh, who claimed to represent the 'young Sikhs' as opposed to 'loyalist' Sikh leaders, was to safeguard the interests of the Sikh community. In pursuit of this, the paper pledged to pursue a programme which included '(i) to get control of our educational and religious institutions, (ii) to advocate justice for the Martial Law and Komagata Maru prisoners, and the recognition of the right to bear Kirpans in the army'. (Mangal Singh, 'The Sikhs and national evolution; what the Akali stands for', *Tribune*, 31 July 1920).

3 *Loyal Gazette* (13–15 Nov. 1921), Punjab Govt, *Selections*, vol. 34, no. 47; Panth Sewak (9 Nov. 1921), Punjab Govt, *Selections*, vol. 34, no. 48.

4 'Akali Dal and SGPC'. See also Summary of News from Colonel C. Kaye to S. P. O'Donnel, 16 Nov. 1921, GOI, Home (Political) proceedings, no. 459 of 1921.

5 'Akali Dal and SGPC'.

6 Note by H. D. Craik, 26 Nov. 1921, GOI, Home (Political) proceedings, no. 459 of 1921. See also Note by W. Vincent, 17 Nov. 1921, GOI, Home (Political) proceedings, no. 459 of 1921.

7 Fortnightly Report, 15 Jan. 1922, GOI, Home (Political) proceedings, no. 18 of Jan. 1922.

8 Fortnightly Report, 15 Jan. 1922.

9 Fortnightly Report, 15 Jan. 1922.

10 J. Maynard, Member (Home) of Governor's Council, in *Punjab Legislative Council Debates*, vol. 3, no. 1; Punjab Government Press Communiqué, *Tribune* (13 Jan. 1922).

11 *Akali*, 21 Jan. 1922, Punjab Govt, *Selections*, vol. 35, no. 4. See also *Punjab Darpan*, 11 Jan. 1922, Punjab Govt, *Selections*, vol. 35, no. 4; *Loyal Gazette*, 15 Jan. 1922, Punjab Govt, *Selections*, vol. 35, no. 3.

12 Fortnightly Report, 31 Jan. 1922, GOI, Home (Political) proceedings, no. 18 of Jan. 1922.

13 'Akali Dal and SGPC'.

14 J. Wilson-Johnston, Home Sec. Punjab Govt, to Sec. Home (Political) Dept, GOI, 10 Mar. 1922, GOI, Home (Political) proceedings,

no. 459/II of 1922. See also Fortnightly Report, 15 Jan. 1922, GOI, Home (Political) proceedings, no. 18 of Jan. 1922.

15 *Tribune* (3 May 1921).

16 *Tribune* (17 Jan. 1922).

17 Fortnightly Report, 28 Feb. 1922, GOI, Home (Political) proceedings, no. 18 of Feb. 1922; Fortnightly Report, 15 Jan. 1922 and 31 Jan. 1922, GOI, Home (Political) proceedings, no. 18 of Jan. 1922.

18 Fortnightly Report, 28 Feb. 1922.

19 'The military aspects of the present situation in the Punjab' prepared by the Army general staff, 24 Feb. 1922, GOI, Home (Political) proceedings, no. 459/II of 1922.

20 'The military aspects of the present situation in the Punjab'.

21 Fortnightly Report, 15 Feb. 1922, GOI, Home (Political) proceedings, no. 18 of Feb. 1922.

22 Fortnightly Report, 28 Feb. 1922.

23 Fortnightly Report, 15 Feb. 1922.

24 Fortnightly Report, 15 Feb. 1922.

25 Telegram, no. 231, 28 Feb. 1922, from Viceroy (Home Dept) to Sec. of State for India, GOI, Home (Political) proceedings, no. 18 of Feb. 1922.

26 Punjab govt Press communiqué, 10 Mar. 1922, GOI, Home (Political) proceedings no. 459/II of 1922.

27 Punjab govt Press communiqué, 10 Mar. 1922; undated SGPC Press communiqué, GOI, Home (Political) proceedings, no. 459/II of 1922; SGPC Press communiqué, *Tribune* (19 Mar. 1922).

28 SGPC Press communiqué, *Tribune* (3 Mar. 1922). See also SGPC Press communiqué, *Tribune* (24 Mar. 1922).

29 SGPC Press communiqué, *Tribune* (4 Apr. 1922). See also Fortnightly Report, 15 Mar. 1922, GOI, Home (Political) proceedings, no. 18 of Mar. 1922; C. W. Gwynne, Dep. Sec., Home Dept, GOI, to E. Joseph, Chief Sec., Punjab Govt, 14 Mar. 1922, J. Wilson-Johnston, Sec., Home Dept, Punjab Govt, to C. W. Gwynne, Dep. Sec., Home Dept, GOI, 23 Mar. 1922, GOI, Home (Political) proceedings, no. 459/II of 1922; Report by Sant Singh, Dep. Supt, Police (Political), 13 Mar. 1922, GOI, Home (Political) proceedings, no. 459/II of 1922.

30 Note by S. P. O'Donnel, 18 Feb. 1922, GOI, Home (Political) proceedings, no. 459/II of 1922.

31 Notes by C. A. Innes and B. N. Sharma, 20 Feb. 1922, GOI, Home (Political) proceedings, no. 459/II of 1922. See also note by W. Vincent, 18 Feb. 1922 and Note by C. Rawlinson, 1 Mar. 1922, GOI, Home (Political) proceedings, no. 459/II of 1922.

32 Note by C. Kaye, 8 Mar. 1922, GOI, Home (Political) proceedings, no. 459/II of 1922.

33 'The military aspects of the present situation in the Punjab'. See also Report by Lt. Col. R. H. Anderson, 45th Sikhs, 6 Feb. 1922, GOI, Home (Political) proceedings, no. 459/II of 1922.

34 J. Wilson-Johnston, Sec. Home Dept, Punjab Govt, to the Commissioners of Jullundur, Lahore, Ambala and Multan Divisions and Dep. Commissioners of Lahore, Amritsar, Gurdaspur, Sialkot, Gujranwala, Sheikhupura, Hoshiarpur, Jullundur, Ludhiana, Ferozepur, Ambala, Lyallpur and Montgomery Districts, Home (General), 6 Mar. 1922, GOI, Home (Political) proceedings, no. 459/II of 1922.

35 J. Wilson-Johnston to the Commissioners of Jullundur ..., 6 Mar. 1922.

36 S. P. O'Donnel, Sec., Home Dept, GOI, to Chief Sec., Punjab Govt, 16 Mar. 1922, Home (Political) proceedings, no. 459/II of 1922.

37 S. P. O'Donnel to Chief Sec. Punjab Govt, 16 Mar. 1922.

38 GOI, Home (Political) proceedings, no. 179/II of 1922. See also Judgement in the Nankana Sahib Case, *Tribune* (9 Mar. 1922).

39 GOI, Home (Political) proceedings, no. 179/II of 1922.

40 GOI, Home (Political) proceedings, no. 179/II of 1922.

41 Note by S. P. O'Donnel, Sec. Home Dept, GOI, 6 June 1922, GOI, Home (Political) proceedings, no. 179/II of 1922.

42 Note by Mohammed Shafi, undated, and Note by E. M. Cook, undated, GOI, Home (Political) proceedings, no. 179/II of 1922.

43 Note by S. P. O'Donnel, 6 June 1922.

44 See Fortnightly Report, 15 Nov. 1920, GOI, Home (Political), Deposit, no. 74 of Dec. 1920; Fortnightly Report, 15 Jan. 1921, GOI, Home (Political), Deposit, no. 41 of Apr. 1921; Fortnightly Report, 31 Jan. 1921, GOI, Home (Political), Deposit, no. 12 of June 1921 and GOI, Home (Political) proceedings, no. 179/II of 1922.

45 Secret circular letter issued to leading *jathedars* of the Akali Dal by Sahib Singh, Joint Sec., SGPC, 19 Mar. 1922, GOI (intercepted), Home (Political) proceedings, no. 18 of Apr. 1922.

46 See Note by H. D. Craik, 22 Mar. 1922 and 25 Mar. 1922, Note by S. P. O'Donnel, 28 Mar. 1922; J. Wilson-Johnston, Sec., Home Dept, Punjab Govt, to S. W. Gwynne, Dep. Sec., Home Dept, GOI, 28 Mar. 1922, Weekly Reports on the Sikh Situation and the Akali Movement of 4 Apr. 1922, 11 Apr. 1922, 18 Apr. 1922, 25 Apr. 1922, 2 May 1922 and 16–17 May 1922, GOI, Home (Political), Deposit, no. 18 of Apr. 1922, and Home (Political), Deposit, no. 18 of May 1922.

47 Telegram no. 336, Viceroy (Home Dept) to Sec. of State for India, 11 Apr. 1922, GOI, Home (Political), Deposit, no. 18 of Apr. 1922.

48 SGPC Press communiqué, *Tribune* (19 Apr. 1922). See also, SGPC Press communiqué, *Tribune*, (31 May 1922); Punjab govt. Press communiqué, 6 May 1922, GOI, Home (Political) proceedings, no. 861 of 1922.

49 Dasaundha Singh, Statement in *Punjab Legislative Council Debates*, vol. 4, no. 7.

50 'Application from four Udasi *mahant* organizations for permission to present a memorial or address regarding the *gurdwara* reform bill to H. E. the Viceroy in person by means of a deputation', GOI, Home (Political) proceedings, no. 179/II of 1922; *Tribune* (28 July 1922, 29 July 1922).

51 See *Tribune* (18 Mar. 1923); Statement by the Punjab Govt regarding Guru-ka-Bagh, GOI, Home (Political) proceedings, no. 914 of 1922.

52 H. D. Craik, Chief Sec., Punjab Govt, to S. P. O'Donnel, Sec., Home Dept, GOI, 26 Aug. 1922, GOI, Home (Political) proceedings, no. 914 of 1922; *Tribune* (18 Mar. 1923).

53 Statement by the Punjab Govt regarding Guru-ka-Bagh, GOI, Home (Political) proceedings, no. 914 of 1922; Note by H. D. Craik, 28 Aug. 1922, GOI, Home (Political) proceedings, no. 914 of 1922.

54 See *Tribune* (8 Sept. 1922, 9 Sept. 1922); Notes in the Intelligence Bureau, Note by Bhagwan Das, 7 Sept. 1922, GOI, Home (Political) proceedings, no. 914 of 1922; Fortnightly Report, 30 Sept. 1922, GOI, Home (Political) proceedings, no. 18 of Sept. 1922.

55 *Civil and Military Gazette* (21 Sept. 1922).

56 *Tribune* (19 Sept. 1922).

57 H. D. Craik to S. P. O'Donnel, 20 Sept. 1922, GOI, Home (Political) proceedings, no. 914 of 1922.

58 Fortnightly Report, 15 Sept. 1922, GOI, Home (Political) proceedings, no. 18 of Sept. 1922.

59 H. D. Craik to S. P. O'Donnel, 20 Sept. 1922, GOI, Home (Political) proceedings, no. 914 of 1922.

60 See SGPC Press communiqué, *Tribune* (27 Oct. 1922, 1 Nov. 1922); Fortnightly Report, 31 Oct. 1922, GOI, Home (Political) proceedings, no. 18 of Oct. 1922; H. D. Craik to S. P. O'Donnel, 31 Oct. 1922, GOI, Home (Political) proceedings, no. 914 of 1922.

61 C. W. Gwynne to S. P. O'Donnel, 31 Oct. 1922, GOI, Home (Political) proceedings, no. 914 of 1922.

62 C. W. Gwynne to S. P. O'Donnel, 31 Oct. 1922; See also Record of proceedings of a conference at Viceregal Lodge, 3 Oct. 1922, and H. D. Craik to W. Vincent, 5 Oct. 1922, GOI, Home (Political) proceedings, no. 914 of 1922.

63 See 'Report of the Select Committee on the Sikh Gurdwaras and Shrines Bill, 1921', *Punjab Gazette Extraordinary*, 8 Apr. 1921; Fazl-i-Husain, statement in *Punjab Legislative Council Debates*, vol. 4, no. 4.

64 'A Bill to provide for the administration and management of certain Sikh gurdwaras and shrines, and for an enquiry into matters connected therewith', *Punjab Gazette*, 17 Nov. 1922, items 5(4).

65 'A bill to provide for the administration and management of certain Sikh shrines . . .', *Punjab Gazette*, 17 Nov. 1922, item 5(2), 5(3).

66 See Record of proceedings of a conference at Viceregal Lodge, 3 Oct. 1922, GOI, Home (Political) proceedings, no. 14 of 1922; Sunder Singh Majithia, 'Sikh Gurdwaras and Shrines Bill and related papers, 1921–1923', (private papers), vol. 35; Record of proceedings of the executive council on the Sikh *gurdwaras* bill, 3 Nov. 1922, GOI, Home (Political) proceedings, no. 914 of 1922.

67 Record of proceedings of the executive council on the Sikh *gurdwaras* bill, 3 Nov. 1922, GOI, Home (Political) proceedings, no. 914 of 1922.

68 See H. D. Craik to S. P. O'Donnel, 31 Oct. 1922, GOI, Home (Political) proceedings, no. 914 of 1922; Raghubir Singh, statement in *Punjab Legislative Council Debates*, vol. 4, no. 4; *Tribune* (25 October 1922).

69 H. D. Craik to S. P. O'Donnel, 31 Oct. 1922.

70 Telegram P, no. 1314, 5 Nov. 1922, Governor, Punjab, to Viceroy, GOI, Home (Political) proceedings, no. 914 of 1922.

71 W. M. Hailey to W. Vincent, 15 Nov. 1922, GOI, Home (Political) proceedings, no. 914 of 1922. See also Telegram P, 2 Nov. 1922, Sec., Home Dept, GOI, to W. Vincent; H. D. Craik to S. P. O'Donnel, 2 Nov. 1922; Telegram P, 3 Nov. 1922, Sec., Home Dept, GOI, to W. Vincent, W. Vincent to S. P. O'Donnel, 3 Nov. 1922; Telegram P, 5 Nov. 1922, Private Sec. to Viceroy to Sec., Home Dept, GOI, GOI, Home (Political) proceedings, no. 914 of 1922.

72 *Tribune* (28 Oct. 1922).

73 Report of the Select Committee on the Sikh Gurdwaras and Shrines Bill, 1922, *Punjab Gazette*, 17 Nov. 1922, item 5(2), 5(3). See also items 1(3), 5(1), 8(2).

74 Note by C. M. G. Oglive, 4 Nov. 1922, GOI, Home (Political) proceedings, no. 914 of 1922.

75 Note by W. M. Hailey, 15 Nov. 1922, GOI, Home (Political) proceedings, no. 914 of 1922.

76 Note by W. M. Hailey, 15 Nov. 1922.

77 S. P. O'Donnel to H. D. Craik, 20 Nov. 1922, GOI, Home (Political) proceedings, no. 914 of 1922.

78 Fortnightly Report, 30 Nov. 1922, GOI, Home (Political) proceedings, no. 18 of Nov. 1922.

79 Fortnightly Report, 30 Nov. 1922. See also Fortnightly Report, 15 Dec. 1922, GOI, Home (Political) proceedings, no. 18 of Dec. 1922.

80 Fortnightly Report, 30 Nov. 1922, GOI, Home (Political) proceedings, no. 18 of Dec. 1922.

81 H. D. Craik to S. P. O'Donnel, 28 Nov. 1922, GOI, Home (Political) proceedings, no. 914 of 1922.

82 S. P. O'Donnel to H. D. Craik, 1 Dec. 1922, GOI, Home (Political) proceedings, no. 914 of 1922.

83 There were exceptions, however, to the lull in militant Sikh activity. The summer of 1923 saw a brief campaign of terrorism in the Punjab by an organization called the Babbar Akali Jatha. Recruited largely from the ranks of ex-Ghadrites and returned emigrants, the group's tactics were similar to those adopted by the Ghadr party. It conducted assasinations of loyal Sikhs and attempted to intimidate unco-operative *mahants*. The SGPC, however, disowned them, and deter-mined official action resulted in the death or imprisonment of the majority of the terrorists within months. See GOI, Home (Political) proceedings, no. 25 of Jan.–May 1923; Note on the Babbar Akali Jatha, GOI, Home (Political) proceedings, no. 134/II of 1923; The Babbar Akali Movement, GOI, Home (Political) proceedings, no. 1 (X), of 1924; Kamlesh Mohan, 'The Babbar Akali Movement and its Ideology', *Proceedings of the Punjab History Conference 1972* (Patiala, 1972).

84 Fortnightly Report, 15 Apr. 1923, GOI, Home (Political) proceed-ings, no. 25 of Apr. 1923.

85 'A brief statement of the present policy of the Punjab government with regard to the Gurdwara question', GOI, Home (Political) proceedings, no. 914 of 1922.

6

Implications of Militancy

Recurring conflict between the SGPC and the government had progressively strengthened the hands of the committee and won it the allegiance of the majority of the Khalsa Sikh community, but the controversy over *gurdwara* management remained unresolved. The summer of 1923 saw the Tat Khalsa once again in dramatic conflict with the government, a conflict which was to continue for almost a year. The SGPC's tactics remained the same, but the essentially political nature of the issue which the committee chose to confront the government on provided the latter with an opportunity for decisive action. The government succeeded in containing Sikh political unrest, but made vital concessions to Tat Khalsa religious sentiment which were tantamount to the recognition and institutionalization of a distinct and separate Sikh identity.

On 9 July 1923 the government of India announced that the Maharaja of the state of Nabha had abdicated in favour of his son, who was a minor.[1] The abdication of the ruler of Nabha, one of the five Sikh rulers of native states, attracted wide interest. The Sikh League immediately passed a resolution in protest and the radical Sikh Press was quick to interpret the 'enforced' abdication of the Maharaja as a direct threat to the Sikh community. Thus the *Akali-te-Pardesi* asked, 'will the bureaucracy succeed in weakening the Panth by putting an end to the Nabha State?'.[2] The SGPC also joined in active denunciation of the Government. In a communiqué issued on 10 July it warned, 'the weakening of Nabha is the thin edge of the wedge of the designs of Government against an important section of the Sikh Community – the ... [native] States'.[3] But in fact the committee was deeply divided as to appropriate action. A militant section of the committee urged immediate drastic action, but other members felt that such a political issue was outside the jurisdiction of the committee. Thus, though the SGPC was severe in its condemnation of the government, its working committe resolved to postpone action in the matter until after the forthcoming elections of the SGPC.

The SGPC's elections, in which all Khalsa Sikhs above the age of 18 were permitted to vote, had been completed by the end of July. The success of the committee's agitation at Guru-ka-Bagh had enhanced the authority and prestige of its more militant members, and the Punjab government noted that, 'The recent elections have returned a Committee which is far more extremist in character than its predecessor'.[4] The new committee was confronted from its own ranks by a campaign for militant action regarding the abdication of the Maharaja of Nabha. The Akali Dal passed a series of resolutions urging the SGPC 'to raise a typhoon of agitation till the Maharaja was restored',[5] and Sikh militants drummed up support through the columns of the radical Sikh Press. In August 1923 a general meeting of the SGPC was held to discuss the issue, and the committee decided with a majority vote that 'the Nabha question was one with which it was entitled to deal'.[6] The SGPC also passed a resolution stating that it believed that,

> the Government of India has deliberately taken advantage of the Patiala-Nabha dispute to wrest the administration of Nabha State from His Highness ... that to effect that purpose threats and intimidation have been used ... and that this decision of Government is vindictive, unjustified and absolutely uncalled for ... [the SGPC] is convinced that this action taken by Government ... is calculated to give a severe blow to the Panthic orthodoxy, organization, and well-being.[7]

The resolution authorized the executive committee to get 'the wrong done to Nabha and the Panth righted by all peaceful and legitimate means'.[8] Under the direction of the SGPC a concerted campaign of protest against the Maharaja's abdication was initiated. Through the Press and a series of *diwans* held throughout the province, militant Akalis stirred up feeling against the government. This campaign was not limited to British Punjab, and agitation quickly spilled into Nabha State.

To cope with the growing tide of disaffection among Sikhs, the administration of Nabha issued an ordinance prohibiting all political meetings in the state. However, the Akalis contended that their *diwan*s were essentially religious, not political, gatherings, and in open defiance of the state authorities continued to hold public meetings in various parts of Nabha at which violently anti-government speeches were made. Sikhs were repeatedly warned of the sinister designs of the government and urged to fight in defence of the organization and unity of the *panth*. One such *diwan* began at the Gangsar *gurdwara* at Jaito on 25 August 1923 at which resolutions were passed expressing sympathy with the former ruler and alleging conspiracy and treachery on the part of the government. The administration of Nabha reported that the organizers of the *diwan* called upon Sikhs 'to assemble and turn out the British dacoits who have seized the State and forcibly expelled the Maharaja'.[9] The Nabha administration responded firmly to this direct challenge to its authority and arrested the Akalis responsible for organizing the meeting. However, the arrest of Akalis at Jaito only increased the determination of the protestors to fight 'oppression'. The *diwan*, originally intended to last for three days, was extended, and, in an effort to attract greater public interest, an *akhand path* (non-stop recitation of the Guru Granth Sahib) was initiated at the *gurdwara*. The Nabha police raided the meeting again and, in the process of arresting leading Akalis, disrupted the *akhand path*.

The interruption of the *akhand path* at Jaito provided the SGPC with an opportunity to put a religious complexion on the entire issue and thus effectively rally support against the government. Popular Sikh agitation might have been difficult to sustain in the name of an abstract threat to the unity of the *panth*, but the forcible interruption of a sacred ceremony could easily be interpreted as an insult to the gurus and the faith. The SGPC freely alleged that the *pujari*s reading the Granth had been manhandled and the sacred book trampled upon, and quickly succeeded in evoking a sense of outrage among a wide segment of the Sikh community. A widely publicized resolution passed by the committee stated,

> The SGPC holds the Government of India responsible for the unbearable insult to Sikh scriptures and the action of challenging the religious liberty of the Sikhs to assemble in congregation and to go on pilgrimage to their Gurdwaras ... [and] therefore ... solemnly declare its determination to fulfill the sacred duty of adopting all peaceful and legitimate means to maintain the dignity of Sri Guru Granth Sahib and to enjoy the unfettered exercise of the religious rights that have been challenged.[10]

Sikh disaffection was effectively channelled by a revival of the *jathabandi* tactics employed at Guru-ka-Bagh. Batches of twenty-five Akalis were formed, and blessed amidst much ceremony at the Golden Temple. They then proceeded daily towards Jaito to 'resume' the unfinished *akhand path*. At Jaito the *jathas* were confronted by the Nabha police who demanded that they make a declaration not to indulge in any political activity at the shrine, upon which they would be permitted to enter the *gurdwara*. The *jathas* refused to make such a commitment on the ground that it represented interference in their religious liberty, and on their insistence on proceeding towards the shrine were arrested. Such *jathas* arrived daily at Jaito and the numbers of Akalis under arrest grew steadily. The stage was set for a repetition of mass conflict between the Tat Khalsa and the government.

The Government of India and the Punjab government viewed this resurgence of Akali militancy with grave apprehension. Officials in Delhi and Lahore had in the past repeatedly voiced their anxiety at the political nature of Akali organization and activity, but the issues behind Sikh unrest had been basically religious ones. Anxious not to alienate the sympathy of Sikhs by confrontation over religious demands which stirred deep feelings among the community as a whole, the Punjab government had proceeded with deliberate restraint. The SGPC's campaign of militant protest against the 'forced' abdication of the Maharaja of Nabha, however, demonstrated beyond a doubt to the local government the ineffectiveness of past conciliatory policy towards the Akalis, and it reinforced their fears as to the 'subversive' nature of the committee's ambitions. The campaign for the reinstatement of the Maharaja of Nabha was seen as a direct political challenge to the British Raj on which there could be no room for flexibility. The administration of Nabha and the Punjab government, in consultation with the government of India, proceeded to meet this challenge firmly. Akali *jathas* were permitted to enter Nabha State without hindrance, for the government preferred to confront them at a place far removed from the heartland of Akali support, but the daily arrest of *jathas* at Jaito was continued. A concerted effort was also made to curb Akali propaganda within the state. The editors and proprietors of newspapers sympathetic to the Akalis were charged with inflammatory writing, Akali meetings were repeatedly raided and leaders and organizers rounded up. But the daily march of *jatha*s to Jaito continued to excite interest and sympathy for the SGPC's programme and ensured a steady supply of recruits to perpetuate the campaign. Thus, in October 1923 the government acted decisively to curb Akali activity. In a Press communiqué the Punjab government stated that

> since the abdication of . . . the Maharaja of Nabha . . . the Prabhan-dak Committee and the allied Akali Dal have openly encouraged bodies of Akalis to invade the Nabha State with the object of intimidating Government, and to interfere with the maintenance of law and order. These associations are in the opinion of Govern-ment, a danger to the public peace. The managing agencies of these associations will now be prosecuted for sedition and conspiracy to overawe Government.'[11]

The SGPC and the Akali Dal were declared unlawful associations, and thirty of the leading office-holders of the committee were arrested and charged with conspiracy to wage war against the King.[12]

The remaining members of the SGPC proved quick to adapt to official repression. The offices of the arrested committee members were filled by men with relatively little standing in the committee, while those who continued to direct its campaign receded from the public eye. Similar tactics were adopted to cope with official action against the pro-Akali Press, and vulnerable editors took refuge behind volunteers willing to court arrest. Two weeks later the Punjab government reported, 'The places of the arrested members of the proclaimed organizations have been taken by non-entities asking for arrest . . . The men now in real charge of the proclaimed organizations remain in the background . . . it is difficult to ascertain who they are.'[13] The daily despatch of *jatha*s to Jaito continued unabated, and official repression provided a sharper edge to Akali propaganda. The *Akali* newspaper, for example, described the campaign as a 'war which is not between Akalis and Government but between God and Satan'.[14] The forthcoming elections to the provincial legislative council, to be held in early December 1923, served temporarily to divert public interest from the campaign at Jaito, but the elections also demon-strated effectively the extent of popular support enjoyed by the SGPC.

The past conduct of Sikh members of the Punjab Legislative Council had emphasized to SGPC leaders the necessity of tighter control over the Sikh Legislators. Thus, in preparation for the elections to the legislative council, a general meeting of the SGPC held in September 1923 had announced that 'bearing in mind the desirability of securing satisfactory Gurdwara Legislation and the changed conditions of affairs the SGPC hereby resolve to run its own candidates for election to the Indian Legislative Assembly and the Punjab Legislative Council'.[15] The committee subsequently announced the nomination of candidates to contest the provincial elections. Each candidate nominated by the SGPC was required to adhere to a declaration which stated,

> (a) I shall abide by the mandate of the SGPC with regard to all matters placed before the Legislative Assembly or the Punjab Legislative Council concerning the welfare of the Panth ... and if necessary I shall resign my seat; (b) I shall not accept any post in or under the Government without the permission of the SGPC ...; (c) If, for any reason, at any time, I find myself unable to carry out the mandate of the SGPC, I will resign my seat; (d) I shall conform to the condition of being an orthodox Amritdhari [Khalsa] and wear the Sikh symbols.[16]

The participation of the SGPC's nominees in the elections evoked widespread interest among Sikhs. The proportion of Sikh electors which turned out to vote in the special Sikh constituencies was a significant increase on that which voted in the 1921 elections.[17] Moreover, the elections proved a stunning victory for the SGPC's candidates. The Punjab government reported to the government of India, 'A special feature of the Sikh election was the overwhelming majority of votes secured by the Gurdwara Committee's nominees over their opponents.'[18] In only one constituency was the SGPC candidate defeated.

The elections secured for the SGPC exclusive control over Sikh representation in the provincial legislative council, and Akali leaders had reason to be pleased by this affirmation of support, but public interest in the campaign at Jaito was beginning to slacken. By the end of November the Punjab government reported that the SGPC was finding it increasingly difficult to recruit Akalis and for the daily dispatch of *jathas* to Jaito.[19] In December 1923, however, a dispute over the management of the Bhai Pheru *gurdwara* in Lahore District provided the committee with an opportunity to rekindle enthusiasm for the Akali campaign. The *gurdwara* at Bhai Pheru had been seized by the Akalis in October 1922. In the middle of December 1923 the Akalis in possession broke into a property claimed by the *mahant*. The *mahant* complained to the police and the Akalis responsible were arrested. The SGPC immediately despatched a *jatha* of twenty-five Akalis to join those at Bhai Pheru. Under instructions from the committee, the *jatha* made another attempt to seize the disputed property, and its members were taken into custody. The dispatch of small Akali *jatha*s to Bhai Pheru and their subsequent arrest for trespassing became a regular feature. Another Akali campaign was thus launched and another front in the conflict with the government opened up. Though the agitation at Bhai Pheru initially contributed to straining Akali resources, it amply served its purpose. Sikhs were reminded of the danger posed to their faith by official interference in their religious affairs, and Akali recruitment proceeded briskly. Within weeks the Punjab government reported that at Bhai Pheru, 'the Akalis, who have presented themselves for arrest do not care about the wisdom or justice of their cause, and when questioned as to their motives usually say "it is the order of the SGPC". This blind obedience to the orders of the Committee and the willingness of men to go to jail under very dreary and depressing circumstances are ... disquieting.'[20] By the end of January more than 500 Akali had been arrested at Bhai Pheru.

The SGPC further intensified the agitation at Jaito. In February 1923 a *shahidi*, or martyrs' *jatha* of 500 Akalis was formed and dispatched from Amritsar. In order to derive maximum benefit from this escalation of *jathabandi*, the *shahidi jatha* was instructed to take a circuitous route to Jaito, passing through areas of potential recruitment of Akalis. The *jatha* stopped at various villages en route and held *diwan*s to stimulate Akali recruitment. The success of the SGPC's strategy was immediately apparent. The Punjab government noted that as a result of the march of this *jatha*,

A tremendous amount of interest has been excited in the countryside. People are coming from miles to see the Jatha and some of them even take up the dust over which the Jatha has passed and smear it over their faces. There is little doubt that by this display, which has been extremely well stage managed, the S. G. P. Committee has succeeded in impressing on non-Akali Sikhs, or at any rate the illiterate majority, that this is a purely religious pilgrimage.[21]

Meanwhile, the government moved to counter the SGPC's tactics. On 10 February it was announced that all *jatha*s visiting Jaito were required to give an undertaking not to indulge in political activity, and further, the state authorities would limit the size of *jatha*s permitted to advance towards Jaito to fifty persons.[23] On 20 February 1924, the anniversary of the Nankana massacre, the *shahidi jatha* arrived at the border of Nabha State. It was met by state officials who announced the new orders in compliance with which only fifty of the *jatha* could proceed to Jaito on giving the required undertaking. The *jatha* ignored the order and continued its advance. It was met by a detachment of police who again asked it to retire; on its continued advance the police opened fire, killing fourteen Akalis and wounding thirty-four others.[24]

If the government had intended to temper Sikh unrest by firm action against the *shahidi jatha*, its strategy failed miserably. The 'massacre' in Nabha served only to contribute to an escalation of Akali activity, and convinced even partial Akali converts that government policy was both dubious and harsh. The Punjab government was forced to admit that 'Most Sikhs believe Government is attacking their religion and even Sikhs of moderate views look at the religious pretext on which the ... jathas are marching and not at the political motives which are behind them'.[24] The SGPC found no difficulty in recruiting and dispatching another *shahidi jatha* of 500 men. The second *shahidi jatha* took a different route from the first one and was eventually arrested while attempting to enter Nabha State. Further *shahidi jatha*s followed the second one, in addition to the dispatch of small daily *jatha*s to Jaito. Meanwhile, at Bhai Pheru the number of Sikhs under arrest had reached 1,600.[25]

The Akali campaign continued, but after six months of *jathabandi* the SGPC was privately beginning to show signs of anxiety at its lack of success. For the moment sufficient enthusiasm prevailed among the Sikh masses to ensure the uninterrupted recruitment of *jatha*s, but the campaign could not be prolonged indefinitely. Moreover, the approaching harvesting season would renew the problem of recruitment. Towards the end of March 1924 the Punjab government reported to the government of India, 'it is definitely known that the SGPC would like to extricate itself from the morcha [campaign] provided it could do so in a manner compatible with its dignity.'[26] Signs of strain among Akali leaders prompted the government to reopen negotiations with the SGPC over the drafting of suitable *gurdwara* legislation. General Birdwood, the officer commanding the Northern Command, who had a reputation of being a friend to Sikhs, was chosen to approach the committee. An eagerness to settle the controversy existed on both sides, but the release of Akali prisoners remained the stumbling block. The SGPC declared its willingness to drop the Nabha agitation provided that all Sikh prisoners were released, and the committee was permitted to perform not one, but one hundred and one, continuous *akhand paths* at Jaito. If government cancelled the notification declaring the SGPC and the Akali Dal unlawful associations, the committee for its part would not dispatch further *jathas* to settle *gurdwara* disputes, pending the passage of acceptable *gurdwara* legislation. But, in view of bitter past experience, the government was unwilling to release Akali prisoners prior to the passage of legislation. In vain General Birdwood assured the committee that on the completion of successful negotiations the Nabha administration would permit free access to the shrine at Jaito for the performance of the *akhand paths* and that once the dispatch of jathas to Jaito ceased the government would remove the declaration against the SGPC and the Akali Dal. The SGPC remained intransigent and by June 1924 the negotiations had been abandoned.[27]

Meanwhile, in May 1924, Malcolm Hailey took over as Government of the Punjab and introduced a new strategy for dealing with Tat Khalsa unrest. Shortly after his transfer to the Punjab, Hailey noted,

I have come to the conclusion that for the moment it would be very unwise to attempt anything of a description which I may call 'dramatic' ... either in the way of conciliation or repression. They [the SGPC] so recently showed themselves unwilling to accept reasonable conditions that I am not inclined to believe that conciliation would yield any results; as for repression I do not think that this is the psychological moment ... All officers whom I have consulted, agree that for the moment enthusiasm is waning ... [and] advise against any attempt at the moment to break up or disperse the jathas ... if we do so we should be giving the extremists just the aid which they require to whip up fresh enthusiasm.[28]

Hailey did not, however, advocate a policy of inaction in dealing with the SGPC. He contemplated a series of measures which, while not arousing public interest, would erode the committee's capability to carry on its campaign. Thus he reported to the government of India,

> I would press on the trial of the leaders of the Committee; if fresh leaders arose of the same complexion, I would prosecute them also. I would resist by all legal means any attempt to use illegal force to gain possession of more gurdwaras or their lands ... I think that we should refuse to consider giving employment, either civil or military, to any person whose family has strongly marked Akali sympathies, and would let this fact be known; I would confiscate civil and military pensions of those who join in the agitation against us. I would ... continue the policy of pressure by all ordinary legal means, only avoiding ... any step which may once more help to bring the extremist section forward as a champion of Sikh interests'.[29]

Accordingly, the Punjab government implemented measures designed to discourage Akali recruitment and activity. Pro-Akali newspapers were repeatedly prosecuted for inflammatory writing, and when elusive editors proved difficult to charge, action was taken against the publishers and proprietors. Akali public meetings were closely watched and individuals singled out for prosecution. Pensions and land grants of persons participating in Akali campaigns were confiscated and recruitment into the army was curtailed from villages and families conspicuous for Akali sympathies. Regarding the agitation in Nabha, the government reverted to its earlier policy of permitting *jathas* to enter the state, but restricting access to the Gangsar *gurdwara* to those willing to make a declaration not to indulge in political activity. The arrest of Akalis unwilling to make the required declaration was quietly continued. Indeed, regarding the entire *jathabandi* campaign, Hailey brought a markedly different perception to government strategy. Commenting on the campaign at Bhai Pheru he noted,

> For myself, I consider this ... a blessing in disguise, for it is clear that we cannot deal with the Akali problem until the mass of people are tired of their present leaders ... Nothing will disgust them so much as futile proceedings of this nature. They cannot even pretend that they cause us any annoyance, for the whole matter causes no more trouble than a prize giving at a girls school.[30]

Government strategy was to let the Akali *jathas* run out of steam. But Hailey also initiated a more insidious policy to counter and undermine the SGPC's influence. District officers with a substantial Sikh population were instructed to encourage the formation of anti-Akali associations by rallying Sikhs with a stake in loyalty to the government. These associations, *sewak* or *sudhar* (reform) committees as they were usually called, were drawn largely from Sikh landlords and landed gentry whose influence had been eclipsed by the authority exercised by the SGPC. In addition they included a number of retired Sikh army men and civil pensioners. With government support, the *sudhar* committees grew rapidly in number and strength. By the middle of August 1924 the Punjab government reported that such anti-Akali associations had been or were in the process of being formed in the districts of Karnal, Hoshiarpur, Ludhiana, Sialkot, Sheikhupura, Rawalpindi, Amritsar and Gujranwala.[31]

The *sudhar* committees launched a campaign to clarify the religious issues behind Sikh unrest and to separate them from the political ambitions of the Akalis. Through widely distributed posters and the publication of newspapers directed at the Sikh peasantry they attacked the SGPC's tactics while urging the fulfilment of Sikh religious aspirations. Its objective, the Punjab government reported to the government of India, 'was by these ... means to create in time a body of opinion which will put pressure on the Akalis to adopt a more reasonable attitude but this is a process which will necessarily take time'.[32]

By the middle of October 1924 the Punjab government was confident that the time had come for direct action to counter the Akali campaign. It was announced that a provincial Sikh *sudhar* committee had been formed, and that it was sending a *jatha* to Jaito to complete the *akhand path*. The *jatha* of the provincial *sudhar* committee, composed of prominent members of the landed gentry and landlords drawn from the various district *sudhar* committees, arrived at Jaito on 20 October, gave the required undertaking not to indulge in political activity and was permitted into the *gurdwara*. By 23 October it had completed the interrupted *akhand path*.[33] The basis of Akali agitation at Jaito had effectively been undermined.

The SGPC had refused to recognize the authority of the Sikh *sudhar* committees, but the dispatch of the *sudhar* committee's *jatha* came as a great shock to Akali leaders. At the last moment the SGPC strove desperately to save the situation. A hastily assembled *jatha* of sixty-one Akalis was dispatched to Jaito, and the SGPC apparently sent an emissary to Malcolm Hailey with an offer to stop the campaign at Nabha if the Governor came to a secret agreement to permit the SGPC's *jatha* to perform the *akhand path* at Jaito without pre-conditions.[34] Hailey refused to come to such an arrangement. The SGPC was left with no alternative but to maintain its public posture and continue the campaign at Jaito.

Government strategy had paid off and much of the sting of the SGPC's allegations had been removed. By undermining the basis on which Akali leaders rallied support for the campaign at Jaito, the government had succeeded, at least temporarily, in weakening the political platform of the Akalis. But the SGPC remained the sole Sikh organization which could legitimately claim to represent the majority of the Sikh community. The *sudhar* committees, created and nurtured by the government, could not present a viable alternative to the SGPC. Hailey himself had no illusions as to the support commanded by these *sudhar* committees. He noted,

> I have never attempted to attach too great importance to them, but they have a great effect for publicity purposes, and I think I can claim that they have had a wide influence on the outside press and have certainly weakened the positions of the Prabhandak Commit- tee. It still remains to be seen whether they can influence the ordinary Sikh in the villages. It is here that our greatest difficulty lies. We can weaken the [Akali] movement by depressing the leaders, but I must admit frankly that I do not think that we have so far succeeded in shifting the allegiance of the ordinary villager from the Prabhandak Committee. The villager is far less enthusiastic than before, nor will he come forward to make the same sacrifices as he was prepared to make a year ago; but it will be some considerable time yet before we can persuade him ... that he has nothing to gain from following the leadership of the Prabhandak Committee.[35]

Thus the moment was seen as opportune to reopen negotiations between the Punjab government and the SGPC over the drafting of permanent legislation for the management of Sikh *gurdwaras*.

On 10 November 1924 Hailey addressed the provincial legisla- tive council and expressed the government's willingness to enter into discussions with the SGPC over the drafting of a permanent *gurdwara* bill. But, anxious not to present the gesture as concess- ion to the Akalis, the government made it clear that any discussion would have to be restricted to *gurdwara* legislation, and no demands for the release of Akali prisoners or other matters would be entertained. Furthermore, Hailey stated that the initiative for drafting another bill must come from the Sikhs themselves.

The more extremist Akalis had been clearly out-manoeuvred and Hailey's assessment of the mood of the SGPC proved correct. Through the Sikh members of the legislative council the SGPC responded promptly to the government's offer. A sub-committee of five Sikh members of the council was appointed to begin discussions with the government. These private discussions proved to be a lengthy and tedious affair, and it was not until the end of April 1925 that the provisions of a draft *gurdwara* bill were made public. In the interim, under pressure from the extremist section of its ranks, the SGPC continued the campaigns at Bhai Pheru and Jaito. During discussions between the government and the SGPC over the preparation of another *gurdwara* bill, the committee, under the guise of claiming 'legitimate Sikh rights', pressed for legislation which would ensure it complete control over all Sikh *gurdwara* and shrines. The government for its part, while meeting some of the SGPC's demands, attempted to minimize the possibility of exclusive Akali control over Sikh religious institutions under the pretext of establishing 'proper procedure'. An examination of the bill which emerged from these discussions reveals clearly the nature and extent of compromises on both sides.

The Sikh Gurdwaras and Shrines Bill of 1925 was based on the principle enunciated by Tat Khalsa reformers over the past two decades, namely, that responsibility for the management and control of all Sikh religious institutions was to lie with the Sikh community. The bill envisaged the establishment of a central board of management of all Sikh *gurdwaras* and shrines. The board was to be constituted of 121 elected members, together with the chief priests of the five important Sikh *gurdwaras*, including the Golden Temple, and twelve members nominated by the rulers of the Sikh princely states. In addition, the board so constituted was to co-opt fourteen persons resident in India, of whom not more than five were resident in the Punjab, to provide representation for the small Sikh communities in other parts of the country. The elected members of the board were to be elected by district-based constituencies. However, districts representing larger proportions of the Sikh population were to elect greater proportions of the elected members of the Board. Thus the districts of Amritsar and Ferozepur were to elect fifteen members each, while Rawalpindi District was to elect two and Multan only one. The franchise qualification laid down for participation in the election was that the elector must reside in the constituency, be a Sikh aged 21 or over, and be on the electoral roll prepared for elections to the special Sikh seats in the provincial legislative council. Members of the board were to hold office for three years and it was incumbent upon the board to meet once annually. At its first such meeting the board was to elect a president and vice-president and an executive council of not fewer than five and not more than eleven members. The central board of management was to exercise supervisory power over a number of local *gurdwara* committees. The Golden Temple and all other *gurdwaras* within the limits of Amritsar municipality were to have one such *gurdwara* committee, as were six other important groups of Sikh shrines, such as those at Nankana, Tarn Taran and Anandpur. In addition, every Sikh *gurdwara* or shrine or groups of them were to have their own committee of management subordinate to the central board. The local *gurdwara* committees were to meet at least three times a year.[36]

The bill included a list of Sikh *gurdwaras* and shrines notified on the basis that a *gurdwara* was a Sikh place of public worship 'established by or in memory of any of the Ten Sikh Gurus, or in commemoration of any incident in the life of the Ten Sikh Gurus and is used for public worship by Sikhs or owing to some incident or tradition connected with one of the Ten Sikh Gurus, is used for public religious worship predominantly by Sikhs'.[37] A Sikh shrine was similarly defined. Furthermore it was laid down that any fifty or more Sikh worshippers above the age of 21 could, within one year of the passage of the bill, apply to the Punjab government for the notification of a particular place of religious worship as a Sikh *gurdwara* or shrine. Such a petition could not, however, apply to an institution specified in a schedule to the bill. Further, when a notification that a particular religious institution was a Sikh *gurdwara* had been published by the government, any heriditary office-holder of that institution, or twenty or more of its worshippers, could within ninety days petition the local authorities against the declaration. These petitions were to be considered by a judicial tribunal established under the bill. The judicial tribunal was to consist of three members, all of whom were to be Sikhs, who were in addition to be district or subordinate judges, or barristers of England or Scotland, advocates, *vakils* or pleaders of ten years' standing. It was to be presided over by a judge of the high court. The three members of the tribunal were to be chosen by the government from a panel of seven names submitted to it by the central board. The judicial tribunal was further responsible for settling disputes regarding the removal of *mahant*s, and specific conditions were laid down under which a *mahant* could be removed from his office. In such an eventuality the proper payment of compensation to the *mahant* was also laid down, which was to be paid from *gurdwara* income.[38]

On the surface the bill seemed an equitable solution to the controversy over *gurdwara* management. But the Punjab government had made a crucial concession to Tat Khalsa opinion. The term 'Sikh' was defined in the bill to mean a person who professes the Sikh faith, and the bill laid down that a person would or would not be deemed to be a Sikh depending on whether or not he makes a declaration stating: 'I solemnly affirm that I am a Sikh, that I believe in the Guru Granth Sahib, that I believe in the Ten Gurus and *that I have no other religion* (my italics).[39] Sahajdhari Sikhs who saw themselves as part of the larger Hindu religious community would thus be forced to declare themselves as separate from the Hindus in order to participate in the management of Sikh religious institutions. Furthermore, for the election of members of the central board of management, the various local *gurdwara* committees, and the judicial tribunal, a disqualification laid down was that the person elected should not be a *patit* (an apostate or fallen man).[40] The term 'patit' was not, however, defined in the bill, and the Sikh judicial tribunal chosen by the government from Khalsa Sikhs was to decide who was or was not a *patit*. In the eyes of the Tat Khalsa, all non-Kesdhari Sikhs, inasmuch as they deviated from the rules prescribed for the Khalsa, were *patits*, or fallen men. The rules laid out under the bill thus ensured that the control over all Sikh religious institutions would effectively pass to the Khalsa Sikhs.

But while making this crucial, though veiled, concession to the SGPC, the government worked towards ensuring that the Akalis would not automatically gain control of all Sikh religious institutions under the bill. From the outset the Punjab government was reluctant even to establish a single central board under the measure. Hailey noted,

I and many others would have been glad if we could have avoided the institution of a central body, and could have placed the shrines entirely in the management of local committees ... [we] dislike the idea of instituting a central Sikh body which is always liable to misuse for political purposes the position derived from religious causes. Nevertheless, those who know the position best assure us that ... the Sikhs will not agree to legislation which does not recognize a central body of some kind ... [thus] I am afraid that our attempts must be limited to giving local committees as strong a position as possible and minimizing the sphere of activity of a central body ... we shall insist that the central body must have a regular constitution under the statute with defined powers and a proper electorate.[41]

Thus an elaborate scheme for the election of local *gurdwara* committees was laid out. The rules for election to the *gurdwara* committees controlling the Golden Temple, for example, stated that four members of the committee were to be elected by the Amritsar District electors, three members by the electors of the municipal area of Amritsar, and five members to be elected by the central board in general meetings.[42] Government strategy was clear. The more varied and smaller the constituencies for election of *gurdwara* committee members, the less was the chance of the Akalis obtaining exclusive control. Explicit rules were further laid down for the use of *gurdwara* income, and each *gurdwara* committee was to publish regular accounts open to the public. Even if the Akalis swamped the elections to the central board, the government hoped to ensure that their access to vast *gurdwara* funds would be limited.

The publication of the Sikh Gurdwaras and Shrines Bill of 1925 brought a storm of protests from the Sahajdhari Sikhs. A spate of resolutions were passed by numerous Udasi organizations alleging that the bill severely trespassed against their rights.[43] In a widely publicized communiqué the Udasi Publicity Bureau, Lahore, expressed the Sahajdhari Sikh point of view clearly. It stated:

Sikhism was never a religion but always a Panth ... a cult ... embracing Hindu religion though laying particular stress on the devotional attachment towards Gurus ... The Bill defines 'Sikh' to be a person who professes the Sikh religion. If it had contented itself with this laconic definition, it would have been all right. But it demands much more ... It ... prescribes a solemn declaration ... The last words in the declaration ... clearly compel a Hindu even though otherwise qualified, to renounce his religion, simply because the Bill aims at creating a separate Sikh community ... The words, 'that I have no other religion' should ... be deleted ... The Central Board must be recruited from amongst all those who believe in Gurus even though they be ... Sikhs who have not adopted five symbols necessary for the volunteer corps organized by the tenth Guru in defence of the Hindu religion.[44]

Criticism of the bill was not limited to Sahajdhari Sikhs. Some Akali leaders saw clearly the government's strategy to limit their control of all Sikh shrines. Mangal Singh, a notable Akali leader, while accepting the fundamentals of the bill expressed his reservations:

The ... defect which appears to me rather serious is the official attempt to weaken the control of the Central Body over their local committees. The power to modify the budgets prepared by the local committees and the right to settle the scheme of administration of Gurdwaras should be given to the Central Body ... the control of Akal Takht and Takht Kesgarh ... should be vested in the Central Body, because they, in addition to being places of worship are seats of authority from which bills [sic] are issued from time to time which are binding upon every Sikh.[45]

The Sikh Gurdwaras and Shrines Bill of 1925 was introduced by Tara Singh, as a private bill, in the Punjab Legislative Council on 7 May 1925, and referred to a select committee of twenty legislators. The bill had been jointly drafted by the government and the Sikh legislators and thus the select committee's deliberations were for Tat Khalsa Sikhs only an arena to clarify the finer points. The membership of the select committee chosen placed the Sahajdhari Sikh representatives in a minority against the combined votes of the five Khalsa Sikh legislators and the ten government nominees, and ensured that they could not hinder its proceedings. Nevertheless, the select committee's proceedings bogged down over details of each of the 148 clauses in the bill. Eventually the bill was passed by the select committee, but Raja Narender Nath and Gokul Chand Narang, representing the Hindus and Shadjhari Sikhs, appended minutes of dissent to its report. Predictably their dissent focused on the definition of the term 'Sikh' employed. Thus Gokul Chand Narang suggested that the last words in the required declaration of a person that he had no other religion be deleted, since 'As it is, the declaration is likely to put an unnecessary strain on the conscience of many people who are true Sikhs in every sense of the term'.[46] Both Gokul

Chand Narang and Raja Narender Nath objected to the disqualification of *patits* since the term was not defined in the bill.

Meanwhile, a clear division of opinion had emerged in the SGPC over the adoption of the bill. A militant section of the Akalis insisted that no bill could be accepted until the Jaito question was settled to its satisfaction and all Akali prisoners were released. To settle the matter, the SGPC held a general meeting at which more moderate counsels prevailed and the Sikh legislators were instructed to continue their co-operation with the government in the passage of the legislation. On 8 July 1925 the Sikh Gurdwaras Bill of 1925 was passed by the Punjab Legislative Council. The Sikh Gurdwara and Shrines Act of 1922 was simultaneously repealed.

Extremist Akalis within the SGPC were not satisfied, however, and the passage of the Act further accentuated divisions among Akalis. Sixteen members of the SGPC resigned in protest at its acceptance of the measure. In June, in an attempt to conciliate the extremist Akalis, the Punjab government had announced that any Akali prisoner who gave an undertaking to work the Act would be released. The SGPC's front-line leadership, in jail since October 1923, differed greatly in their response to this offer. A group led by Mahtab Singh agreed to the undertaking, but another led by Kharak Singh refused to make such a declaration as a matter of principle. Mahtab Singh and his supporters were accordingly released and they resumed their offices in the SGPC. A few months later Kharak Singh and his companions were also released but without pre-conditions. They condemned Mahtab Singh's party as collaborators and ousted them from the SGPC. Meanwhile, the Punjab government took the opportunity to make preparations to field a large number of *sudhar* Committee candidates for the forthcoming elections to the central board of management of Sikh shrines and the various local *gurdwara* committees. But in the *gurdwara* elections which followed, the militant Akalis won an overwhelming majority. One of the first resolutions adopted by the newly constituted central board of management of Sikh shrines was to change its name officially to the Shiromani Gurdwara Prabhandak Committee.

The Sikh Gurdwaras Act of 1925 was of immense significance for the Sikh community. The Act marked a turning point in the movement towards the reformulation of Sikh identity and the development of a distinct Sikh communal consciousness. The Tat Khalsa had been instrumental in drawing communal boundaries with the Hindu community and building a spirit of internal solidarity among Sikhs, and the agitation over *gurdwara* management had witnessed the mass expression of this new Sikh consciousness. The overlapping of the identities of the Sikh and Hindu communities remained a subject of theological debate for Hindus and Sahajdhari Sikhs, but, by effectively debarring them from representation in a body responsible for the control and administration of all Sikh religious institutions, the Act provided, by statute, recognition of the claims of the Tat Khalsa to a cohesive and separate Sikh identity. The SGPC became an institutional framework for a separate Sikh communal consciousness which remains valid to this day. The Sikh Gurdwaras Act of 1925 has since undergone thirty amendments, but its basic principles and the institutions established under it have remained the same.

Notes to Chapter 6

1 The Maharaja of Nabha had a long-standing dispute with the Maharaja of Patiala. In the eyes of the government this sordid dispute was further coloured by the Maharaja of Nabha's conspicuous support for nationalist activity and for the Akalis. In January 1923 a committee of inquiry was set up to look into the matter and its findings were against the Maharaja of Nabha. Subsequently, the Maharaja was persuaded by the British government to abdicate. See Report of the special commission on disputes between Nabha and Patiala States, 1923, GOI, Home (Political) proceedings, no. 201 of 1923.

2 Quoted in Fortnightly Report, 15 July 1923, GOI, Home (Political) proceedings, no. 25 of 1923.

3 Fortnightly Report, 15 July 1923.

4 Fortnightly Report, 30 July 1923, GOI, Home (Political) proceedings, no. 25 of 1923.

5 Quoted in GOI, Foreign (Political) proceedings, no. 628–3–P of 1924.

6 Quoted in GOI, Foreign (Political) proceedings, no. 628–3–P of 1924.

7 *Tribune* (8 Aug. 1923).

8 *Tribune* (8 Aug. 1923).

9 J. Wilson-Johnston to C. A. H. Townsend, Chief Sec., Punjab Govt,

7 Sept. 1923, GOI, Foreign (Political) proceedings, no. 628–3–P of 1924.

10 Published SGPC Press communiqué, undated, Ruchi Ram Sahni private papers.

11 Punjab Govt Press communiqué, *Tribune* (16 Oct. 1923).

12 Punjab Govt Press communiqué, *Tribune* (16 Oct. 1923).

13 Fortnightly Report, 31 Oct. 1923, GOI, Home (Political) proceedings, no. 25 of Oct. 1923.

14 Quoted in Fortnightly Report, 15 Nov. 1923, GOI, Home (Political) proceedings, no. 25 of Nov. 1923.

15 SGPC Press communiqué, *Tribune* (3 Oct. 1923).

16 SGPC Press communiqué, *Tribune* (3 Oct. 1923).

17 Return showing the result of elections in India, 1924, Cmd 2154, 18: 497 (86), pp. 501, 503–4, 543–64.

18 Fortnightly Report, 15 Dec. 1923, GOI, Home (Political) proceedings, no. 25 of Dec. 1923.

19 Fortnightly Report, 30 Nov. 1923, GOI, Home (Political) proceedings, no. 25 of Nov. 1923.

20 Fortnightly Report, 15 Jan. 1924, GOI, Home (Political) proceedings, no. 25 of Jan. 1924.

21 Fortnightly Report, 15 Feb. 1924, GOI, Home (Political) proceedings, no. 25 of Feb. 1924.

22 *Tribune* (12 Feb. 1924).

23 *Tribune* (24 Feb. 1924).

24 Fortnightly Report, 29 Feb. 1924, GOI, Home (Political) proceedings, no. 25 of Feb. 1924.

25 Anxious to limit the number of Akalis under arrest, the government resorted to new tactics. The Akalis arrested at Jaito were taken to Bhawal, a few hundred miles away and released. For details of govt and SGPC tactics, see Report on the Akali Movement, GOI, Home (Political) proceedings, no. I/II of 1924; Reports on the Sikh Situation from Lahore District, GOI, Home (Political) proceedings, no. 15/II of 1924; Report on the progress of Akali *jatha*s to Jaito, GOI, Home (Political) proceedings, no. 67 of 1924; Report on Akali *jatha*s, GOI, Home (Political) proceedings, no. 67 (III–IV) of 1924.

26 Fortnightly Report, 31 July 1924, GOI, Home (Political) proceedings, no. 25 of July 1924.

27 Based on Ganda Singh (ed.), *Some Confidential Papers of the Akali Movement* (Amritsar, 1965), pp. 69–71; The Birdwood Committee, GOI, Home (Political) proceedings, no. 297 of 1924.

28 W. M. Hailey to Gen. W. Birdwood, 20 June 1924, private papers of William Malcolm Hailey, Governor of the Punjab 1924–8, Mss, EUR,E,220,6A.

29 Memo by W. M. Hailey on the Akali situation, 20 June 1924, Hailey private papers, Mss,EUR,E,220,6A.

30 W. M. Hailey to W. Howard, 23 Aug. 1924, Hailey private papers, Mss,EUR,E,220,6B.

31 Fortnightly Report, 15 Aug. 1924, GOI, Home (Political) proceedings, no. 25 of Aug. 1924. In July 1924, for example, Hailey wrote to G. de Montmorency, Private Sec. to the Viceroy, 'We have lately issued an order to District Officers asking them to give as quietly as possible any support in their power to the anti-Akali organizations. We are considering the means by which we can place ourselves in funds for helping in the publicity campaign against the Akalis (W. M. Hailey to G. de Montmorency, 8 July 1924, Hailey private papers, Mss,EUR,E,220,6A).

32 Fortnightly Report, 31 July 1924, GOI, Home (Political) proceedings, no. 25 of July 1924. See also Fortnightly Report, 31 Aug. 1924, GOI, Home (Political) proceedings, no. 25 of Aug. 1924; W. M. Hailey to W. Vincent, 12 Aug. 1924, Hailey private papers, Mss, EUR,E,220,6B.

33 *Tribune* (21 Oct. 1924, 25 Oct. 1924). See also Fortnightly Report, 15 Oct. 1924, GOI, Home (Political) proceedings, no. 25 of Oct. 1924.

34 W. M. Hailey to A. Muddiman, 29 Oct. 1924, Hailey private papers, Mss,EUR,E,220,6C.

35 W. M. Hailey to A. Muddiman, 29 Oct. 1924.

36 Sikh Gurdwaras and Shrines Bill of 1925, clauses 43, 44 Schedule IV, clauses 49, 53, 56, 62, 85, 91, 100, *Punjab Gazette* (26 June 1925).

37 Sikh Gurdwaras and Shrines Bill of 1925, clause 16.

38 Sikh Gurdwaras and Shrines Bill of 1925, clause 11, schedule II, clauses 16, 72.

39 Sikh Gurdwaras and Shrines Bill of 1925, clause 11.

40 The bill stated, 'no persons shall be prevented from standing as a candidate at an election of the Board on the grounds that he is a patit, but if the person elected is thereafter ... found to be a patit his election shall be void' (Sikh Gurdwaras and Shrines Bill of 1925, clause 45). Similar rules were laid down for the elections of members of the local *gurdwara* committees and the Sikh judicial commission.

41 W. M. Hailey to A. Muddiman, 25 Nov. 1924, Hailey private papers, Mss,EUR,E,220,6C.

42 Sikh Gurdwaras and Shrines Bill of 1925, clause 85.

43 See *Tribune* (12 May 1925), and also *Tribune* (6 May 1925, 9 May 1925, 16 May 1925).

44 *Tribune* (27 May 1925).

45 *Tribune* (28 Apr. 1925).

46 Sikh Gurdwaras and Shrines Bill of 1925, select committee report, *Punjab Gazette* (26 June 1925).

7

Power for the Faithful

While the Sikh Gurdwaras Act of 1925 provided an institutional structure for Sikh communal separatism, it also created, in the new SGPC, a unique organization of authority and influence within the Sikh community. During the formulation of the legislation, the Punjab government had attempted to minimize the possibility of Sikh militants using the central board of management of Sikh shrines for political purposes. The broad and detailed constituency basis for elections to the board, and close government association with the working of the Act, had been provided for in the legislation for this reason. Ironically, these factors served only to enhance the authority of the board, or the SGPC as it was now called. The majority of the SGPC's membership, elected exclusively by Sikh voters from numerous small electoral constituencies, provided it with unimpeachable authority to claim to represent the Sikh community as a whole. This claim was further legitimized by the close involvement of the government in the preparation and maintenance of electoral rolls, the delineation of electoral constituencies, and the supervision and management of *gurdwara* elections. Indeed, therefore, in later years official suggestions to establish a trust for the management of Sikh religious institutions and do away with the necessity for government-supervised *gurdwara* elections were repeatedly rejected by the SGPC.[1]

Under the 1925 Act as it was originally enacted, the SGPC exercised jurisdiction over some 300 historic Sikh *gurdwara*s and shrines in the Punjab. Later, however, a large number of Sikh *gurdwara*s and shrines were notified by the government as being connected with Sikh history and tradition and brought under the authority of the SGPC. Today there are several hundred such non-scheduled Sikh *gurdwara*s and shrines under the SGPC's jurisdiction, in addition to those scheduled in the original legislation. The arrangements established under the 1925 Act gave the SGPC the power of direction of, and general superintendence over, the numerous local *gurdwara* committees. This gave the SGPC access to substantial financial resources, for the local *gurdwara* committees were required to pay an annual contribution to it.[2] Their income derived from religious property and estates associated with the shrines and the daily offerings of devotees. The annual budget of the SGPC from these sources was considerable and was estimated to be more than Rs120 million in 1985.[3] Access to substantial funds enabled the SGPC to establish a centralized bureaucracy to assist its executive committee and thereby develop a highly organized system of control over the local *gurdwara* committees.

The 1925 Act laid down that the *gurdwara* committees were, in the first instance, to utilize *gurdwara* income for the improvement of the religious institutions under their charge, the maintenance of religious worship, and the payment of the salaries of their employees. If the management committees were still left with surplus finances, this income could be utilized for 'a particular religious, educational or charitable purpose'.[4] This surplus income enabled the SGPC to undertake a variety of acts for the benefit of the Sikh community. Numerous schools and colleges were established, hospitals and medical dispensaries were set up and *gurdwara*s for backward groups opened up. The staffing of these institutions, in addition to the hundreds of personnel necessary for the management of Sikh religious institutions and their property, created a significant network of patronage for the SGPC. The use of the SGPC's considerable financial resources and its patronage, in turn, provided it with enormous leverage in seeking and maintaining support from important groups within the Sikh community.

The 1925 Act also provided the SGPC with a formidable platform from which to reach the Sikh community. The SGPC administered a fund for the propagation of the Sikh religion through which an army of wandering preachers, missionary workers and folk musicians was recruited to tour the rural areas and spread its ideology. Through the head priests of important Sikh *gurdwara*s, the SGPC also issued religious edicts binding upon all Sikhs and utilized the *granthi*s (scripture readers) of hundreds of local *gurdwara*s to spread its word on various matters. Moreover, the guardianship of all Sikh religious institutions in the Punjab conferred a quasi-religious authority on the SGPC. Just as the old SGPC had used its religious authority in 1922 to excommunicate Sikh members of the Punjab Legislative Council for not falling in line with its directives, to the new SGPC from time to time declared those it considered to be its opponents as *tankhaiya*, to be ostracized by the Sikh community. A recent example of this was in 1984, when the SGPC, through the priests of the Golden temple, threatened to excommunicate the Sikh President of India, who had ordered Indian army action against Sikh extremists inside the Golden Temple.

As a result of its unparalleled institutional authority within the Sikh community, the SGPC rapidly became both a forum and a power base for Sikh political action. The elections of the SGPC and of its leading office-holders became primary political battles, for leadership and control of the SGPC contributed powerfully to determine leadership of the Sikh community.[5] As one scholar put it, 'The SGPC became a sort of parliament of the Sikhs ... a government within the government'.[6]

Since its establishment, the Akali Dal had been active in nationalist political activity. Following the passage of the 1925 Act, the Akali Dal emerged as the dominant Sikh political party, and it has maintained this position to the present day.[7] The Akali Dal's political strength derived significantly from its ability to dominate the SGPC. In the first *gurdwara* elections held under the 1925 Act, the Akalis gained complete control of the SGPC. The Akali Dal has won in virtually all subsequent elections to the SGPC and maintains its control of the SGPC today. The Akali Dal's enormous success in dominating the SGPC and its political strength is understandable. As a political party, the Akali Dal simply extended the religious appeal it had developed with such success during the campaign for *gurdwara* reform into the political arena. Thus, in its election campaigns the Akali Dal has appealed to the strong sentiment among Sikhs on the achievements of the agitation over *gurdwara* reform. It has projected itself as the saviour of Sikh religious institutions from the corruption of control by the government or by non-Sikhs. It has constantly stressed that there is a danger of the sacrifices and sufferings of the Sikhs during the agitation for *gurdwara* reform being undone. Further, during the agitation for *gurdwara* control, the Akalis were highly successful in portraying each government action against Sikh agitators as interference in the Sikh religion. This tactic was continued by the Akali Dal in its political campaigns and in elections to the SGPC. Indeed, the numerous provisions of the 1925 Act requiring government involvement in its functioning provided the Akali Dal with ample opportunity for alleging official interference during elections to the SGPC or to local *gurdwara* committees, thereby raising a spectre from the past and reinforcing its own election campaign.[8]

The highly organized cadre of Akali workers established during the 1920s, and since maintained, also provided the Akali Dal with a powerful machinery to canvass the Sikh community. Due to the close historical evolution of the SGPC and the Akali Dal, Akali leaders did not hesitate to employ the SGPC's cadre of preachers and missionary workers for Akali campaigns and considered such tactics as normal and justified. One senior Akali leaders explained the use of the SGPC's religious preachers by the Akali Dal, stating, 'it does not make any difference if the preachers engage in political work. The Akali Dal and the preachers say the same thing. So what the Akali Dal says they say. All of them have been in the Akali Dal. All those who are chosen have been through the Akali Dal. We have given them employment. This is all they can do. There is no misuse of money.'[9]

But perhaps the greatest asset of the Akalis, which has ensured their political strength, has been their continued ability to equate themselves with the Khalsa *panth*, the community of the devout made supreme in all temporal matters by the Sikh Guru, Gobind Singh. During the agitation for *gurdwara* reform, the Akalis had presented themselves as the representatives of the *panth*. It was in the name of the *panth* that they had formed the *gurdwara* committee in 1920, forcibly taken over shrines and argued for the maintenance of their control. The association of the Akali Dal with the *panth* through the turbulent, but eventually successful, period of *gurdwara* reform provided them with an immensely powerful religious appeal. The Akalis continued to make use of this appeal for political purposes with considerable effect. In elections to the SGPC or to legislative bodies, the Akali Dal has presented its candidates as *panth*ic candidates, and opponents of Akali Dal have been labelled as traitors to the *panth*. Appealing in the name of the *panth* has given Akali candidates an enormous edge over Sikh candidates from other organizations contesting *gurdwara* elections or elections to legislative bodies. While Sikh candidates put forward by political parties with a secular ideology or a cross-communal following have only been able to contest these elections on issues related to them, the Akali Dal has used an essentially religious platform and appeal in what have been basically non-religious contests. Further, through tactics similar to those developed in the 1920s, each Akali campaign has been based on the holding of hundreds of ostensibly religious *diwan*s often in the precincts of Sikh *gurdwara*s. The campaigns themselves have been conducted in a shroud of powerful religious and historical symbolism and ritual, casting the whole issue into the guise of a sacred function in the cause of the brotherhood.

These Akali tactics have been the subject of several appeals to the election tribunal over the years. In the 1952 elections to the Punjab legislative assembly, for example, an election petition was filed against Hukum Singh, then president of the Akali Dal, by candidates from the Congress party. The petitioners charged that the Akali candidate had made political appeals to the electorate on the grounds of his religion and community by identifying the Akali Dal with the Sikh *panth*, by identifying Sikh religious symbols with his party and by accusing the Congress party of interfering in the Sikh religion. The election of Hukum Singh was not set aside for technical reasons, but the election tribunal stated in its judgement that there had been an attempt 'to rouse the religious sentiments of the Sikh community to a high pitch and to tell the Sikh people that they gain spiritual advantage and become defenders of the faith by voting for the Akali party candidates and by refraining from voting for the Congress candidate'.[10] Similarly, in the 1962 elections to the provincial assembly, the Punjab high court overturned the election of an Akali candidate on the ground that the political campaign of the Akali candidate suggested that 'every Sikh vote should go to the Akali Dal', because 'he was the proper representative of the Sikh Panth', while the Congress candidate, 'represented the Hindu-ridden party'.[11] Further, the court found that the intent of the posters and speeches on behalf of the Akali candidate was to communicate the message that 'You must all vote for me, because I alone am the true representative of the Sikh religion while my opponent, being a non-Akali candidate, is an enemy of the Sikh Panth'.[12]

The Akali Dal's control over the SGPC and its political appeal combined to make it a formidable force in Sikh politics. But Akali leaders remained acutely aware of the vulnerability of a separate Sikh communal entity. In religious terms, a separate Sikh identity was no longer in doubt. But, despite the development of a Sikh consciousness and the drawing of communal boundaries between Sikhs and Hindus over several decades, there remained much in common between the Sikhs and a large body of Punjabi Hindus. A common identification with the same caste groups, a shared spoken language and culture, social and historical traditions and inter-marriage, all bound the Sikhs and Punjabi Hindus together. Sikh communal separatism had been based essentially on religious differentiation. Even in religious matters, though, Sikh and Hindu religious thought and traditions had much in common, and Punjabi Hindus continued to pay homage at Sikh shrines in their thousands. Indeed, for the Akalis the implementation of the provisions of the 1925 Act in itself served as a vivid reminder of this. The examination and declaration of places of worship as being either Sikh or Hindu religious institutions by the judicial tribunal established under the Act served as occasions for acute recrimination between Khalsa Sikhs, Sahajdhari Sikhs and Hindus which was to last for several years. Many religious institutions were predominantly connected with either Sikh or Hindu history and tradition and widely regarded as such. With a number of other religious institutions, however, a common tradition of worship by Khalsa Sikhs, Sahajdhari Sikhs and Hindus made the issue far more complex. In such cases, the judicial tribunal's declaration of a place of worship as being essentially Sikh or Hindu inevitably brought strong protests from either side. Various Udasi organizations vehemently objected to shrines historically under their charge being designated as Sikh shrines and placed under the authority of the SGPC.[13] Sikh militants, on the other hand, insisted that shrines at which they had worshipped for generations should rightfully be declared Sikh shrines.[14] Similarly, the census report of 1931 noted, 'As far as Sikhs go, the criteria that separate them from the Hindus are not very marked on the social side, whatever they may be doctrinally ... Indeed there are apparent cases in which a father may bring up one son as a Hindu, another as a Sikh.'[15] Thus, in the enumeration of Punjabis by religion, the census commissioners found it necessary to instruct enumerators that 'a return of Sikh–Hindu would not be acceptable and that the person enumerated must decide in which body he would be returned'.[16]

Not surprisingly then, the Akali Dal's persistent concern following the passage of the 1925 Act became the maintenance of Sikh communal distinctiveness. While Akali leaders were ideologically committed to the maintenance of a separate Sikh communal identity, their belief was reinforced by the fact that the political fortunes of the Akali Dal derived from the existence and political position of the Sikh community as a separate entity. Sikh communal separatism provided a political base and an appeal for the Akali Dal. Besides, Akali leaders believed that without political power in the hands of the Sikhs as a community, the disintegration of an independent Sikh community and its absorption into the mass of Hinduism was inevitable. The Akali Dal's primary political objective thus became the pursuit of greater political leverage for the Sikhs as a community. This political objective has remained essentially the same today. Such political consistency on the part of the Akali Dal is not surprising, for several of the young Tat Khalsa who had made their political début with the Akali Dal in the 1920s remained at the centre stage of Akali politics for the rest of their lives. Tara Singh, for example, a young Akali leader and member of the SGPC in the 1920s, was elected vice-president of the new SGPC after the 1925 elections, and continued to dominate the Akali Dal until 1962.

In pre-independence India, the Akali Dal's concern with securing a position of political leverage for the Sikhs as an entity was manifest both in its relations with the Indian National Congress and in its political demands. The decades prior to India's independence witnessed mass movements of non-co-operation and civil disobedience by the Indian National Congress over a number of issues related to greater Indian participation in government. The nationalist demand evolved from being for greater self-government for India as a dominion within the Empire to being for complete independence and a campaign for the British to quit India. Akali participation in the nationalist campaign and its co-operation with the Congress was sporadic and was governed essentially by the Akalis' perception of Sikh communal interest. The Akali Dal was careful to maintain its own organization and political identity while participating in campaigns led by the

Congress, and also served as a pressure group which attempted to ensure that the Congress included Sikh demands in its platform. At the same time, the Akali Dal engaged in independent political activity aimed at securing political privileges for the Sikh community. In 1928, for example, the Congress called an all-parties conference to discuss the formulation of a constitutional proposal for India. The conference appointed a committee led by Motilal Nehru to determine the principle of the constitution. Its report, the Nehru report, as it was called, recommended the abolition of separate communal representation as being detrimental to the interests of a united India and urged the introduction of mixed or joint electorates for all communities.[17] However, it agreed to make an exception in the case of the Muslim community in view of their relative economic and educational backwardness which would otherwise adversely affect their representation in the legislatures. Muslim representation was to be ensured through separate communal electorates and the reservation of seats for them in legislatures in proportion to their population in the province.[18] Though in various nationalist forums the Akalis had repeatedly asserted their support for joint electorates and condemned the reservation of seats as a communal evil, they strongly opposed the Nehru report, since it did not foresee special minority representation for the Sikhs. The Central Sikh League, with the powerful Akali leader Tara Singh as its general secretary, adopted a resolution which declared the Nehru report unacceptable to the Sikhs.[19] Later, in 1929, under strong pressure from the Akalis the Congress modified its stand and assured the Sikhs that no constitutional proposal would be acceptable to the Congress which did not give 'full satisfaction' to Sikh demands.[20]

Similarly, when Gandhi launched a civil-disobedience campaign in 1930, the president of the SGPC refused Akali cooperation with the Congress on the grounds that the Sikh colour was not included in the Congress flag. Jawaharlal Nehru, the Congress president, refused to consider a proposal to include the Sikh colour in what had become the national flag since he maintained the colours in the flag had not been designed to represent various Indian communities. After much debate over the question of Sikh participation in the nationalist campaign, the Akali Dal made a declaration urging Sikhs to join in the struggle, but under their own flag.[21] In 1939 the Congress resigned from provincial ministries in protest at not being consulted over India joining the Allies in the Second World War and subsequently adopted a policy of non-co-operation with the Government over the War effort. Akali leaders, however, were primarily concerned with the adverse political impact of a Sikh boycott of the war effort, and helped organize a Khalsa Defence League to engage actively in the recruitment of Sikhs for the British Indian Army.[22]

The 1930s and 1940s witnessed a series of negotiations between the colonial authorities and representatives of Indian political opinion on various schemes of constitutional reform for greater Indian self-government. At every stage, the Akalis insisted on provincial political representation for the Sikhs far in excess of their population. The Sikhs were certainly of greater importance than their numbers alone would indicate. They supplied a significant contingent to the Indian army and, though only some 14 per cent of the provincial population, contributed almost one third of the provincial land revenue. But while the 'historic importance' of the community and its 'substantial contributions' to colonial India were the themes used to justify the demand for substantial Sikh political representation, the Akalis' insistence on a one-third share of political power in a multi-communal province of Muslims, Hindus and Sikhs, stemmed from a belief that anything less would be ineffectual in maintaining or promoting the Sikhs' separate political existence. In the eyes of the Akalis, Punjabi Hindus would never be reconciled to a separate Sikh communal entity, and historical Sikh animosity towards the Muslims made them deeply mistrustful of Muslim intentions. Thus political parity at the provincial level with the Hindus and Muslims, or at least a position of political leverage, became an Akali demand from which they would not be deterred. Indeed, their inability to achieve a position of political authority for the Sikh community only drove them further towards political extremism.

The first opportunity for the Akali Dal to press for greater Sikh political representation in the legislative bodies came in 1928. The Government of India Act of 1919 had foreseen a decennial review of the working of the constitutional reforms embodied in it. Accordingly, in November 1927 the British government announced that an Indian Statutory Commission headed by Sir John Simon would visit India to review the working of the 1919 Act and suggest measures or extend or to modify the existing application of responsible self-government. Since the commission had no Indian representative, the Congress decided to boycott its proceedings in protest. As a result of the nationalists' stance, an all-parties Sikh conference was called at Amritsar in January 1928 to consider the Sikh attitude to the commission. The conference, dominated by the Akalis, decided to join the nationalists in not co-operating with the commission. It passed a resolution condemning the principle of communal representation, but insisted that if separate electorates were maintained, the rights of the Sikhs could only be protected if they were granted a one-third share in any scheme of provincial administration.[23]

The Sikh view was presented to the commission by the Chief Khalsa Diwan. The Diwan's memorandum on Sikh representation also stated its willingness to participate in a form of administration based on joint electorates. But, if separate communal representation in the legislative bodies was to continue, the Chief Khalsa Diwan demanded that communal representation in the Punjab Legislative Council should be fixed at 40 per cent for the Muslims, 30 per cent for the Hindus and 30 per cent for the Sikhs.[24] Since the population of the Punjab was 52 per cent Muslim, 30 per cent Hindu and 14 per cent Sikh,[25] the intention of the scheme was clearly to place the Sikhs in a powerful position of political leverage in relation to both the Hindu and the Muslim communities.

Representatives of the Muslim League understandably objected strongly to this proposal. They insisted that, as the majority community in the Punjab in numerical terms, they should not be made into a statutory minority in the provincial legislature, which the introduction of joint electorates or the Chief Khalsa Diwan's scheme would imply. Furthermore, they stated, 'the distinction which of late has been drawn for political purposes between the Hindus and Sikhs is non-existent'.[26] The Muslim League argued that the distinction between Sikhs and Hindus was 'artificial', and since they in fact belonged to the same community, which together constituted about 45 per cent of the population, they did not merit special political safeguards.[27] Predictably, there was a sharp reaction from the Sikh representatives. The leader of the Chief Khalsa Diwan's deputation, Sunder Singh Majithia, remarked, 'Sikhs have been a distinct community. Since the Gurus they have been a distinct community, and I cannot accept the statement from a rival community that we are not a distinct community ... Religiously and socially we are a distinct community, and as such our interests are not identical with those of any other community at all.'[28] The Chief Khalsa Diwan's position on Sikh representation was supported by the Central Sikh League, which adopted a resolution in October 1928 stating,

> In view of the peculiar conditions prevailing in the Punjab, and in view of the admitted political, historical and economic importance of the Sikhs in the province, it is absolutely necessary to provide adequate and effective representation [for] them ... their rights can only be safeguarded by reservation of at least 30 per cent of seats in the local legislature and the same proportion in the provincial representation in the central legislature.'[29]

The next phase of discussions relating to constitutional reforms in India took place in the form of three sessions of a round-table conference held in London between the British government and Indian political representatives. Discussions at the conference began with the report of the Indian Statutory Commission published in May 1930. The commission had proposed a federal constitution for India with greater provincial autonomy and Indian self-government at the provincial level. The system of dual responsibility between an elected legislature and a British executive introduced at the provincial level under the 1919 Act was now reproduced at the central level. However, the major issue confronting the conference became the question of communal representation: the maintenance of separate communal electorates and the reservation of seats for minority communities versus the introduction of joint electorates. In the absence of an agreement among the Indian representatives, the British government assumed the right to decide on this thorny issue. Meanwhile, a joint committee of the two houses of the British parliament was established to work out a scheme for the future administration of India. The outcome of their deliberations was later embodied in a new set of constitutional reforms introduced in the form of the Government of India Act of 1935.

In 1932 the British government announced its decision to maintain separate electorates and the reservation of seats in legislatures for minority communities. This decision, or the communal award as it was called, granted the Sikhs thirty-three of 175 seats in the Punjab Legislative Assembly and special representation at the centre.[30] Though special representation for Sikhs in proportion to their population would have entitled them to only 14 per cent of the seats in the Punjab, the Sikhs were granted almost 19 per cent of the seats in the provincial assembly. However, the Akali Dal was bitterly critical of the communal award. In July 1932 a Sikh conference was called at Lahore representing the Akali Dal and the Central Sikh League in strength. The conference rejected the proportion of seats allocated to the Sikhs as unacceptable and 'voiced its grim determination not to allow the successful working of any constitution which does not provide full protection to the Sikhs by guaranteeing an effective balance of power to each of the three principal communities in the Punjab'.[31]

In March 1942 Sir Stafford Cripps arrived in India with another set of constitutional proposals aimed at creating a new Indian Union after the end of the war. The mission ended in failure due to a deadlock between the colonial authorities and the nationalists. But the Cripps mission was of considerable significance for another reason. Earlier, at its annual conference at Lahore in March 1940, the Muslim League had declared that the Muslims of British India were a separate nation. They demanded that areas in which the Muslims were in a majority should be constituted into a sovereign Muslim state of Pakistan. The Punjab formed the core of this demand. The Cripps mission made the Muslim League's demand for Pakistan seem an impending reality, for his proposals for an Indian federation included the right of non-accession for Indian provinces.[32]

The possibility of the creation of a sovereign Muslim state of Pakistan greatly perturbed Sikh leaders, for a division of the Punjab along Muslim–Hindu communal lines would split the Sikh population in two. Consequently, the Akali Dal formulated a counter-scheme of territorial adjustment which foresaw the creation of a new territorial unit of Azad, or free Punjab, through a re-demarcation of the boundaries of Punjab. Under the scheme, the Muslim majority areas would be detached from Punjab and a new province constituted in which no religious community had a majority. In June 1943 the Akali Dal issued a statement outlining this proposal in which it declared that 'in the Azad Punjab the boundaries shall be fixed after taking into consideration the poulation, property, land revenue and historical traditions of each of the communities'.[33] The Akali Dal also published a pamphlet explaining its proposal to its constituents in detail. The demarcation of the boundaries of Azad Punjab, the pamphlet stated, would create a province in which the Muslim population was only 40 per cent, the Hindu population also 40 per cent and the Sikhs, being 20 per cent, would serve to maintain the political balance between the two communities. The Sikhs, the pamphlet said, would be able to take sides and maximize their political advantage. Moreover, in time the Sikh princely states would be merged into the new province and thereby raise the Sikh population to 24 per cent. Finally, the Akali Dal argued that as Sikh population growth had been quite rapid during the previous years, in time the Sikh population would rise to 30 per cent of Azad Punjab, which would be even better.[34]

The Azad Punjab scheme of the Akali Dal was not taken seriously by other Indian political leaders, and Akali leaders' apprehensions at political developments were compounded by the announcement by a veteran Congress politician of a formula to appease the Muslim League. In July 1944 C. Rajagopalachari put forward a proposal that if the Muslim League supported the Congress demand for immediate independence, after the war the Congress would agree to the establishment of a commission to demarcate contiguous districts with Muslim majorities in north-western and north-eastern India, and a plebiscite would be held to determine whether the inhabitants wanted a separate Muslim state or to remain within India. The Rajagopalachari announcement was not accepted by the Congress leaders, but it brought an immediate reaction from the Akalis. A Sikh conference, dominated by the Akalis, was held in August 1944 which suggested that a committee be established to look into the possibility of the creation of an independent Sikh state. The Akali leader, Tara Singh declared that the Sikhs, too, were a nation and that they would not be made slaves of Pakistan or Hindustan.[35]

In 1946 a team of British Cabinet ministers visited India to seek agreement with Indian leaders on the constitutional issue. In a memorandum to the Cabinet mission, Tara Singh stated that the Akali Dal preferred a united India since the creation of Pakistan would divide the Sikh community. However, if Pakistan was to be formed, the Sikhs would insist on a separate Sikh state, with the right to federate with either India or Pakistan.[36] The objective of a separate Sikh State of Sikhistan or Khalistan was officially adopted by the Akali Dal in March 1946. A resolution adopted by the executive committee of the Akali Dal stated,

> Whereas the Sikhs being attached to the Punjab by intimate bonds of holy shrines, property, language, traditions, and history claim it as their homeland and holy land and which the British took as a 'trust' from the last Sikh ruler during his minority and whereas the entity of the Sikhs is being threatened on account of the persistent demand for Pakistan by the Muslims on the one hand and of danger of absorption by the Hindus on the other, and Executive Committee of the Shiromani Akali Dal demands, for the preservation and protection of the religious, cultural and economic rights of the Sikh nation, the creation of a Sikh state.[37]

While the Akalis battled for critical political advantage in what was for them an unsympathetic world, their ideology was also developed to enhance and justify their authority. Drawing on an interpretation of Sikh history and traditions, they argued that religion and politics were essentially combined in Sikhism. It was for this reason that the sixth guru, Hargobind, had worn two swords, *miri* and *piri*, one emphasizing his religious, the other his political authority. Further, he had used the spiritual centre of Sikhism, the Golden Temple, to dispense both spiritual guidance and temporal orders. Guru Gobind Singh had carried this process further by founding an essentially political organization of his religious followers in the form of the Khalsa *panth*. Thus the Akali leader Tara Singh wrote in 1945, 'there is not the least doubt that the Sikh religion can live only as long as the Panth exists as an organized entity.'[38] The Akali Dal presented itself as providing this critical organization for the Sikh community, the Khalsa *panth*. Moreover, it was argued by a prominent Akali leader that since membership of the *panth* brings Sikhs together in 'Kinship which transcends distance, territory, caste, social barriers and even race',[39] 'a member of the Panth cannot become, over its head, a member of some other body, e.g. the Indian National Congress, without violating his loyalty to the Panth, for their spheres clash – the Panth itself being a religious cum political organization of the Sikhs'.[40] Further, the Akalis believed that as the sole representative of the Sikh *panth*, the presence of Sikhs in any area gave the Akali Dal an automatic right to represent them irrespective of their political views. Thus in 1948, when a new state of PEPSU, or Patiala and the East Punjab States Union, was formed by bringing the small princely states within the boundaries of Punjab together into one administrative unit, the Akali Dal's executive committee promptly demanded that the Akali Dal should be called upon to form a government to represent the Sikh majority in the new unit.[41]

The independence of India in 1947, and the partition of British Punjab between India and Pakistan on the basis of Hindu and Muslim majority areas, totally changed the political picture. As widespread communal riots broke out, virtually the entire Hindu and Sikh population of the western districts of Punjab, now to form a part of Pakistan, moved to India. Punjabi Muslims similarly fled Indian East Punjab for West Punjab. This mass movement of refugees significantly altered the communal composition of Indian Punjab. The position of the Sikhs in Punjab changed dramatically from that of a small minority in a multi-communal province to a significant proportion of a province essentially of Hindus and Sikhs. In undivided Punjab in 1941 the Hindus comprised some 26 per cent and the Sikhs 13 per cent of the population.[42] But in 1951, 61 per cent of all Indian Punjabis were Hindu and 35 per cent were Sikhs.[43] The Sikhs had increased their proportion of the population of Punjab two and half times, but this brought little solace to Akali leaders. For, in a free India committed to secularism, there would be no separate communal political representation. The Sikhs were dominant in six districts and in a large majority in five others, but as a community they would have little political leverage in provincial politics.

The prospect of a Hindu-dominated Punjabi society and no special political safeguards for the Sikhs raised Akali apprehensions that the Sikhs as a separate entity would in time disappear. In colonial India, Sikh communal representation in the political bodies had been guaranteed through the establishment of separate communal electorates and the reservation of seats on a communal basis. This formula had ensured a degree of Sikh political representation, but it had also served, through the electoral process, as a powerful form of mass identity reaffirmation for Sikhs. Separate Sikh communal electorates in a wider political arena highlighted the distinction between Sikh candidates and Hindu candidates and between Sikh voters and Hindu voters. The reservation of posts in government service especially for Sikhs reinforced Sikh separatism from the Hindus. With the abolition of separate Sikh communal representation, a resulting motivation and a periodic reaffirmation of a separate Sikh communal identity would no longer exist. Moreover, Sikh leaders believed that with the advent of an industrial age and a consequent dilution of religious values, religious unorthodoxy among Sikhs in the form of the non-observance of Khalsa symbols, was on the increase. Sikhs it was widely believed, no longer regularly read the holy scriptures in their homes nor observed Sikh religious traditions with the same diligence. Sikh *gurdwara*s were no longer the centres of community life.[44] A general laxity in religious matters was bound to lead to religious unorthodoxy. The shedding of Khalsa symbols was thought to be particularly prevalent among the younger generation of Sikhs. The process, it was believed, began with the trimming of their beards by young Sikhs which led to the cutting of their hair, and a visible symbol of Khalsa distinctiveness was gone. As one contemporary writer put it,

The educated youth feel no emotional concern for Sikhism because it embodies no values that he recognizes. His values are different. You appeal to him in the name of the Guru; the Guru of his ancestors; you take him to Gurdwara; you quote Gurbani to impress him but everything leaves him cold. Nothing carries force with him. You fail to enlist his emotions because you fail to illuminate his valuational sense.[45]

In fact, the Sikh population of India grew from 3.7 million in 1941 to 5.5 million in 1959,[46] but Akali fears were moulded by their perception and not by statistics.

For Akali leaders, in independent India, there could be only one solution to their political impotence and the threat of fragmentation of the Sikh community and its consequent absorbtion into the mass of Hinduism. If an independent Sikh entity was to be preserved, they believed, a formula had to be found which would provide the Sikhs with political leverage as a community. This concern was initially manifested in a demand that the Sikhs must have a territorial unit in which they were the dominant population. Sikh numerical superiority in such a unit would also ensure political power for the Akalis. Political power in the hands of the Akalis, it was believed, would in itself reinforce the separate Sikh entity and also permit the Akalis to undertake a variety of acts to strengthen Sikh communal solidarity. In more recent times, this Akali objective has been presented in a different form.

Moreover, as the Akalis pressed for fulfilment of their demands, they consistently used symbols and issues which reinforced Sikh communal solidarity and also resurrected the tested agitational tactics of the 1920s. Thus, the Akalis continued to utilize a religious appeal to raise support for non-religious demands, chose issues which highlighted the distinctiveness of the Sikh community and launched mass agitations through Akali *jatha*s breaking the law, courting arrest and thereby attempting to pressurize the government to concede their demands.

Even before the trauma of partition and the resulting mass relocation of the Sikh population had subsided, the Akali leader Tara Singh declared in February 1948, 'we want to have a province where we can safeguard our culture and our tradition'.[47] Accused of being a communalist, he responded, 'I want the right cf self determination for the Panth in matters religious, social and political. If to ask for the existence of the Panth is communalism, then I am a communalist'.[48] A demand for a Sikh majority state within the Indian union was submitted in the form of a memoradum by Sikh members of the Punjab Legislative Assembly to the Constituent Assembly, then framing the constitution of independent India. The memorandum demanded that there be special communal representation for the Sikhs to the extent of 50 per cent in the Punjab legislature and 40 per cent in government services. More importantly, the memorandum stressed that if these demands were not acceptable, the Sikhs should be permitted to form a separate province comprising the districts in which they were in a majority.[49] The Constituent Assembly refused to accept either of the Sikh demands.

The first general election in India under the new constitution in 1952 provided an occasion for the Akali Dal to resurrect the issue. The Akalis had realized, however, that a second division of the Punjab along communal lines would be totally unacceptable to the government of India. Since the demand for the reorganisation of states on a linguistic basis had been raised in other parts of the country, the Akalis now cloaked their demand for a Sikh majority province in linguistic terms.[50] As the Punjabi language was the mother tongue of all Sikhs, while Hindi was the first language of a large body of Punjabi Hindus, a demand for a Punjabi-speaking state coincided closely with the demand for a Sikh majority state. Thus the Akali Dal's election manifesto in 1952 stated,

The true test of democracy, in the opinion of the Shiromani Akali Dal, is that the minorities should feel that they are really free and equal partners in the destiny of their country ... to bring home this sense of freedom to the Sikhs it is vital that there should be a Punjabi speaking language and culture ... The Shiromani Akali Dal is in favour of the formation of provinces on a linguistic and cultural basis throughout India, but it holds it is a question of life and death for the Sikhs for a new Punjab to be created immediately.[51]

The formal presentation of this case was made to the States Reorganization Commission established by the government of India in 1953. The Akali Dal, in a memorandum to the commission, urged the formation of a Punjabi *suba* or a Punjabi-speaking state by the joining together of the Punjabi-speaking areas of existing Punjab, PEPSU and the state of Rajasthan. At the same time the Hindi-speaking areas of Punjab and PEPSU were to be merged with neighbouring Hindi-speaking areas. The Akali Dal argued that a unilingual state was necessary to provide for education and administration to be carried out in the language of the area. Further, they reasoned that since a language corresponds to a specific culture, a unilingual Punjabi-speaking state would allow for the development of Punjabi culture.

This Akali demand developed into a subject of major controversy between Sikh and Hindu Punjabis, for Hindu organizations opposed the demand and saw it as an attempt to establish Sikh domination in the state. The Hindus demanded instead the amalgamation of the overwhelmingly Hindu state of Himachal Pradesh with Punjab. The government of India for its part resisted the Akali demand, which it considered to be contrary to the principles of a secular India and a threat to the unity of the country. Certainly, during the Akali agitation for Punjabi *suba* which was to span more than two decades, Akali leaders repeatedly made statements acknowledging that what they really wanted was a Sikh majority state. In an article discussing the objectives of the demand for Punjabi *suba*, the Akali leader Tara Singh stated that the Akali Dal had decided that the creation of a Punjabi-speaking state was the best way to maintain the independent existence of the Sikhs.[52] In such a state, the Sikhs would be in a majority and would thereby escape from Hindu dominance in the legislatures. Tara Singh stressed that the demand for Punjabi Suba stemmed from a desire for a territorial unit, where on the birthdays of the gurus armies of Sikhs might march in the streets and the Sikh flag fly with the national flag. Therefore, he concluded, 'for the sake of religion, for the sake of culture, for the sake of the Panth, and to keep high the flag of the Guru, the Sikhs have girded their loins to achieve independence'.[53] In another statement, Tara Singh admitted that the primary motive for the demand for a Punjabi Suba was to 'protect the Sikh religion and improve the position of the Sikhs'.[54] 'You might declare [Punjabi] language of the whole of India, would that help the Sikhs?', he asked.[55] Similarly, a leading Indian journalist reported in 1961,

> During a talk we had ... Master Tara Singh made no secret of his motive in asking for a Punjabi Suba. The Sikhs as a distinctive community, he emphasised, must be preserved, and they could be preserved only in a 'home land' of their own. Left in their present position, he asserted, the Sikhs would be gradually 'absorbed' by the majority community ... The Sikhs with their exterior symbols of distinction can last as a separate community only if they enjoy power and can extend patronage for the continuance of the symbols.[56]

Finally, in an interview with the chief minister of Punjab in 1955, Tara Singh admitted that the establishment of a Punjabi-speaking state was not his intention. When asked if he really wanted Sikh dominance, he replied,

> This is exactly what I have in mind ... This cover of a Punjabi-speaking-state slogan serves my purpose well since it does not offend against nationalism. The Government should accept our demand under the slogan of a Punjabi-speaking state without a probe – what we want is Azadi [*independence*]. The Sikhs have no Azadi. We will fight for our Azadi with full power even if we have to revolt for our Azadi. We will revolt to win our Azadi.[57]

While the States Reorganization Commission was still deliberating the question, the Akali Dal launched an agitation to pressurize the government into conceding its demand. To rally the Sikhs, a spate of charges of discrimination against Sikhs in government service and of official interference in Sikh religious affairs were made. The 1954 elections to the SGPC provided the Akali Dal with an opportunity to seek a mandate for its campaign. The Akali Dal's overwhelming victory in the elections led to an intensification of Akali agitation. Akali *jathas* undertook widespread political demonstrations in favour of Punjabi *suba*. Rival

demonstrations by Hindu organizations followed. As the shouting of blatantly communal slogans on both sides made the
atmosphere increasingly tense, the Punjab government declared,
in April 1955, a ban on the shouting of slogans relating to the
reorganization of the state. In response, the Akali Dal gave an
ultimatum to the government to lift the ban or face an intensified
Akali campaign. In May 1955, in response to the government's
refusal to do so, a new Akali campaign was launched. Tara Singh
addressed a huge gathering of Sikhs inside the Golden Temple and
urged them not to give in to official tyranny. The message to the
gathering ran,

> O Singhs! We ask for freedom and they want to ensnare us deeper
> into slavery. We are not satisfied with the present situation and ask
> for Punjabi Suba, but they stop us even from propagating the
> demand for Punjabi Suba. They have imposed a ban on raising
> slogans for the demand. Khalsa Ji! Understand this that this is to
> finish our honour. This is all we have, if this gone then all is gone. So
> stake everything to maintain our honour. In the present time we
> should offer our heads peacefully like Guru Tegh Bhadur. The
> rivals are haughty rulers, but we have faith in the Guru.[58]

As the first group of Akalis marched out of the Golden Temple
shouting slogans in defiance of the ban, they were arrested. Their
arrest led to greater Akali organization and propaganda urging
Sikhs to fulfil their religious duty. The Akalis declared the date of
the martyrdom of the ninth guru, Tegh Bhadur, as Punjabi *suba*
day, and the message of their campaign was spread throughout the
province through the SGPC's network of *gurdwaras*.

Akali propaganda was remarkably successful and Sikh volunteers gathered in Amritsar from all over the province. They were
blessed at the Golden Temple and continued their agitation. After
nearly two months and the arrest of some 12,000 Sikhs, there
seemed little sign of the Akali campaign abating. The Punjab
government decided that their only course of action was to arrest
the Akali leaders directing the campaign from the sanctuary of the
Golden Temple. Accordingly, the police entered the temple and
arrested the Akali organization within, in the process using tear
gas to counter an attack on them. Government action was easily
interpreted as being directed against the Sikh religion, and the
Akalis pointed to the fact that some tear-gas shells had landed
inside the temple and screamed sacrilege. The Akali campaign was

flooded with volunteers. Finally, two days before the government's prohibitory order on slogan shouting was to lapse it was lifted. The Akalis ended their agitation, portraying it as a great victory.

Meanwhile, in October 1955 the States Reorganisation Commission had issued its report and rejected the demand for Punjabi *suba* on the ground that the minimum measure of agreement necessary for making a change did not exist. Tara Singh denounced the report 'as the decree of Sikh annihilation',[59] but negotiations over the issue with the government were begun. While these were in progress, the Congress party held its annual session at Amritsar in 1956 and provided the Akali Dal with an opportunity to demonstrate its strength again. The Akali Dal organised an enormous procession of Sikhs marching in military formation with shining swords and axes. The demonstration was led by Tara Singh riding on an elephant.

Negotiations between Akali leaders and the government resulted in what was known as the regional formula. Under it, PEPSU was merged with Punjab, but the overwhelmingly Hindu province of Himachal Pradesh was retained as a separate entity. In the new Punjab, a limited measure of internal autonomy was to be given to two committees of the provincial legislature representing the Punjabi and Hindi-speaking regions. These committees could formulate legislation on certain subjects for consideration of the legislature as a whole. Further, under an agreement between the Akalis and the ruling Congress party, the Akali Dal amended its constitution and agreed to limit its future activity to religious and cultural affairs concerning the Sikhs.[60]

Having seemingly reached a settlement, the Akali Dal renewed its demand for Punjabi *suba* during the 1959 elections of the SGPC. Its enormous victory in these elections was interpreted by Akali leaders as a mandate to begin agitation on the question again. At the first general meeting of the newly constituted SGPC in March 1960, it adopted a resolution which stated clearly, 'The only solution of the linguistic trouble in the Punjab is to bifurcate Punjab on the basis of Punjabi and Hindi'.[61] The Akali Dal now decided to organize a *shahidi*, or martyrs, *jatha* which would take a religious oath at the Golden Temple not to be deterred in its objective and then march to Delhi to press for the formation of a Punjabi *suba*. In preparation for this campaign, the Akali Dal issued posters warning Sikhs that the Hindus wanted to destroy them and asked them to prepare for a *dharm yudh*, or religious war.[62] Once the *shahidi jatha* had been formed, Fateh Singh, the senior vice-president of the SGPC, personally blessed each Akali volunteer at the Golden Temple and asked him to declare his father's name as Guru Gobind Singh if arrested.[63]

The Punjab government reacted firmly to this new campaign. Tara Singh and other Akali leaders were arrested and charged with incitement to communal violence. Akali *jatha*s attempting to march to Delhi were gaoled. Initially, firm government action only increased Sikh unrest, but after the arrest of thousands of Sikh agitators, the Akali campaign began to wane. In an apparent attempt to divert the attention of the rural Sikh masses, the Punjab government called elections to village councils, and to demonstrate that the agitation has lost its momentum released thousands of Akali prisoners.[64] By November 1960 the Akali Dal's campaign was on its last legs, and Fateh Singh, in charge of the agitation during Tara Singh's imprisonment, announced his intention to undertake a fast until death for the Punjabi *suba*. Meanwhile, as a gesture of conciliation towards enraged Sikh opinion, the Punjab government released Tara Singh who convinced his lieutenant to abandon the fast. Some months later, however, in August 1961, amidst much publicity, Tara Singh took an oath at the Golden Temple and began his own fast until death. Tara Singh demanded that the government accept the formation of a Punjabi *suba* and appoint a commission to inquire into Akali allegations of discrimination against Sikhs. As Tara Singh's fast progressed, it gave rise to considerable apprehension among Sikhs, and dire warnings were issued of the consequences if the Akali leader died. The Prime Minister of India, Jawaharlal Nehru, called the Akali demand for a Punjabi *suba* a communal demand in parliament, but agreed to the appointment of a commission to investigate Akali allegations of discrimination against Sikhs in government service. After forty-three days Tara Singh ended his fast, and an Akali campaign in which 26,000 Sikhs had courted arrest ended in failure. The government appointed a commission to look into Akali allegations of discrimination against Sikhs the same day. Significantly, the Akali Dal refused to submit evidence before this commission.[65]

The aftermath of this unsuccessful Akali agitation was bitter

acrimony between Tara Singh and Fateh Singh and a revolt of
Akali Dal members against their leaders for having broken a
sacred oath. The next SGPC elections in 1965 thus became a
contest between the two leaders to determine control of the Akali
Dal. Fateh Singh emerged from these elections as the clear leader
and subsequently announced that he would undertake yet another
fast for the Punjabi *suba*, followed by self-immolation within
forty days. The stage seemed set for another long-drawn-out
confrontation between the Akalis and government.

However, Fateh Singh's fast was postponed due to an agreement with the government to appoint a sub-committee of the
Cabinet, of which Indira Gandhi was a member, to resolve the
Punjabi *suba* question. Later it was again postponed due to the
outbreak of war between India and Pakistan. In the meantime,
with the death of Prime Minister Nehru, significant changes had
taken place in the central government. In the Punjab too, Pratap
Singh Kairon, who had dominated the provincial government
between 1956 and 1964 had been removed from office. In March
1966, the Indian Cabinet accepted the Akali demand for a Punjabi
suba. The Punjab State Reorganization Bill was enacted in September 1966, under which the state was trifurcated. The southern,
predominantly Hindi-speaking, Hindu areas, were formed into a
new state of Haryana, and other Hindi-speaking parts of Punjab
detached and merged with neighbouring Himachal Pradesh. The
new state of Punjab thus created had a population which was
some 54 per cent Sikh and 44 per cent Hindu. The Akalis had
achieved their long-cherished goal of a Sikh majority in the
Punjab. This Sikh majority, they believed, would provide the
essential security for the maintenance of the Sikh communal
entity, and also the possibility of the Akali Dal emerging as a
governing party in the province.

In the reorganized state of Punjab, the Sikhs were in a majority,
but they had to share political power with the Hindus. Since the
Akali Dal's political appeal to Hindus was non-existent, its
political constituency was limited to the Sikh majority. The Akali
Dal's strong support from the Sikh community had been amply
demonstrated in its various agitational campaigns, but Akali
leaders found to their chagrin that in electoral politics, Sikhs did
not vote exclusively along communal lines. The Congress party,
with its cross-communal following, had always had enough Sikhs

in positions of leadership to make it a powerful contender for electoral support from Sikhs. Thus, in the five elections to the Punjab legislative assembly held between 1967 and 1980, the Congress party was able to command support from a significant body of Sikh voters, and as a result the Akali Dal was unable to get more than 30 per cent of the total vote.[66] The presence of non-Akali Sikh legislators in the Punjab assembly was not regarded by the Akalis as being of any value to the Sikh community. Thus a leading Sikh newspaper sympathetic to the Akali Dal commented,

> There are, undoubtedly many Sikhs in the ruling Congress party, some of them hold high positions in the party as well as in the government at the centre and in the Punjab. But they do not represent the political aspirations of the Sikhs, nor do they work for the economic, social, educational and religious advancement of the Sikhs. This job is solely and squarely that of the Shiromani Akali Dal.[67]

In fact, some Akali leaders regarded Sikh allegiance to non-Sikh political parties as a more sinister development. Thus a prominent Akali politician argued that the Sikhs could not be considered as a group of individuals but must be seen as an indivisible community whose loyalty to a secular state was contingent upon the state's recognition of the Sikhs as a 'collective group' with a historic 'theo-political status'.[68] He further stated that 'the State must deal with [the Sikhs] as one people, and not by atomising them into individual citizens,[69] and that the government of independent India had been determined 'to atomise and absorb' the Sikh community in political terms.[70]

In the first elections in reorganized Punjab, the Akali Dal was able to form a coalition government in an alliance with the Jan Singh and the Communist party. But the Congress party succeeded in electing more Sikh legislators than the Akali Dal.[71] Moreover, the Akali Dal's alliance with the Jan Sangh, a party with an essentially Hindu communal appeal, must have been a bitter pill for Akali leaders to swallow. Throughout the campaign for a Punjabi *suba*, the Jan Sangh had been bitterly opposed to a division of the Punjab, and its president had gone on record stating that, 'The Jan Sangh regards the Sikhs as part and parcel of the Hindu Society'.[72] For the Akalis, having to share power and then with the Jan Sangh significantly diluted the benefits of an

Akali government for the Sikh community. From the establishment of the Punjabi *suba* to 1980, the Akalis have been able to govern the Punjab only with the assistance of a coalition government, and at the same time have had to contend with the Congress party's support from Sikh voters in the Punjab. In the mid-term elections of 1969, the Akali Dal was again able to form a government with the assistance of the Jan Sangh. However, in the next elections of the Punjab assembly in 1972, the Akali Dal was ousted from power by the Congress party. Following the Congress party's historic defeat nation-wide by the Janata party in 1977, the Akali Dal again formed a government in the Punjab through an alliance with the Janata party. But, after the Congress resumed power at the centre, it called fresh elections to provincial assemblies and won 54 per cent of the seats in the Punjab legislature. Moreover, in elections to the lower house of Parliament held in 1980, the Congress won twelve out of thirteen seats from the Punjab and again vividly demonstrated its political appeal to Hindu and Sikh voters.

Moreover, to compound problems of Sikh communal solidarity, significant changes in the distribution of the Sikh population in India had taken place during the previous few decades. As early as 1931, the census report for India had commented, 'A noticeable feature in connection with the Sikhs is their appreciable increase in centres distant from the Punjab to which they migrate largely for the sake of employment.'[73] In post-independence India this process was accelerated, and between 1951 and 1961 the number of Sikhs in India outside the Punjab increased by 62 per cent.[74] By 1981 some 3.3 million or 25 per cent of the Sikh population of India was living outside the Punjab.[75] However, this migration did not adversely affect the Sikh majority in the Punjab. Due to an unusually rapid Sikh population growth and an abnormally slow Hindu population increase, the proportion of Sikhs in the Punjab in fact increased to 60 per cent of the population by 1971, and they maintained this majority in 1981.[76]

Between 1981 and 1984 the Akali Dal launched a series of mass agitations against the central government. Earlier, following elections to the Akali Dal in 1980, the party had split into two principal factions, the dominant group led by the Akali Dal's president, Harchand Singh Longowal, and the other led by the Akali leader and former president of the party, Jagdev Singh

Talwandi. The two groups at times joined forces in the campaign, but it was marked by rivalry between them which led to a spate of escalating and contradictory demands and statements, as each politician sought to demonstrate his leadership.

The core of the Akali Dal's demands derived from a resolution outlining the policy and programme of the party adopted by its working committee in October 1973 at Anandpur Sahib. The text of the Anandpur Sahib resolution itself became a subject of considerable debate and confusion, for due to the subsequent formation of the two rival factions, several versions of the resolution existed. As a result, in 1982 the president of the Akali Dal issued an authenticated version of the 1973 resolution. This version reiterated that 'The Shiromani Akali Dal is the very embodiment of the hopes and aspirations of the Sikh Nation and as such is fully entitled to its representation'.[77] It stated that one of the principal purposes of the Akali Dal was to strive 'To preserve and keep alive the concept of distinct and independent identity of the Panth and to create an environment in which national sentiments and aspiration of the Sikh Panth will find full expression, satisfaction and growth'.[78] The primary political goal of the Akali Dal, the resolution further stated, was the 'pre-eminence of the Khalsa through creation of a congenial environment and a political set up'.[79] To achieve this the resolution outlined seven basic objectives. The more important of these were that Punjab's capital city of Chandigarh, which it shared with neighbouring Haryana State, and certain 'Sikh populated Punjabi speaking areas' presently outside and contiguous to Punjab be merged with it. In the new Punjab thus formed, the interests of the Sikhs and Sikhism were to be specifically protected.[80] Besides, the resolution stated that the new Punjab and other Indian states should be granted a degree of provincial autonomy beyond that governing relations between the state and central governments under the existing constitution of the country. The resolution also stated that the Akali Dal would strive for the enactment of an all-India *gurdwaras* Act.

The primary political objective stated in the Anandpur Sahib resolution was not in itself new. Before the Akali Dal amended its constitution in an agreement with the Congress party in 1956, its constitution included a clause stating, 'The Shiromani Akali Dal stands for the creation of an environment in which the Sikh national expression finds its full satisfaction'.[81] This objective, it has been pointed out, was more clearly stated in the original Punjabi version by the use of the term *desh–kaal*, literally country and era.[82] Moreover, while this clause had in the negotiations prior to India's independence been invoked as the basis for the Akali Dal's demand for a separate Sikh state, it was also cited by a leading Akali politician as the basis for the demand for a Punjabi *suba*. In 1956 Hukum Singh wrote,

> The constitution provides that the objective of the Akali Dal would be to create environment (area and atmosphere) wherein the Sikh religion culture and traditions could survive and grow unhampered. The Akali Dal believed that the formation of a Punjabi speaking state in North India could bring such an atmosphere and the desired environment. It was in pursuance of these aims in the constitution that the demand for a Punjabi Suba was made and sacrifices offered to achieve this.[83]

The new objective of seeking the enactment of an all-India *gurdwaras* Act was clearly intended to increase the Akali Dal's reach over the now substantial Sikh population of the country as a whole. The passage of such legislation would vastly increase the SGPC's network of patronage to Sikhs outside Punjab and its annual income from Rs70 million in 1982 to Rs170 million.[84] Thus the pro-Akali newspaper the *Spokesman*, commenting on the central government's apparent reluctance to expedite the passage of an all-India *gurdwaras* Act, noted, 'The naked truth is that the Centre does not want the Akalis to capture a wider platform and more funds, which shall be theirs when all historic and main gurdwaras in the country come under their control. This is deciding a purely religious issue on political considerations.'[85]

The Akali Dal was a coalition partner with the Janata party in the Punjab government between 1977 and 1980, but despite its affinity with the central Janata party government it did little to raise demands based on the Anandpur Sahib resolution with the central government. An Akali meeting in 1978 endorsed the principles and objectives of the 1973 resolution, but it was not until September 1981 that the Akali Dal presented a series of demands based partly on the 1973 resolution to the central government.

Meanwhile, in February 1981, the working committee of the Akali Dal had met and its president, Harchand Singh Longowal, reiterated that the implementation of the Anandpur Sahib resolution was the long-term objective of the party.[86] In response, a prominent member of the Talwandi group asserted that, since the Sikhs were a nation, they must have a sovereign state of their own.[87] In March the annual session of the all-India Sikh Educational Conference was held under the auspices of the Chief Khalsa Diwan. The conference was attended by all major Sikh political leaders and proved to be a forum for an outburst of Sikh consciousness. In his address to the gathering, the president of the conference reminded the Sikhs that the 'Sikh nation is unique in refusing to be absorbed in the Brahmanical traditions and modes of the Hindu nation' and that the 'Sikhs were still struggling for asserting our rightful claim to our identity and nationhood'.[88] He warned the gathering that if even the slightest deviation from the true beliefs and traditions of the Sikhs was permitted, 'after some time, we will hardly be able to recognise the face of our faith'.[89] The conference adopted a resolution calling for the establishment of a sovereign Sikh state and the seeking of consultative status for the Sikh nation within the United Nations.[90] Later, at an annual meeting of the SGPC in April, a resolution stating that the Sikhs were a separate nation and calling for the implementation of the Anandpur Sahib resolution was adopted.[91]

Once the euphoria of the conference had subsided, however, the organizer of the meeting, the Chief Khalsa Diwan, disassociated itself from the demand for a separate Sikh state. A few weeks later, the president of the Akali Dal stated that his party's concept of the Sikhs as a nation was a purely religious one. The rival, Talwandi, group for its part issued a statement stating that it was not in favour of a separate Sikh state but demanded the creation of a *desh* Punjab, or Punjab country, within the Indian union. To demonstrate its commitment to this demand, the Talwandi group launched a small-scale civil-disobedience movement in Delhi by Akali volunteers violating a prohibitory order against public gatherings outside parliament and courting arrest. The shifting stance of Akali leaders perplexed even their supporters. Commenting on the statements of the Talwandi group, the *Spokesman* noted in an editorial,

> In the beginning, they supported the demand for Khalistan, which meant an independent and sovereign State outside the Indian Union ... when they found that there was little support for this demand ...

the Talwandi faction contended that it was asking for a 'Desh Punjab' within the Indian Union ... but no one bothered to pinpoint what they meant by 'Desh Punjab', what its boundaries would be and what its constitutional status would be. Now this faction is insisting on the implementation of the Anandpur Sahib resolution.[92]

Akali leaders now launched an intensive publicity campaign alleging discrimination against Sikhs by the government and official interference in Sikh religious affairs. The president of the Akali Dal announced that a number of Akali *jathas* would begin touring the rural areas to educate the people against such discrimination. In August 1981 an All World Sikh Convention was called to draw up plans for a *dharm yudh*, or religious war, against the Government. A set of forty-five grievances was drawn up and submitted to the central government in September. Meanwhile, while the Talwandi group continued sending token volunteers to court arrest in Delhi, the Longowal group organized a protest march of Sikhs in the capital.

The list of forty-five grievances submitted to the central government was a strange mixture of the core objectives stated in the Anandpur Sahib resolution, grievances obviously intended to appeal to various segments of the Sikh population and others intended simply to lend credence to Akali allegations and reinforce Sikh communal solidarity. The central government's failure to settle the grievances was portrayed as indifference and discrimination towards the Sikh community. Thus the list stated that the government had kept the city of Chandigarh and certain Punjabi-speaking areas outside Punjab, denied internal autonomy to the state and not enacted an all-India Sikh *gurdwaras* Act. Further, the government was accused of discrimination against Sikhs by reducing the recruitment quota of Sikhs in the armed forces, of being responsible for the paucity of heavy industry in the Punjab, for the denial of loans to farmers at the rates given to industrialists and for the non-remunerative prices of agricultural produce, and of failing to safeguard the rights of weaker sections of the population. The list also complained that the government had shown apathy towards the safety of life and property of Sikhs settled abroad and in other states in India, had failed to name any railway train the Golden Temple Express, and had not granted 'holy city' status to Amritsar or permitted the installation of a radio transmitter in the Golden Temple for broadcasting Sikh religious hymns and teaching. Further, it had not recognized a separate Sikh personal law, and had interfered in the Sikh tenets and violated the sanctity of Sikh traditions. It had projected Sikhs in an improper way in films and on television and had encouraged anti-Sikh literature.[93] As negotiations between the Akalis and the government over the grievances began, the forty-five grievances were reduced to fifteen demands. The major demands reflected the core objectives of the Anandpur Sahib resolution, including a demand for a special status for the Sikhs in the Punjab. The nature and ramifications of this special status were not spelt out. In addition, the Akali Dal demanded the annulment of earlier agreements on the use of river water between Punjab and neighbouring states and the establishment of new guidelines on the use of river water.

Negotiations between Akali leaders and the central government began in October 1981 and though little information is available on them, they continued intermittently for two and a half years, with each side accusing the other of intransigence, bad faith and deliberate delaying tactics. While the negotiations continued sporadically, the Akali Dal launched a series of agitations to pressurize the government and to demonstrate its following. In April 1982 a campaign to obstruct the digging of a canal linking the Sutlej and Yamuna rivers was begun by the Akali Dal. Akali leaders alleged that by diverting water to the neighbouring state of Haryana, the construction of this canal would deprive the Punjab's peasantry of vital water resources, and they urged them to take a firm stand against such discrimination. Farmers were also urged to stop the repayment of loans due to the government in protest. As the propaganda campaign progressed, an Akali *jatha* proceeded to the site of the canal, attempted to prevent construction work and was arrested. This *nahar-roko*, or 'stop the canal', campaign was escalated a few weeks later when a *jatha* of 1,000 Akali volunteers led by the SGPC president Gurcharan Singh Tohra joined in the agitation. Thereafter, for a period, small batches of Akalis proceeded daily to the site and courted arrest. The Punjab government responded to this increase in Akali activity by continuing to arrest the agitators but releasing them shortly thereafter at a distance from the site.

In June 1982 the two Akali factions announced that they would join forces against the 'repressive policies' of the government, and in August a new Akali campaign was launched in the city of Amritsar. For some time past, the Akalis had been holding public meetings and demonstrations in the city in pursuit of their demand that it be declared a 'holy city'. Akali leaders pointed to the presence of tobacco merchants in the vicinity of the Golden Temple, which was a grave insult to their faith, and demanded a ban on smoking within the city. As public passions, demonstrations and counter-demonstrations on this issue increased, the local authorities imposed a ban on public gatherings within the old city. This declaration provided an appropriate opportunity to escalate the agitation. A group of 4,000 Akali volunteers was formed, blessed at the Golden Temple for their participation in a righteous struggle and marched through the city in defiance of the order. Predictably, their arrest only helped to intensify Akali propaganda of gross disregard for the religious sensibilities of the Sikhs on the part of the government and led to the formation of additional volunteer groups to continue the agitation. The dispatch of Akali *jathas* and their subsequent arrest became a daily affair and generated much interest and sympathy among local Sikhs. By the end of September, it was reported that some 20,000 Sikh agitators had been thus arrested.[94] The same month the death of some Akali prisoners in a railway accident provided an additional issue for agitation. Akali leaders stated that this was a deliberate attempt to kill the prisoners and organized a mass demonstration in Delhi which resulted in violence. For the faithful, the hostility of the government towards the Sikhs was becoming increasingly apparent.

Disaffection among Sikhs was beginning to spread rapidly, and in October 1982 the Punjab government released 25,000 Akali prisoners as a gesture of conciliation. Some weeks later the government of India also strove to appease Sikh religious sentiment and to clarify its position on some Akali demands. It was announced that the government was willing to relay Sikh religious hymns from the Golden Temple through a local radio station and that Sikh passengers on domestic flights would be allowed to carry *kirpans* of a certain length. Further, to meet Sikh concern, the sale of tobacco, liquor and meat would not be permitted in a demarcated area around the Golden Temple. On the Akali demand for the enactment of an all-India *gurdwaras* Act, the government stated that the provincial administrations of states in which Sikh *gurdwara*s were located, and the managements of these institutions, would be consulted on the proposed legislation. The government also announced that the issue of relations between the central and state governments would be referred to an independent commission which was to make recommendations on the question within the existing framework of the constitution. The essential Akali demands relating to the merger of Chandigarh and other areas with Punjab, the granting of a special status to the Sikhs and the sharing of river waters remained unresolved.

The government's announcement had little impact on the determination of Akali leaders to continue their agitation. Indeed, the Akali Dal's president, Harchand Singh Longowal, warned that 'The country [would] be on fire if Government rejected the Akali demands'.[95] In April 1983 a one-day *rasta roko*, or traffic-obstruction campaign was initiated, and Akali groups attempted to stop traffic on the states national highways. A fracas with the police ensued and forty Sikhs were killed. In response, Akali leaders announced their intention to raise an army of 100,000 Akalis who would serve as suicide squads willing to do or die for a decisive war against the government.[96] In June a similar one-day *rail roko* campaign to disrupt railway traffic in the state was announced. Fearing a repetition of violence, the government suspended all railway services on that day. Undeterred, the Akali leaders announced plans for a similar *kam roko*, or work-stoppage, in August in which Akali volunteers would attempt to disrupt the functioning of the provincial administration. This campaign also resulted in violence between Sikh agitators and the police. Also in August it was announced that, at a meeting of the Akali high command with district Akali leaders, it had been decided to celebrate the anniversary of the Akali agitation against the government as a day of prayer for its success and that such prayer meetings would be organized in all Sikh *gurdwara*s in the province. In September 1983 the annual meeting of the militant All India Sikh Students' Federation held in Amritsar, which was attended by all leading Akali politicians, provided an opportunity for bitter allegations against the government and dire warnings of the consequences of not meeting Akali demands. Jagdev Singh Talwandi in addressing the gathering suggested that the Akalis should form a parallel government in the Punjab and begin collecting taxes.[97] He was arrested. However, widespread Sikh unrest was by now clearly beyond the ability of the Punjab government to deal with. Thus in October 1983, under a presidential ordinance, the Punjab legislative assembly was dissolved and the administration of the province placed directly under the central government.

Meanwhile, as the Akali agitation progressed, other significant developments affecting the Sikhs had also occurred.[98] The most important of these was the rise of a young militant fundamentalist Sikh preacher, Jarnail Singh Bhindranwale. Born in a peasant family closely associated with the Dam dama Taxal, a small centre for Sikh orthodoxy and religious teaching, Jarnail Singh joined the institution at an early age. In 1971 he became its head priest and in accordance with the custom of the order adopted the honorific Bhindranwale. From the outset of his new responsibilities Bhindranwale emerged as a rigid champion of Sikh orthodoxy. He toured Sikh villages, exhorted his congregation not to discard Khalsa symbols and baptized hundreds. An essential feature of his preaching was that, in keeping with Sikh traditions, all Sikhs should bear weapons. Bhindranwale's crusade for Sikh orthodoxy focused on the Nirankari Sikhs. Since the Nirankaris worshipped a living guru, contrary to orthodox Sikh teaching, they had in 1973 been declared enemies of the Sikh *panth* by the priests of the Golden Temple. In April 1978 some of Bhindranwale's followers clashed violently with a group of Nirankari Sikhs. The Nirankaris arrested in the incident were subsequently found to have acted in self-defence. In April 1980 the Nirankari guru was assassinated, and the murder of several Nirankaris followed. In September 1981 Lala Jagat Narain, a prominent local Hindu leader and editor of a newspaper critical of the new Sikh fundamentalism, was murdered and Bhindranwale was arrested for alleged involvement. But by then Bhindranwale had gathered around him a loyal and extremist group of armed followers, and his arrest provoked a violent clash with the police in which seventeen Sikhs were killed. Two months later Bhindranwale was released, and although his complicity in the murder could not be proved he publicly applauded the killers. Later he moved to the sanctuary of a building in the Golden Temple complex.

Bhindranwale rapidly assumed the role of a militant messiah.

He took to carrying a silver arrow reminiscent of the martial Sikh guru, Gobind Singh, and surrounded himself with a retinue of heavily armed guards. He began to hold court and urged his congregations to be wary of the designs of the government. Elaborating on the familiar theme of discrimination against Sikhs, he said, 'The Hindus are trying to enslave us; atrocities against the Sikhs are increasing day by day under the Hindu imperialist rulers of New Delhi; the Sikhs have never felt so humiliated, not even during the reign of the Moghul emperors and British colonialists. How long can the Sikhs tolerate injustice?'[99] But for Bhindranwale the solution to this grievance was obvious. 'It should be clear to all Sikhs', he stated, 'whether living in urban or rural areas that we are slaves and want liberation at any cost. To achieve this end, arm yourself and prepare for a war and wait for orders.'[100] In other statements he was more explicit about what was to be done: 'I had earlier directed that each village should raise a team of three youths and one revolver each and a motorcycle'.[101] and 'There is a need to raise motorcycle-groups in order to take revenge against perpetrators of crime against the Sikhs'.[102]

While details of the nature and extent of Bhindranwale's extremist following remain unclear, he found vocal support from the All Indian Sikh Students Federation and his incitements to violence were followed by an apparently well-conceived wave of terrorist activity in the Punjab. Initially, local banks and jewellery shops were attacked and a home guard armoury looted. Selective killings of Nirankaris and minor government officials and bomb explosions at random followed. Between September 1981 and April 1983 there were nearly a hundred such incidents. In most cases the pattern followed was similar, and motorcycle groups were identified with extremist action. In April 1983 extremist violence took a more brazen form and a Sikh deputy inspector general of police was killed as he emerged from the Golden Temple in the heart of Amritsar City. In September 1983 a new dimension of extremist activity began with the indiscriminate killing of Hindus. The terrorists' intention was apparently to create panic among Hindus and thereby trigger an exodus of Hindu punjabis from the province. If such violence would prompt reprisals against Sikhs outside the Punjab, it could only lead to Sikh emigration to the Punjab from other parts of India. By this process, the Punjab would become a Sikh state. Thus, in

October a local bus was stopped at a remote location, and the Hindu passengers isolated and shot. In November this incident was repeated. As incidents of terrorism and violent encounters between Sikh extremists and the security forces escalated, the Akali leadership was affected by this radicalization of Sikh agitation and blamed the government for the bloodshed. In May 1983 the SGPC president warned that there had been a 'sustained conspiracy of the Punjab Government to foment communal trouble',[103] and in July the president of the Akali Dal stated that the central government wanted to liquidate the Sikhs.[104] Moreover, while the government remained hesitant to arrest Bhindranwale from within the Golden Temple complex, the president of the Akali Dal reacted sharply to an official appeal to him to force Bhindranwale to leave. In fact Harchand Singh Longowal stated that this appeal was a clear indication of the government's intentions against the Sikhs since Bhindranwale was involved in baptizing and proselytizing activities.[105] To forestall further action, Bhindranwale moved to the sanctuary of the Akal Takht inside the Golden Temple.

By the beginning of 1984 the atmosphere in the Punjab had become exceedingly tense. A vigorous Akali propaganda campaign, mass agitation and increasing terrorist activity had left many Sikhs and Hindus feeling resentful and vulnerable. In January 1984 the Akali Dal's leadership launched a new agitation against the government. In 1983 the party had circulated a pamphlet enumerating their grievances to members of the Indian Parliament. This pamphlet, entitled, 'You owe us justice', stated

> India is a multi-lingual, multi-religious and multi-national land. In such a land, a micro-scopic minority like the Sikhs has genuine forebodings that ... they may also lose their identity in the vast ocean of overwhelming Hindu majority. Their misgivings are heightened by arbitrary manner in which they are defined as Hindus under Article 25 of the Constitution.[106]

Article 25 of the Indian constitution relates to the freedom of religious worship guaranteed to all citizens. Two explanations follow the clause. The first states that the wearing and carrying of *kirpan*s is deemed to be included in the profession of the Sikh religion, and the second states that reference to Hindus or to Hindu religious institutions should be construed as including persons professing the Sikh, Jain or Buddhist religions. In January

1984 the Akali Dal's grievance against the wording of article 25 of
the constitution was resurrected, and prominent Akali leaders led
a campaign in which this portion of the constitution was burnt in
protest. The Akalis involved were arrested but released a few
months later.

In February 1984 negotiations between Akali leaders and the
central government resumed. While these negotiations were in
progress the Akali Dal organized a one-day general strike in the
Punjab. Moreover, the onset of fresh discussions between the
authorities and the Akali leadership was followed by a fresh
outburst of terrorist activity in the province. In February, in
separate incidents, thirty-five people were killed in three days. In
March a dozen masked motorcycle riders entered a village and
killed Hindu residents at random. In April, in a well co-ordinated
show of strength, extremists simultaneously attacked thirty-nine
local railway stations located in twelve different districts. While
terrorist activity escalated, the president of the SGPC stated that
the central government had hatched a conspiracy to arrest and
eliminate Bhindranwale, and the president of the Akali Dal denied
rumours that there was any fundamental difference of views
between him and Bhindranwale.[107]

It was by now becoming apparent that Sikh extremists were
using some Sikh *gurdwaras* as a secure base. In April security
forces traced some terrorists to a *gurdwara* in Moga. Their
attempt to cordon off the *gurdwara* resulted in heavy firing from
within the shrine. There were also clear indications that extremists
within the Golden Temple were involved in fortifying it. Meanwhile, the Akali Dal announced a new campaign of mass non-co-
operation to begin on 3 June 1984. Sikhs were urged to stop the
movement of food grains out of the province and the payment of
land revenue and water rates to the government from that day. On
2 June, however, the central government moved decisively. The
Punjab was completely sealed off from the rest of the country by
the Indian army, and troops equipped with tanks and heavy
armour surrounded the Golden Temple. To emphasize that this
military action was in the interests of national unity, the soldiers
were commanded by Hindu and Sikh officers. An appeal to the
extremists to surrender brought a heavy barrage of firing from
them from well-entrenched positions. However, the Akali leaders
who were also inside the temple complex at the time gave

themselves up and were detained. The first phase of Operation Bluestar, as the Indian army's action against Sikh extremists was code-named, focused on an assault on the Golden Temple and its surrounding buildings. Within a few days the army was in complete control, and Bhindranwale and many of his followers had been killed. Inside the temple, the army found substantial quantities of arms and ammunition and a grenade factory.

Notes to Chapter 7

1 Baldev Raj Nayar, *Minority Politics in the Punjab* (Princeton, NJ, 1966), p. 187.
2 Sikh Gurdwaras Act of 1925, *Punjab Gazette*, 7 Aug. 1925, par. 107 (I).
3 *The Times of India* (26 Mar. 1985).
4 Sikh Gurdwaras Act of 1925, *Punjab Gazette*, par. 106 (2).
5 See, for example, Tara Singh, *To All Men of Good Conscience* (New Delhi, 1959), pp. 2–3, 607, for comments on the 1953 and 1958 SGPC presidential elections. Also for this reason, non-Sikh political parties have repeatedly sponsored Sikh candidates for the SGPC's elections. For some such instances see Balbir Singh Mann, *The Punjabi Suba Morcha: A Plea for Sympathy* (Patiala, undated), p. 11; Kailash Chander Gulati, *The Akalis Past and Present* (New Delhi, 1974), pp. 162, 168–9.
6 Khushwant Singh, *History of the Sikhs*, vol. 2, pp. 214–5. See also Nayar, *Minority Politics*, pp. 177–80; Paul R. Brass, *Language, Religion and Politics in North India* (Cambridge, 1974), pp. 311–14.
7 As already noted, the passage of the 1925 Act accentuated divisions among Akalis over tactics. This subsequently led to the formation of a rival Central Akali Dal. The original Shiromani Akali Dal, however, remained the dominant group and the Central Akali Dal eventually ceased to exist. In this study, reference to the Akali Dal is to the Shiromani Akali Dal. In post-independence India, the Shiromani Akali Dal has from time to time had rival factions, but their differences have been tactical rather than ideological. In post-independence India, the Indian National Congress party also split into rival groups. Reference in this study is to the dominant Congress party, later known as the Congress (I) party.
8 See Nayar, *Minority Politics*, p. 186.
9 Quoted in Nayar, *Minority Politics*, pp. 179–80.
10 Sardul Singh Caveesher vs Hukum Singh and Others, GOI, Election

Law Reports, vol. 6, edited by A. N. Aiyar (Delhi, undated), p. 329, quoted in Brass, *Language, Religion*, p. 353.

11 Kultar Singh vs Mukhtiar Singh, GOI, Election Law Reports, vol. 24, edited by R. K. P. Shankardass (Delhi, 1968), p. 419, quoted in Brass, *Language, Religion*, p. 354.

12 Kultar Singh vs Mukhtiar Singh, p. 429, quoted in Brass, *Language, Religion*, p. 354.

13 See, for example, several protests by Udasi and Hindu organizations in the *Tribune* (May and June 1925).

14 See, for example, GOI, Home (Political) proceedings, nos 16/I to 16/III of 1926.

15 GOI, Census of India, 1931, vol. 1, *India*, pt 1, report by J. H. Hutton (Delhi, 1933), p. 382.

16 GOI, *1931 Census Report India*, pp. 388–9.

17 All Parties Conference, 1928, *Report of the Committee Appointed by the Conference to Determine the Principles of the Constitution of India* (Allahabad, 1928), pp. 30, 123.

18 All Parties Conference, 1928, *Report*, p. 52.

19 *Tribune*, 26 Oct. 1928.

20 Resolution adopted by the Indian National Congress at its annual session at Lahore in December 1929, quoted in Gulati, *Akalis*, p. 50.

21 Gulati, *Akalis*, pp. 55–6.

22 Gulati, *Akalis*, p. 80; Khushwant Singh, *History of the Sikhs*, vol. 2, p. 240.

23 Gulati, *Akalis*, p. 37.

24 Selections from memoranda and oral evidence by non-officials, Indian Statutory Commission (London, 1930), pt 1, pp. 135–47.

25 GOI, *1931 Census Report*, vol. 17, Punjab, by Khan Ahmad Hasan Khan, Part 1 (Lahore, 1933), p. 290.

26 *Selections, Memoranda and Evidence*, pt 1, p. 125.

27 *Selections, Memoranda and Evidence*, pt 1, p. 125.

28 *Selections, Memoranda and Evidence*, pt 1, p. 138.

29 *Tribune* (26 Oct. 1928).

30 Khushwant Singh, *History of the Sikhs*, vol. 2, p. 232.

31 Quoted in Gulati, *Akalis*, pp. 62–3.

32 Reginald Coupland, *The Indian Problem: Report on the Constitutional Problem in India* (New York, 1944), pt 2, pp. 262–86.

33 Nripendra Nath Mitra, *Indian Annual Register*, 1943 (Calcutta, 1944), vol. 1, p. 298.

34 Bhagat Singh Tangh, *Azad Punjab Ke Mutalaq Pothohari Nuktanigah*, Shiromani Akali Dal (Amritsar, 1943), pp. 16–21, quoted in Nayar, *Minority Politics*, p. 84.

35 Mitra, *Indian Annual Register*, 1944 (Calcutta, 1945), vol. 2, pp. 212–13.

36 Khushwant Singh, *History of the Sikhs*, vol. 2, p. 258.

37 Quoted in Harbans Singh, *The Heritage of the Sikhs* (Bombay, 1964), p. 302.

38 Tara Singh, foreword to Sarup Singh, *The Forgotten Panth* (Amritsar, 1945).

39 Sarup Singh, *Forgotten Panth*, p. 10. Sarup Singh was a prominent Akali leader who also served as vice-president of the Akali Dal.

40 Sarup Singh, *Forgotten Panth*, p. 20.

41 Nayar, *Minority Politics*, p. 170.

42 GOI, Census of India, 1941, vol. 1, *India*, pt 1, tables by M. W. M. Yeatts (Simla, 1943), pp. 98–100.

43 GOI Census of India, 1951, paper no. 1, 1959, *Religion and Livelihood Classes by Educational Standards of Reorganised State* (New Delhi, 1959), pp. 7–8.

44 This view was expressed by several contemporary writers. See, for example, Kartar Singh, *Rekindling of the Sikh Heart* (Lahore, 1945), pp. 29–30; Khushwant Singh, *The Sikhs*, pp. 180, 184–5; Ratan Singh, *The Revolt of the Sikh Youth* (Lahore, 1943), pp. 132–3.

45 Ratan Singh, *Revolt*, pp. 132–3.

46 GOI, *1941 Census Report, India*, vol. 1, pt 1, pp. 98–100; GOI, *1951 Census Report*, paper no. 1, 1959, pp. 7–8.

47 Quoted in Nayar, *Minority Politics*, p. 98.

48 Nayar, *Minority Politics*, p. 98.

49 Gulati, *Akalis*, p. 147.

50 Baldev Raj Nayar in his major study of the Punjabi *Suba* demand concludes, 'the linguistic argument is considered to be merely a camouflage for the eventual creation of a Sikh theocratic State' (Nayar, *Minority Politics*, pp. 322–3). Similarly, Khushwant Singh stated, 'The demand for the Suba was in fact for a Sikh State, language was only the sugar coating' (Khushwant Singh, *History of the Sikhs*, vol. 2, p. 295).

51 Quoted in Khushwant Singh, *History of the Sikhs*, vol. 2, p. 296.

52 Tara Singh, 'Punjabi Suba', quoted in Nayar, *Minority Politics*, p. 36.

53 Tara Singh, 'Punjabi Suba'.

54 Quoted in Khushwant Singh, *History of the Sikhs*, vol. 2, p. 299.

55 Khushwant Singh, *History of the Sikhs*, vol. 2, p. 299.

56 Prem Bhatia, 'Prospects and retrospects: alternatives before Akalis', *The Times of India* (16 May 1961), quoted in Nayar, *Minority Politics*, pp. 107–8.

57 Quoted in Nayar, *Minority Politics*, p. 37.

58 Quoted in Nayar, *Minority Politics*, p. 242.

59 Quoted in Khushwant Singh, *History of the Sikhs*, vol. 2, p. 297.

60 Gulati, *Akalis*, p. 165.

61 Quoted in Gulati, *Akalis*, p. 169.

62 Nayar, *Minority Politics*, p. 249.

63 Nayar, *Minority Politics*, p. 250.

64 Nayar, *Minority Politics*, p. 251.

65 Gulati, *Akalis*, p. 176. Indeed, earlier in 1956, in response to repeated Akali allegations of discrimination against Sikhs in government service, the government of India had offered to establish a commission to look into these allegations if the Akali Dal would provide some evidence to this effect; the Akali Dal provided no such evidence (Nayar, *Minority Politics*, pp. 261–2).

66 Figures for elections in 1967, 1969 and 1972 from Brass, *Language, Religion*, p. 371, and for 1977 and 1980 from Kuldip Nayar and Khushwant Singh, *Tragedy of the Punjab, Operation Bluestar and After* (New Delhi, 1984), p. 50. The one exception was the election to the Punjab legislative assembly in 1977, when the Akali Dal got 31.4 per cent of the vote.

67 *Spokesman* (17 Aug. 1981).

68 Gurnam Singh, *A Unilingual Punjabi State and the Sikh Unrest* (New Delhi, 1960), pp. 10–11.

69 Gurnam Singh, *Unilingual Punjabi State*, p. 17.

70 Gurnam Singh, *Unilingual Punjabi State*, p. 41.

71 Brass, *Language, Religion*, p. 360.

72 Brass, *Language, Religion*, p. 333.

73 GOI, *1931 Census Report, India*, vol. 1, pt 1, p. 389.

74 GOI, Census of India, 1961, vol. 13, *Punjab*, pt 1–A(i), general report by R. L. Anand (Delhi, 1969), p. 422.

75 Census of India, 1981, series 1, *India*, paper no. 3, 1984, *Household Population by Religion of Head of Household*, report by V. S. Verma (New Delhi, 1984), pp. xii–xiii, xvi.

76 GOI, Census of India, 1971, series 17, *Punjab*, pts II–C(i) and VA, *Distribution of Population by Religion and Schedule Castes*, report by P. L. Sondhi and H. S. Kwatra (Punjab, undated), p. 3; GOI, *1981 Census Report, India*, paper no. 3, pp. xii–xiii, xvi.

77 The resolution as authenticated by Harchand Singh Longowal in 1982 is reproduced in several works, including Chand Joshi, *Bhindranwale, Myth and Reality* (New Delhi, 1984), pp. 45–66.

78 Joshi, *Bhindranwale*, pp. 45–66.

79 Joshi, *Bhindranwale*, pp. 45–66.

80 Joshi, *Bhindranwale*, pp. 45–66.

81 Quoted in Nayar, *Minority Politics*, p. 40.

82 Nayar, *Minority Politics*, p. 40.

83 *Spokesman* (3 Dec. 1956), quoted in Nayar, *Minority Politics*, p. 40.

84 *Spokesman* (11 Oct. 1982).

85 *Spokesman* (Baisakhi No., 1982).

86 *Spokesman* (23 Feb. 1981).

234   *Sikh Separatism: The Politics of Faith*

87 *Spokesman* (23 Feb. 1981).
88 *Spokesman* (23 Mar. 1981, 30 Mar. 1981).
89 *Spokesman* (23 Mar. 1981, 30 Mar. 1981).
90 *Spokesman* (23 Mar. 1981, 30 Mar. 1981).
91 *Spokesman* (23 Mar. 1981, 30 Mar. 1981).
92 *Spokesman* (Baisakhi No., 1981).
93 Quoted in Government of India, *White Paper on the Punjab Agitation* (New Delhi, 1984).
94 *Spokesman* (27 Sept. 1982).
95 *Spokesman* (17 Jan. 1983).
96 *Spokesman* (25 Apr. 1983).
97 *Spokesman* (26 Sept. 1983).
98 Although little information is available on extremist Sikh individuals and organizations based outside India and their activities in the Punjab, they certainly appear to have had an impact on the central government's appraisal of Sikh unrest in the state. Jagjit Singh Chauhan, a former minister in an Akali government, urged the formation of a sovereign Sikh state of Khalistan from his base in London and canvassed support among Sikhs in the Federal Republic of Germany, Canada and the United States. Sikh terrorist organizations such as the Dal Khalsa and the Babbar Khalsa with branches in Britain and Canada advocated an armed struggle in the Punjab, took responsibility for several murders in the province and attempted to organize an army of liberation. For details, see GOI, *White Paper on Punjab*, and an undated note in the home ministry, reproduced in Kuldip Nayar and Khushwant Singh, *Tragedy*.
99 Quoted in Kuldip Nayar and Khushwant Singh, *Tragedy*, p. 73.
100 Quoted in GOI, *White Paper on the Punjab*.
101 Quoted in GOI, *White Paper on the Punjab*.
102 GOI, *White Paper on Punjab*.
103 *Spokesman* (9 May 1983).
104 *Spokesman* (8 Aug. 1983).
105 *Spokesman* (12 Dec. 1983).
106 Quoted in *Spokesman* (1 Aug. 1983).
107 *Spokesman* (23 Jan. 1984, 13 Feb. 1984).

Epilogue

Three years of growing unrest in the Punjab had an enormous impact on Sikh communal perception. A concerted Akali propaganda campaign, official action against Akali agitations and the intransigence of the government in conceding seemingly legitimate Akali demands had won the Akalis the tacit support of a broad cross-section of the Sikh community. As Sikh communal solidarity with the Akali campaign grew, escalating competition for leadership among Sikh politicians and a resulting multiplication of the grievances and demands espoused by them had rapidly radicalized Sikh unrest. The emergence of Sikh extremism had also brought little condemnation from Sikhs. While few Sikhs publicly supported the terrorist campaign of the extremists, the ambiguity and constant shifting of Sikh demands prevented opposition to extremist violence from crystallizing. Besides, moderate and extremist Sikh activists used the same idiom to enlist support and made similar allegations. A widespread belief that the central government had not dealt firmly with extremist violence from the outset and that Bhindranwale had initially risen to prominence through the support of the ruling Congress party, added credence to Akali allegations of an official conspiracy against the Sikh community. The assault on the Golden Temple at Amritsar in July 1984 was therefore widely seen by Sikhs as a deliberate attempt to humiliate their community rather than as a necessary step to curb extremist violence. For many Sikhs, substantial damage to sacred property became a powerful symbol of official repression.

Military action in the bastion of Sikhism provoked a wave of deep anguish and resentment among Sikhs. But, the detention of all prominent Akali leaders, the declaration of the militant All India Sikh Students Federation as an illegal organization and rigorous control over the Punjab prevented the outbreak of widespread public reaction in the state. However, news of the

Indian army's action prompted the desertion of some Sikh troops in other parts of the country and rebellious soldiers attempted to reach Amritsar to defend the faith. Moreover, in the Punjab, extremist activity was not completely muffled. Within days of the action in the Golden Temple, a major irrigation canal in the Punjab was breached twice and in two separate incidents an Indian aircraft was hijacked by Sikh extremists. In the months following the assault on the Golden Temple, the central government's attempts to control extremism in the Punjab inevitably increased Sikh cries of victimization. The detention and interrogation of thousands of Sikhs deeply affected the Sikh community. The Indian army's continued presence in the Golden Temple complex, while extensive repairs were carried out, served to perpetuate resentment among Sikhs. In October 1984 the Golden Temple complex was handed back to the SGPC. The same month the Prime Minister of India, Mrs Indira Gandhi, was assassinated, reportedly by two of her Sikh bodyguards.

Widespread public condemnation by Sikh leaders of the assassination of the Indian Prime Minister was notably missing and their reaction was a clear indication of the deep alienation of the community from the mainstream of Indian politics. Many Sikhs saw the assassination simply as an inevitable consequence of actions taken against their community, and their quiet resentment provided legitimacy to what was regarded as an act of revenge. Although the crisis in the Indian government was quickly resolved by the unanimous selection of Mrs Gandhi's son, Rajiv Gandhi, as the leader of the ruling Congress party and the Prime Minister, for the Sikh community their sense of alienation was dramatically compounded by the outbreak of anti-Sikh riots in several parts of the country following the assassination. For three days, before the Indian army imposed control, the Sikh community in Delhi and a few other areas became the target of unchecked mob violence. Sikh individuals were singled out and lynched and Sikh property destroyed. Over 2,000 Sikhs were killed and some 10,000 rendered homeless in Delhi and its suburbs according to official estimates. Thousands of Sikhs found themselves refugees in a city they had fled to in 1947.

For the Sikh community, the civil authorities' inability to control the situation quickly, and a general belief that violence directed at Sikhs was not merely an outburst of popular anger, only made matters worse. The Indian press published a spate of allegations charging the administration and the Congress party with complicity in the violence. It was alleged that local Congress party leaders had incited, organized and led mob violence against Sikhs, while the civil administration and police had chosen to remain inactive. A widely publicized report on the violence by two local human rights organizations, for example, concluded that, 'the attacks on members of the Sikh community in Delhi ... far from being spontaneous expressions of "madness" and of popular "grief and anger" at Mrs Gandhi's assassination as made out by the authorities, were the outcome of a well-organized plan marked by acts of both deliberate commission and omission by important politicians of the Congress ... and by authorities in the administration.'[1] The report further claimed that, 'the police all over the city uniformly betrayed a common behavioural pattern marked by (i) a total absence from the scene, or (ii) a role as passive spectators, or (iii) direct participation or abetment in the orgy of violence against the Sikhs.'[2] As Sikh leaders cried for justice, the central government refused to order an official inquiry into the anti-Sikh violence on the grounds that such an investigation would only inflame communal passions further. For many Sikhs, the government's attitude was a confirmation of their worst fears.

With the continued detention of leading Akali politicians and the Indian army's control of the Punjab, an uneasy calm settled on the Sikh community for the next four months. The second rung leadership of the Akali Dal passed a series of resolutions calling for the immediate release of their leaders and the punishment of those responsible for the anti-Sikh riots, and threatened to resume agitation if their demands were not conceded; but no concrete programme of action was formulated. However, the migration to the Punjab of some Sikhs rendered destitute in the anti-Sikh violence, the initiation of court martial proceedings against Sikh deserters by the Indian army and the establishment of extraordinary judicial procedures to examine cases of suspected Sikh extremists, served to maintain Sikh communal solidarity at an intense pitch.

Meanwhile, the new Prime Minister moved to consolidate his own position by calling general elections to parliament and for the various state legislatures. Elections were, however, temporarily postponed in the Punjab and the state continued to be governed directly by the central government. The situation in the Punjab inevitably became a major issue during the general elections and the Congress party's election campaign emphasized its firm handling of Sikh unrest. The Prime Minister vigorously attacked the Anandpur Sahib resolution of the Akali Dal as secessionist and maintained that a dialogue with the Akali leadership was only possible if they disowned the Sikh extremists. The outcome of these elections was an unprecedented victory for the Congress party which secured an absolute majority in the Indian parliament and control of the majority of state assemblies. Rajiv Gandhi emerged as the most powerful Prime Minister in India's history. The new government declared that a solution to the unrest in the Punjab was its highest priority, but continued its criticism of the Akali Dal. The Akali Dal, for its part, refused to hold any discussions with the central government until its leaders were released.

Once the election rhetoric had subsided the central government realized that a solution to Sikh unrest was not possible without a settlement with the Akali Dal. Therefore, in March 1985, through a carefully co-ordinated series of actions, it moved to break the stalemate and set the stage for renewed negotiations with the Akalis. In stages, the Akali leaders were unconditionally released and the ordinance declaring the All India Sikh Students Federation an illegal organization was rescinded. A package of economic assistance and concessions was announced for the Punjab. The Prime Minister muted his criticism of the Anandpur Sahib resolution and declared his willingness to resume discussions with the Akalis provided that their demands were within the framework of the Indian constitution. A close aide of the Prime Minister was appointed as the governor of the Punjab with a specific mandate to prepare the groundwork for discussions with Sikh leaders. A month later, as another gesture of conciliation towards enraged Sikh opinion, the central government ordered a judicial inquiry into the anti-Sikh violence in Delhi.

The release of Akali politicians began a renewed and intensified phase of competition for leadership among them. Having voluntarily surrendered to the military authorities during the confrontation at the Golden Temple, they now sought to establish their credibility within their community by rapidly adopting militant postures on a variety of issues. Immediately after his release, the president of the Akali Dal, Sant Harchand Singh Longowal, began a tour of the Punjab and launched a bitter attack on the central government which was portrayed as being solely responsible for unrest in the Punjab through its 'anti-Sikh' policies. He refused to condemn Sikh terrorists or the assassins of Indira Gandhi, insisted that the central government should apologize to the Sikh community for the storming of the Golden Temple and expressed his sympathy and support for the families of those killed during Operation Bluestar. His militant stance was clearly expressed in an interview with a leading Indian journalist. 'The Sikh has begun to wonder after the assassination – and even before it – whether he can live in India and what his future will be', he stated.[3] Longowal further spelled out a set of conditions which the central government must meet before dialogue on Akali demands could begin. These included the immediate abolition of the special judicial procedures instituted for examining cases of persons charged with extremist acts, the withdrawal of anti-terrorist legislation, the release of all Sikh detainees and the rehabilitation of Sikhs who had deserted from the army. Even on the demand for a separate Sikh state of Khalistan, which he had earlier refuted, Longowal now adopted an attitude of confrontation. He stated, 'We do not want a separate country, we don't want to separate ourselves from the country ... But if the government were to force us, then we would think and say, "let's settle the price".'[4]

The Akali leader, Jagdev Singh Talwandi, on his release, quickly became another apostle of Sikh militancy. He called for an acceptance of the Anandpur Sahib resolution by the central government and demanded autonomy for the Punjab. Talwandi projected himself as the successor to Bhindranwale and launched a vigorous attack on Longowal, who he charged with cowardice for having surrendered at the outset of the assault on the Golden Temple. Emboldened by the release of Akali leaders, the SGPC's budget session in Amritsar in April proved to be another forum for expressions of militancy. The general secretary of the SGPC lauded Bhindranwale as a martyr for the faith and charged the central government with the 'genocide' of Sikhs. The budget proposed by the SGPC's executive committee had allocations for the establishment of a martyrdom fund and a relief fund. Each family which had a member killed during Operation Bluestar was to receive a grant-in-aid and funds were set aside for the legal defence of Sikhs charged with extremist activities and for Sikh deserters from the army. Later, following his release, the president of the SGPC, Gurcharan Singh Tohra, proposed that the sacred Akal Takht in the Golden Temple complex should be demolished and rebuilt since it had been repaired with official support and not through voluntary work from the Sikh community in accordance with Sikh tradition.

The race for militant credibility among Akali leaders brought a new figure into Sikh politics. The octogenarian father of Bhindranwale, Baba Joginder Singh, emerged as a leader of radical Sikh youth drawn from the All India Sikh Students Federation, and rapidly became a focus of public attention as each Akali leader sought his symbolic support. In May 1985, Sikh politics took a bizarre turn and Joginder Singh announced that since both Longowal and Talwandi had sought his intervention, in the interests of the *panth* he was unilaterally dissolving the two factions of the Akali Dal and forming a United Akali Dal. Joginder Singh also announced that this United Akali Dal would be run by an *ad hoc* committee of nine men and that he was nominating Longowal, Talwandi and Tohra and the former Akali chief-minister of the Punjab, Prakash Singh Badal, to it. From the radical nature of the other nominees to the *ad hoc* committee, and Joginder Singh's statements, it was apparent that he was attempting to succeed his son as the militant messiah of the Sikh community.

While Talwandi clearly welcomed this new found support, the other Akali leaders refused to be associated with the United Akali Dal and quickly moved to rally support for their leadership. Longowal resigned as president of the Akali Dal, Tohra quit the SGPC's presidency and Badal refused to serve any longer as the unofficial leader of the former Akali legislators. Their moves to precipitate a crisis of leadership in the Sikh community brought the desired result. Within two weeks of their decision, the district Akali *jathedars* and the presidents of the Akali units outside the Punjab, the executive committee of the SGPC, and the former Akali legislators, had all met and induced each of their leaders to withdraw their resignations as the head of their respective constituencies. The immediate threat to their leadership having been surpassed, the Akali leaders continued their efforts to consolidate their support. Longowal called for the Akali Dal to organize a week of prayers and peaceful protests in June 1985 to observe the anniversary of the storming of the Golden Temple. In response, the United Akali Dal declared ten days of mourning for the martyrs of Operation Bluestar. For its part, the SGPC's executive committee amid much publicity announced its intention to serve a legal notice on the central government demanding compensation of Rs 10,000 million for damage and loss to sacred Sikh property. It also charged that the launching of Operation Bluestar was due to the 'clandestine political motives of the ruling group which was at the helm of affairs during the period'.[5]

While Akali leaders jockeyed for position, Sikh extremists had not been inactive. Isolated incidents of terrorist activity directed at the police and at members of the ruling Congress party had continued in the Punjab in March and April 1985. In May the extremists dramatically demonstrated their ability to reach outside the Punjab. A series of bombs were concealed inside portable radios and planted in Delhi and in towns in the neighbouring states of Haryana, Rajasthan, and Uttar Pradesh, in addition to Hindu majority areas of the Punjab. In Delhi the bomb explosions took a particularly heavy toll and over eighty people were killed. Moreover, in an equally serious development, the assassination of a prominent Hindu political leader in Hoshiarpur in the Punjab provoked a reaction against Sikhs. Led by a militant Hindu communal organization, Hindu mobs went on a rampage following the murder. They burnt Sikh shops and attacked Sikh passers-by. In May, during a visit of Prime Minister Rajiv Gandhi to the United States, the American security authorities uncovered a conspiracy to assassinate him involving Sikh extremists. In June, an Indian aircraft crashed, killing its 329 passengers. Preliminary investigations into the disaster revealed the possibility of a bomb explosion on board and two radical Sikh organizations based in Canada took responsibility for the incident.

The future of Sikh unrest in the Punjab seemed grim. The Akali leaders were at a loss as to future tactics and their efforts to consolidate their own position were leading the Sikh community towards another confrontation with the government. The resurgence of Sikh terrorism had further increased the probability of an outbreak of mass communal violence between Sikhs and Hindus if Akali agitation were to be revived. But the president of the Akali Dal, Sant Harchand Singh Longowal, seemed to realize that a continued radicalization of Sikh politics could overwhelm the leadership role of the Akali Dal and lead to serious consequences for the future of the Sikh community in India. Following his reinstatement as the head of the Akali Dal in May 1985, he therefore announced that he would launch a 'peace offensive' in the Punjab. Although he maintained a militant stance on Sikh demands, he gradually began to direct Sikh animosity away from communal recrimination and emphasized that the Akali Dal's grievances were with the central government and not with the Hindu community. Through a series of public meetings across the Punjab he reiterated the importance of Hindu–Sikh amity, condemned acts of violence by Sikh extremists, and repeatedly declared that the Akali Dal was not in favour of the pursuit of a separate Sikh state of Khalistan.

The central government was quick to react to signs of moderation from Longowal. The Governor of the Punjab began cautious indirect approaches to Longowal indicating the central government's willingness to resume negotiations on Akali demands. In July this was followed by a letter from the Prime Minister to Longowal suggesting a meeting between the two men. To safeguard this fragile peace initiative, these approaches were undertaken in complete secrecy. Given the volatile mood of the Sikh community, Longowal also proceeded with extreme caution. Shortly after receiving the Prime Minister's offer he convened a meeting of the Akali Dal's district *jathedars* and the former Akali legislators and called for a resumption of the 'holy war' against the central government in August 1985. But he then proceeded on a tour of Delhi and the neighbouring states of Rajasthan and Uttar Pradesh, addressed Hindu and Sikh audiences and stated that the Akali Dal was seeking a settlement with the central government within the framework of the Indian constitution. He insisted, however, that prior to any discussions, Sikh detainees must be released and the special judicial procedures must be abolished.

A few days later the Governor of the Punjab announced the release of 600 Sikh detainees and indicated that other detainees against whom serious charges had not been made would be released. The central government also indicated its willingness to limit the jurisdiction of the special judicial procedures. Longowal accepted the Prime Minister's invitation to a meeting and the two men met on 23 July 1985. After a brief period of intense discussions it was announced that the Prime Minister and the president of the Akali Dal had agreed to a memorandum of settlement. With this development, Longowal declared that the period of confrontation with the central government was over.

The memorandum of settlement agreed to between the Indian Prime Minister and the president of the Akali Dal was aimed at beginning the process of negotiation. It conceded the basis of some of the demands which the Akali Dal considered an essential prerequisite to discussions and set the parameters within which other demands would be addressed. Thus the agreement stipulated that the central government would provide compensation to the families of innocent persons killed in agitation or actions which took place after August 1982 and would also pay compensation for damage to property. However, the modalities for determining the extent of the compensation and to whom it was to be paid were not spelt out. Further, the memorandum stated that the government would curtail the extraordinary powers given to the Indian army in the Punjab and endeavour to rehabilitate Sikhs discharged from the army. But, no promise of leniency towards Sikh troops charged with mutiny and waging war against the country was made.

Regarding the demands submitted by the Akali Dal to the central government in 1981, it was agreed that the federally administered city of Chandigarh, which was the shared capital of both Punjab and Haryana states, would be transferred to the Punjab. A commission would however be established to determine what territory Punjab would transfer to the state of Haryana in return. Other territorial claims between Punjab and Haryana State were to be referred to a boundary commission which was to examine the question on the basis of the linguistic affinity of the areas under dispute and whose decision would be binding on the concerned states. The Akali Dal's demand for a reapportionment of river waters between the two states was similarly addressed and it was agreed that this issue would also be referred to an independent tribunal whose decision would be binding. In addition, the central government reiterated its commitment to consider the formulation of an all-India *gurdwara* bill in consultation with the Akali Dal. The question of greater autonomy for the Punjab and the controversial Anandpur Sahib resolution was dealt with in a similar spirit of compromise. The memorandum declared that since the Akali Dal 'states that the Anandpur Sahib resolution is entirely within the framework of the Indian Constitution', and 'that the purpose of the resolution is to provide greater autonomy to the state with a view to strengthening the unity and integrity of the country ... ',[6] the portion dealing with centre-state relations in the Anandpur Sahib resolution would be referred to an independent commission which was to make recommendations to the central government on the question. The demand for a special status for the Sikhs contained in the Anandpur Sahib resolution was not addressed.

By accepting some of the Akali Dal's demands and promising to have others reviewed, the central government hoped to initiate a new spirit of mutual compromise and provide the basis for an end to Sikh unrest; but the agreement had yet to be endorsed by rival Akali leaders. Longowal was himself conscious of the pitfalls ahead and in an attempt to appease Akali militants immediately portrayed the agreement with the Prime Minister as a great victory for the Sikh community. At an emergency meeting of the Akali Dal's district *jathedars* he cited the agreement as one between the Sikh community and India and likened it to past treaties between the sovereign Sikh monarch Ranjit Singh and British India. Moreover, he threatened to resign as the president of the Akali Dal if the agreement was not unanimously endorsed by his party. Longowal succeeded in getting the Akali Dal's district *jathedars* to endorse the agreement, but the secret negotiations which had led to it accentuated divisions with Akali politicians who had not been consulted. The former Akali chief-minister, Prakash Singh Badal termed the agreement a 'sellout' and declared that he was 'dissatisfied with every point in the accord';[7] the president of the SGPC expressed his resentment at not being party to the discussions by stating that Longowal had acted as though he had no faith in other Akali politicians.

Predictably, the United Akali Dal also expressed its strong opposition to the agreement on the grounds that it was the only Sikh body competent to negotiate on Sikh demands, and Baba Joginder Singh declared that Longowal was a traitor to the *panth* for his unilateral discussions with the central government. In July, militant supporters of the United Akali Dal clashed violently with Longowal supporters in Amritsar and a flag bearing the insignia of the 'armed forces of Khalistan' was raised on the Golden Temple complex. Opposition to the agreement was also expressed through an immediate increase in terrorist activity. On 28 July a sub-inspector of police was killed by Sikh extremists and in a daring raid the next day a prominent Indian trade unionist leader and member of parliament for the ruling Congress party was gunned down in a middle-class neighbourhood in Delhi.

The central government viewed growing dissension over the settlement with concern, and as a means to consolidate the peace process it considered calling early elections in the Punjab. An initiation of the electoral process could serve to force a closing of Akali ranks, but it was also fraught with considerable danger. If Akali leaders boycotted the elections their non-participation would place the central government in a difficult position and undermine further its credibility with the Sikh community. Besides, campaigning among rival groups during elections could rekindle communal passions and Sikh extremists would certainly attempt to disrupt the electoral process. In the event the central government chose what it believed to be the only course open to it and pressed ahead with arrangements for the formation of a representative government in the Punjab.

The central government's strategy proved to be correct. The announcement of early elections for the 117 member Punjab legislative assembly and for the 13 parliamentary seats from the Punjab was initially opposed by all Akali leaders, but once the schedule for elections was set there was a flurry of activity in Akali ranks. While the United Akali Dal announced that it would advocate a boycott of the elections, the president of the Akali Dal announced that his party would contest the elections and began intensive discussions with other Akali leaders in an effort to form a common electoral platform. By 20 August 1985, Longowal had succeeded in convincing Badal and Tohra to participate in the Akali Dal's election effort. The same day, Longowal was assassinated by Sikh extremists while addressing a public meeting.

The assassination of Sant Harchand Singh Longowal created a wave of sympathy for his party and reinforced the fragile unity in Akali ranks that he had only just achieved. Within days of the murder the Akali Dal had selected Surjit Singh Barnala, a confidant of the slain leader, as the acting president of the Akali Dal and, as a concession to the supporters of Prakash Singh Badal, elected his nominee, Sant Ajit Singh, as the chairman of the party's parliamentary board. Attention within the Akali Dal now quickly turned to the laborious process of selecting candidates from among the many aspirants of the Longowal, Tohra and Badal camps and to working out an election strategy.

Meanwhile, extraordinary steps were taken by the central government in anticipation of attempts by Sikh extremists to sabotage the elections. Thousands of policemen and para-military forces were deployed in the Punjab and all candidates were offered bullet proof jackets and individual security personnel. To reduce the potential for a disruption of the electoral process, the rules governing elections were exceptionally amended so that the death of a candidate who did not belong to an established political party would not require fresh elections in a consituency. But, the possibility of election violence did not deter those who aspired for political office and by early September, 848 persons had announced their candidature for the 117 seats in the provincial legislative assembly and over 70 had filed their nominations for elections to the 13 parliamentary seats from the Punjab.

The Akali Dal's candidates were a mixture of Longowal, Badal and Tohra supporters. The party's election campaign focused on the settlement with the central government which was portrayed as a great victory for the Sikh community. Its election manifesto stated that 'The accord is a vindication of the Akali stand and it restores to the Sikhs a place of pride and dignity in the Indian mainstream.'[8] The Akali Dal argued that peace could only return in the Punjab through a policy of conciliation towards aggrieved sections of the Sikh community and promised the immediate release and rehabilitation of detained Sikhs and financial assistance to families of Sikhs killed in Akali agitations and in 'false encounters' with the police. While the Akali Dal's election propaganda was clearly directed at the Sikh community, it also emphasized the importance of Hindu-Sikh amity and steered clear of raising issues which might aggravate communal bitterness. Thus, no mention was made of the assault on the Golden Temple, of subsequent events affecting the Sikh community, or of acts of violence by Sikh extremists. The party also included a few Hindus, a Muslim and a Christian among its candidates. Further, to deflect criticism of its agreement with the central government, which it had earlier denounced for its anti-Sikh policies, the Akali Dal now chose to attack the policies pursued by the previous Congress party government in the Punjab rather than the existing Congress government at the Centre.

The other main contender in the elections, the Congress party, also emphasized the settlement which was presented as evidence of the new central government's commitment to seeking an equitable solution to Sikh unrest. In addition, it stressed the need to bring peace and stability to the Punjab and to deal firmly with extremism. The Congress party also attempted to present a new image to the electorate and to disassociate itself from past policies of the Congress government in the Punjab and at the centre. Thus, a large number of former Congress legislators in the Punjab were not presented as candidates, and no mention of the former leader of the party, Indira Gandhi, was made in its election campaign. Beside candidates from the Akali Dal and the Congress party, candidates of other political parties and a few Sikh militants contested the elections, but the United Akali Dal launched an extensive campaign advocating a boycott of the elections on the grounds that they were based on an unsatisfactory agreement with the central government.

The elections in the Punjab were essentially a straight contest between the Akali Dal and the Congress party, but the outcome of the elections was also crucial for another reason. Both the Akali Dal and the Congress party were committed to proceed with negotiations within the framework of the settlement reached and in the face of strong opposition from Sikh militants, the level of popular support for the settlement remained unclear. The extent of public participation in the elections therefore became a referendum on the settlement. In the event, Punjabis overwhelmingly rejected appeals to boycott the elections and, despite the threat of extremist violence and sporadic terrorist activity, 66 per cent of the electorate participated in elections for the Punjab legislature as against 64 per cent in the provincial elections of 1977 and 1980.[9] Moreover, the elections resulted in an unprecedented demonstration of Sikh communal solidarity with the Akali Dal. Figures on the communal composition of electoral constituencies are not released, but it appears that the substantial number of low caste Sikhs, who had in the past viewed the Akali Dal as essentially a party of Sikh *jats* and considered the Congress party as a champion of their interests, this time swung heavily behind the Akali Dal. The Akali Dal secured an overwhelming victory and an absolute majority in the Punjab legislature for the first time in its history. In addition, the Akalis won 7 of 13 parliamentary seats from the Punjab. The elections revealed broad support for the Akali Dal and for its settlement with the central government, but pockets of popular militancy were also apparent. Bimal Khalsa, for example, the wife of one of the alleged assassins of Mrs Gandhi, who had become a symbol of Sikh militancy, stood as an independent candidate for elections from two constituencies and was defeated by only a narrow margin of 415 votes in one and by 1794 votes in another.[10]

The Akali Dal had finally achieved its long cherished dream of forming a government in the Punjab on its own. The euphoria of this dramatic victory initially overcame differences among its members and resulted in the unanimous selection of the acting president of the party, Surjit Singh Barnala, as the leader of the new provincial government. However, negotiations over the nature and level of representation in the government for each of the principle factions within the party brought internal rivalry to the forefront. As a result, Badal and his supporters refused to serve on the provincial ministry. The Akali Dal government established on 29 September 1985 consisted of the supporters of Barnala and Tohra.

Beside dissension from a powerful group within the party, the Barnala government was immediately faced with formidable challenges to its commitment to bring peace to the Punjab. In keeping with its election pledge the new government released the majority of persons who had been detained in the interests of national security and reiterated its intention to rehabilitate detainees and compensate those who had suffered during the past years of unrest. Barnala stated that by this process his government would 'try to tackle the reasons responsible for extremism'.[11] But, this conciliatory attitude had little impact on terrorist activity and in separate incidents five persons were killed within a month of the formation of the Akali government. Moreover, the provincial security forces believed that Sikh extremists had reverted to using the Golden Temple complex as a sanctuary. The Akali government was thus placed in the awkward position of having to pursue a policy they had earlier vehemently condemned and authorize police entry into Sikh places of worship.

As was to be expected, Sikh militants immediately began to exploit the new government's handling of highly emotional issues confronting the Sikh community. At a meeting in Amritsar shortly after the establishment of the Akali government, the All India Sikh Students Federation called for a continuation of the struggle for Sikh demands and adopted a resolution stating that 'the emergence of the Barnala government is not because of the traitorous act of Sant Harchand Singh Longowal but because of the policies of Sant Jarnail Singh Bhindranwale and the continuous struggle of his supporters.'[12] A few days later, the United Akali Dal vigorously condemned the provincial government for permitting the police to search the Golden Temple complex and announced its determination to launch an agitation if Sikh deserters from the army and those charged with mutiny were not reinstated and the few remaining detainees not released.

Acrimony between the Akali government and its Sikh opponents also led to expressions of militancy from within the Akali Dal. In November 1985, attention focused on elections for the powerful presidency of the SGPC. The contest between the Akali Dal's candidate, Gurcharan Singh Tohra, and the candidate of the United Akali Dal brought assertions of radicalism from both sides. Tohra addressed public meetings of his constituents and paid tribute to Bhindranwale as an exemplary martyr for the faith. He condemned the recent searches of the Golden Temple complex and declared that Operation Bluestar was 'an ill thought action designed to crush the Sikhs and their religion.'[13] Tohra was re-elected as the president of the SGPC for the fourteenth time and his election provided the Akali government with a powerful instrument of political leverage, but given the fragile unity within the Akali Dal, it also provided Tohra and his followers with considerable independence of action.

The tasks confronting the Akali government in the Punjab are thus daunting. It must maintain unity within the government and the party, deal with terrorist activity and counter the threat posed by Sikh militants. Besides, as the SGPC's elections revealed, issues concerning the Sikh community can quickly overcome the new spirit of moderation in the Akali Dal. By the end of 1985, growing acrimony between the Akali government and the administration of Haryana over the various terms of the settlement with the central government promised to provide a series of issues for Sikh militancy in the future. Unless there is a dramatic shift in the communal ideology governing Sikh politics or in the political arithmetic within the Sikh community, the prospect of peace in the Punjab could therefore remain elusive.

NOTE: This epilogue was completed on 24 January 1986. On 26 January, it was reported in the *Guardian*, London, that Sikh extremists in control of the Golden Temple had begun to demolish the Akal Takht. It was further reported that young Sikhs, equipped with self-loading rifles, Sten guns, 12-bore guns and hand grenades, had occupied vantage positions all over the Temple.

Notes to Epilogue

1 People's Union for Democratic Rights and People's Union for Civil Liberties, *Who are the Guilty?: Report of a Joint Inquiry into the Causes and Impact of the Riots in Delhi from 31 October to 10 November* (Delhi, 1984), p. 1. For similar views see also, Citizen's Commission, Delhi, *Delhi, 31 October to 4 November 1984, Report of the Citizen's Commission* (Delhi, 1984).

2 *People's Union for Democratic Rights and People's Union For Civil Liberties*, p. 4.

3 Kuldip Nayar, 'Interview with Sant Harchand Singh Longowal', *Sunday*, Vol. 12, No. 21 (Calcutta, 1985).

4 *Nayar*, 'Interview with Sand Harchand Singh Longowal'.

5 *Spokesman* (24 June 1985).

6 Text of the memorandum of settlement agreed to between the Indian Prime Minister and the president of the Akali Dal, quoted in *Indian Express* (25 July 1985).

7 *Indian Express* (27 July 1985).

8 *Indian Express* (12 September 1985).

9 *Indian Express* (12 October 1985).

10 *Indian Express* (28 September 1985).

11 Kanwar Sandhu, 'Interview with Surjit Singh Barnala', *Indian Express* (6 October 1985).

12 Quoted in *Spokesman* (14 October 1985).

13 Quoted in *Spokesman* (8 November 1985).

Bibliography

The fragmentary nature of source material available for this study posed special problems. The two major Sikh organizations, the Shiromani Gurdwara Prabhandak Committee (SGPC) and the Shiromani Akali Dal, have not preserved the bulk of their historical records. I have, therefore, also relied on an examination of the records of the Punjab government and the government of India, together with an extensive study of newspapers published in the Punjab, collections of private papers and official and non-official published literature. Sikh political literature which was banned or proscribed by the government at the time has also been studied.

OFFICIAL SOURCES

1 Records of the Government of India

NATIONAL ARCHIVES OF INDIA, NEW DELHI
Home Department, political proceedings, 1907–21.
Home/Political Department proceedings, 1921–22.
Home Department, political proceedings, 1923–31.
Home Department, Reforms Office proceedings, 1919–35.
Home Department, general proceedings, 1900–31.
Foreign/Political Department proceedings, 1923–25.

2 Records of the Punjab Government

INDIA OFFICE LIBRARY AND RECORDS, LONDON
Punjab Administration Reports, 1915–30.
Punjab Gazette and *Punjab Gazette Extraordinary*, 1919–30.
Punjab Legislative Council Debates, 1917–30.

NATIONAL ARCHIVES OF INDIA, NEW DELHI
Selections from Indian Newspapers Published in the Punjab, later entitled *Punjab Press Abstract*, 1890–1930.

3   Parliamentary Papers

BODLEIAN LIBRARY, OXFORD

Draft and approved rules for election to provincial legislative councils and the Indian Legislative Assembly and Rules for business in the provincial legislative councils and the Indian Legislative Assembly, 1920, Cmd, 757, 764, 768, 812, 813, Cmd, 814, 35:169 (142).

Return showing the results of elections in India, 1920, 1921, Cmd 1261, 26:11 (26).

Return showing the results of elections in India, 1923, 1924, Cmd 2154, 18:497 (86).

Return showing the results of elections in India, 1925 and 1926, 1927, Cmd 2923, 18:393 (30).

LIBRARY OF CONGRESS, WASHINGTON DC

Report of the Reforms Enquiry Committee, 1924, and connected papers 1924–5, Cmd 2360, 10:1 (v, 203).

Report of the local governments on the working of the reformed constitution, 1923, and connected papers 1924–5, Cmd 2361, 10:215 (iv, 250).

4   Private Papers

INDIA OFFICE LIBRARY AND RECORDS, LONDON

Chelmsford, Frederic John Napier Thesiger, Viceroy of India, 1916–21.

Hailey, William Malcolm, Governor of the Punjab, 1924–8.

Halifax, Edward Frederick Lindley Wood, Viceroy of India, 1926–31.

Lytton, Victor, Alexander, George, Robert, Bulwer, Acting Viceroy of India, Apr.–Aug. 1925.

Reading, Rufus Daniel Isaac, Viceroy of India, 1921–6.

5   Official and Semi-Official Reports

Bamford P. C., *Histories of the Non-Cooperation and Khilafat Movements* (Delhi, 1925).

Barstow, A. E., *Sikhs: Handbook for the Indian Army* (Calcutta, 1928).

Bingley, A. H., *Handbook for the Indian Army* (Calcutta, 1899).

Bingley, A. H., *Handbook for the Sikhs* (Simla, 1899).

Falcon, R. W., *Handbook on Sikhs for the Use of Regimental Officers* (Allahabad, 1896).

GOI, Census of India, 1868, *Report on the Census of the Punjab* (Lahore, 1870).

GOI, Census of India, 1881, *Report on the Census of the Punjab*, report by Ibbetson, Denzil Charles Jelf (Calcutta, 1883).

GOI, Census of India, 1891, vol. 20, *The Punjab and its Feudatories*, report by Maclagan, E. D. (Calcutta, 1892).

GOI, Census of India, 1901, vol. 17, *The Punjab, its Feudatories and the North-West Frontier Province*, report by Rose, H. A. (Simla, 1902).

GOI, Census of India, 1911, vol. 14, *Punjab*, report by Kaul, Harkishan (Lahore, 1912).

GOI, Census of India, 1921, vol. 15, *Punjab and Delhi*, report by Middleton, L. (Lahore, 1923).

GOI, Census of India, 1931, vol. 1, *India*, pt 1, report by Hutton, J. H. (Delhi, 1933).

GOI, Census of India 1931, vol. 17, *Punjab*, pt 1, report by Khan, Khan Ahmad Hasan (Lahore, 1933).

GOI, Census of India, 1941, vol. 1, *India*, pt 1, tables by Yeatts, M. W. M. (Simla, 1943).

GOI, Census of India, 1941, vol. 6, *Punjab*, tables by Fazl-i-ilahi, Khan Bhadur Sheikh (Simla, 1941).

GOI, Census of India, 1951, vol. 8, *Punjab, PEPSU, Himachal Pradesh, Bilaspur and Delhi*, pt II–A, report by Vashishta, Lakshmi Chandra (New Delhi, 1953).

GOI, Census of India, 1951, paper no. 1, 1959, *Religion and Livelihood Classes by Educational Standards of Reorganized State* (New Delhi, 1959).

GOI, Census of India, 1961, vol. 13, *Punjab*, pt I–A(i), general report by Anand, R. L. (New Delhi, 1969).

GOI, Census of India, 1971, series 17, *Punjab*, pts II–C(i) and V–A, *Distribution of Population by Religion and Scheduled Castes*, report by Sondhi, P. L., and Kwatra, H. S. (Punjab, undated).

GOI, Census of India, 1981, series 1, *India*, paper no. 3, 1984, *Household Population by Religion of Head of Household*, report by Verma, V. S. (New Delhi, 1984).

GOI, *White Paper on the Punjab Agitation* (New Delhi, 1984).

Indian Statutory Commission, Report (London, 1930).

Indian Statutory Commission, *Report of the Committees Appointed by the Provincial Legislative Councils to Cooperate with the Indian Statutory Commission* (London, 1930).

Indian Statutory Commission, *Extracts from Official Oral Evidence* (London, 1930).

Indian Statutory Commission, *Selections from Memoranda and Oral Evidence by Non-Officials* (London, 1930).

Isemonger, F. C. and Slattery, J., *An Account of the Ghadr Conspiracy* (Lahore, 1921).

Ker, James Campbell, *Political Trouble in India 1907–1917* (Simla, 1917).

Leigh, M. S., *The Punjab and the War* (Lahore, 1922).

Petrie, D., *Confidential report on Developments in Sikh Politics 1900–11* (Simla, 1911).

Report of the Komagata Maru Committee of Inquiry, 1914 (Calcutta, 1914).

Report on Indian Constitutional Reforms, 1918 (London, 1918).

Report of the Committee Appointed by the Government of India to Investigate the Disturbances in the Punjab, Delhi and Bombay (Calcutta, 1920).

Report of the Committee Appointed by the Secretary of State for India to Inquire into Questions Connected with the Franchise and Other Matters Relating to Constitutional Reforms (London, 1919).

Report of the Committee Appointed by the Government of India to Investigate Revolutionary Conspiracies in India (Calcutta, 1918).

Report of the Punjab Reforms Committee, 1929 (Lahore, 1929).

Rose, H. A., *A Glossary of Tribes and Castes of the Punjab and North-West Frontier Province* (Lahore, 1911–19).

Terrorism in India, 1917–36 (Simla, 1937).

The Sikh Gurdwaras Act of 1925, as amended, in Nijhawan, Vinod.

The Encyclopaedia of Punjab and Haryana Local Acts, vol. 7, *Civil and Criminal* (Delhi, 1972).

UNOFFICIAL SOURCES

1 Private Papers

NEHRU MEMORIAL LIBRARY, NEW DELHI

All India Congress Committee, 1917–40.
Caveesher, Sardul Singh.
Majithia, Sunder Singh.
Sachar, Bhim Sen.

PUNJAB STATES ARCHIVES, PATIALA

Sahni, Ruchi Ram, comprising unpublished MSS of 'A history of my own times', 'Autobiography of an octogenarian', 'History of the Press in the Punjab' and 'Special volumes on the Akali movement'.

2 Newspapers

Indian Express, Delhi, 1981–5.
Spokesman, Delhi, 1981–5.

NEHRU MEMORIAL LIBRARY, NEW DELHI
Tribune, Lahore, 1916–30.
Khalsa Advocate, Lahore, 1919–30.

BRITISH MUSEUM NEWSPAPER COLLECTION, LONDON
Civil and Military Gazette, Lahore, 1919–30.

SIKH ITIHAS RESEARCH BOARD LIBRARY (SGPC), AMRITSAR
Collection of published Press communiqués issued by the SGPC, 1921–30.

PUNJAB STATES ARCHIVES, PATIALA
Collection of newspaper cuttings relating to the Sikh agitation in the Punjab, 1920–5, in the private papers of Sahni, Ruchi Ram.

3 Interviews

Interviews by the author with Sikhs and British officials active in the period under study.

NEHRU MEMORIAL LIBRARY, NEW DELHI
Interviews recorded by the oral-history section: Tegh, Amar Singh; Sachar, Bhim Sen; Narang, Gokul Chand; Musaffir, Gurmukh Singh; Gill, Niharanjan Singh; Sobha Singh.

4 Unpublished Manuscripts

Barrier, N. Gerald, 'Punjab politics and the disturbances of 1907', PhD Dissertation, Duke University, 1966.
Brief, David, 'Recruitment and the Punjab, 1914–1917', a paper presented to the South Asia History Seminar, Oxford University, 1977.
Gursharan Singh, 'Akali movement in the Phoolkian States', MA thesis, Punjabi University, Patiala, 1967.

5 Books and Articles

Adhikari, G., *Sikh Homeland through Hindu–Muslim–Sikh Unity* (Bombay, 1945).
Ahluwalia, M. L., and Kirpal Singh, *The Punjab's Pioneer Freedom Fighters* (Calcutta, 1964).
Ahluwalia, M. M., *Kukas, The Freedom Fighters of the Punjab* (Bombay, 1965).

Ahmad, Waheed (ed.), *Letters of Mian Fazl-i-Husain* (Lahore, 1976).

Ajit, Singh, *The Gurus Prescribed Duties of the Sikhs to the British Empire* (Lahore, 1914).

Akbar, M. J., *India, The Siege Within* (London, 1985).

All Parties Conference, 1928, *Report of the Committee Appointed by the Conference to Determine the Principles of the Constitution of India* (Allahabad, 1928).

Amarjit Singh, 'The Ghadr Party trial and the United States of America', *Punjab Past and Present*, vol. 4, pt 2, (1970).

Amarjit Singh, 'Akali Movement of the Sikhs', *Nation*, vol. 119, (July 1924).

Archer, E. C., *Tours in Upper India* (London, 1833).

Archer, John Clark, *The Sikhs in Relation to Hindus, Muslims, Christians and Ahmadiyyas* (Princeton, N. J., 1946).

Arnold, E. L., *The Marquess of Dalhousie's Administration of British India* (London, 1862–5).

Ashta, Dharam Pal, 'Sikhism as an off-shoot of traditional Hinduism and a response to the challenge of Islam', in *Sikhism and Indian Society, Transactions of the Indian Institute of Advanced Study*, vol. 1 (Simla, 1967).

Avtar Singh, *Ethics of the Sikhs* (Patiala, 1970).

Bains, J. S., 'Political ideas of Guru Nanak', *Indian Journal of Political Science*, vol. 23 (Oct.–Dec. 1962).

Baird, J. G. A. (ed.), *Private Letters of the Marquess of Dalhousie* (Edinburgh, 1911).

Balbir Singh Mann, *The Punjabi Suba Morcha: A Plea for Sympathy* (Patiala, undated).

Bannerjee, Indubhusan, *Evolution of the Khalsa* (Calcutta, 1972).

Bannerjee, Indubhusan, 'A short history of the origin and rise of the Sikhs', *Indian Historical Quarterly*, vol. 18 (1942).

Barrier, N. Gerald, 'The Punjab Disturbances of 1907; the response of the British government in India to agrarian unrest', *Modern Asian Studies*, vol. 1, no. 4 (1967).

Barrier, N. Gerald, 'Literature of confrontation: an introduction to banned publications of British Punjab', *Indian Archives* (Jan.–June 1972).

Barrier, N. Gerald, 'Quantification in Punjab social and political history: sources and problems', *Punjab Past and Present*, vol. 8, no. 1 (1974).

Barrier, N. Gerald, *Punjab History in Printed British Documents* (Columbia, Mo., 1969).

Barrier, N. Gerald, *The Sikhs and their Literature* (Delhi, 1970).

Barrier, N. Gerald and Wallace, Paul, *The Punjab Press, 1880–1905* (Mich., 1970).

Barrier, N. Gerald, *Controversial Literature and Political Control in British India, 1907–1947* (Delhi, 1976).

Barrier, N. Gerald, 'The Arya Samaj and Congress politics in the Punjab, 1894–1908', *Journal of Asian Studies*, vol. 26, no. 3 (1967).

Barrier, N. Gerald, 'The Punjab government and communal politics, 1870–1907', *Journal of Asian Studies*, vol. 27, no. 3 (1968).

Barrier, N. Gerald, 'The Formulation and Enactment of the Punjab Alienation of Land Bill', *The Indian Economic and Social History Review*, vol. 2, no. 2 (1965).

Barrier, N. Gerald, *The Punjab Alienation of Land Bill of 1900* (Durham NC, 1966).

Bhagat Singh, 'The Kuka movement', *Punjab Past and Present*, vol. 7, no. 1 (1973).

Bhattacharya, N. N., Indian Revolutionaries Abroad, 1891–1919, *Punjab Past and Present*, vol. 3, no. 2 (1974).

Birdwood, Field Marshal W., *Khaki and Gown: An Autobiography* (London, 1941).

Bondurant, Joan V., *Regionalism versus Provincialism, A Study in the Problem of Indian National Unity* (Berkeley, 1958).

Bosworth-Smith, R., *Life of Lord Lawrence* (London, 1883).

Brass, Paul R., *Language, Religion and Politics in North India* (Cambridge, 1974).

Brown, Giles T., 'The Hindu conspiracy', *Pacific Historical Review*, vol. 17 (1953).

Brown, W. Norman, 'Religion and practical politics in India', *Asia*, vol. 24, no. 3 (1926).

Calvert, H., *The Wealth and Welfare of the Punjab* (Lahore, 1927).

Campbell-Johnson, A., *Mission with Mountbatten* (London, 1951).

Candler, Edmund, *The Sepoy* (London, 1919).

Chand, Duni, *The Ulster of India or An Analysis of the Punjab Problem* (Lahore, 1936).

Charan Singh and Darbara Singh, *The Work of the Sikh Educational Conference* (Amritsar, 1944).

Chhabra, G. S., *Advanced Study in History of the Punjab* (Ludhiana, 1960).

Chhajju Singh, *The Ten Gurus and Their Teachings* (Lahore, 1903).

Chief Khalsa Diwan, 'Fifty years of service, 1902–1951', *Punjab Past and Present*, vol. 7, no. 1 (1973).

Chirol, Valentine, *Indian Unrest* (London, 1919).

Chopra, V. D., Mishra, R. K., and Nirmal Singh, *Agony of Punjab* (New Delhi, 1984).

Citizen's Commission, Delhi, *Delhi, 31 October to 4 November 1984; Report of the Citizen's Commission* (New Delhi, 1985).

Colvin, Ian, *The Life of General Dyer* (London, 1929).

Congress Punjab Enquiry, 1919–1920, *Report of the Commissioners appointed by the Punjab Sub-Committee of the Indian National Congress* (Lahore, 1920).

Coupland, Reginald, *The Indian Problem: Report on the Constitutional Problem in India* (New York, 1944).

Court, Henry, *History of the Sikhs or Translation of the Sikhan Di Raj Di Vikhia* (Lahore, 1888).

Cunningham, Joseph Davy, *A History of the Sikhs from the Origin of the Nation to the Battles of the Sutlej* (London, 1849).

Dalip Singh, 'Evolution of the Khalsa', *Sikh Review*, vol. 7, no. 6 (1960).

Daljeet Singh Sethi, 'Guru Gobind Singh's aim in forming Khalsa', *Sikh Review*, vol. 7, no. 4 (1959).

Darling, M. L., *The Punjab Peasant in Prosperity and Debt* (Bombay, 1925).

Darling, M. L., *Rusticus Loquitar or The Old Light and the New in the Punjab Village* (London, 1930).

Darling, M. L., *Wisdom and Waste in the Punjab Village* (London, 1934).

Das, Thakur, *Sikh Hindu Hain* (Hoshiarpur, 1899).

Desai, A. R., *Social Background of Indian Nationalism* (Bombay, 1966).

Durlab Singh, *Sikh Leadership* (Delhi, 1950).

Durlab Singh, *The Valiant Fighter: A Biographical Study of Master Tara Singh* (Lahore, 1942).

Dwyer, R. E. H., *Disturbances in the Punjab* (London, 1920).

'Exemption of Kirpans from restrictions', *Punjab Past and Present*, vol. 7, no. 1 (1973).

Farquhar, J. N., *Modern Religious Movements in India* (London, 1929).

Fauja Singh, 'Foundation of the Khalsa commonwealth: ideological aspects', *Punjab Past and Present*, vol. 5, no. 1 (1971).

Fauja Singh (ed.), *Who's Who Punjab Freedom Fighters* (Patiala, 1972).

Fauja Singh et al., *Sikhism* (Patiala, 1969).

Field, Dorothy, *The Religion of the Sikhs* (London, 1901).

Forster, George, *A Journey from Bengal to England* (London, 1798).

Furneaux, Robert, *Masssacre at Amritsar* (London, 1963).

Ganda Singh, *A Brief Account of the Sikh People* (Delhi, 1971).

Ganda Singh, *The British Occupation of the Punjab* (Patiala, 1955).

Ganda Singh (ed.), *A Bibliography of the Punjab* (Patiala, 1966).

Ganda Singh, *A History of the Khalsa College* (Amritsar, 1949).

Ganda Singh (ed.), *Some Confidential Papers of the Akali Movement* (Amritsar, 1965).

Ganda Singh (ed.), *Bhai Jodh Singh Abhinandan Granth* (Patiala, 1962).

Ganda Singh, 'Sikh educational conference', *Punjab Past and Present*, vol. 7, No. 1 (1973).

Ganda Singh, *Early European Accounts of the Sikhs* (Calcutta, 1962).

Gandhi, Mahatma, *Collected Works* (Ahmedabad, 1958).

Gangulee, N., *Indians in the Empire Overseas* (London, 1947).

G. B. Singh, *The Morcha of Nabha: An Appeal to all Indian Leaders* (Lahore, undated; proscribed).

Gopal, Ram, *Indian Muslims, A Political History* (London, 1959).

Gopal, S., *Jawaharlal Nehru, A Biography*, vol. 1, 1889–1947 (Bombay, 1976).

Gopal, S. (ed.), *Selected Works of Jawaharlal, Nehru* (Delhi, 1972).

Gordon, General J. H., *The Sikhs* (Edinburgh, 1904).

Government Allegations Against the Sikhs Refuted (Sind, 1924; proscribed).

Griffin, Lepel H., *Chiefs and Families of Note in the Punjab* (Lahore, 1940).

Griffin, Lepel H., *The Rajas of the Punjab, being the History of the Principal States in the Punjab and their Political Relations with the British Government* (London, 1873).

Gulati, Kailash Chander, *The Akalis Past and Present* (New Delhi, 1974).

Gupta, Hari Ram, *History of the Sikhs* (Lahore, 1944).

Gurbachan Singh and Lal Singh, *The Idea of the Sikh State* (Lahore, 1946).

Gurbux Singh Jhabalia, *Shahidi Jiwan* (Nankana, 1938).

Gurdarshan Singh, 'Origin and development of the Singh Sabha movement', *Punjab Past and Present*, vol. 7, no. 1 (1973).

Gurdit Singh, *The Voyage of the Komagata Maru* (Calcutta, undated).

Gurdit Singh, *Biography of Baba Gurdit Singh* (undated; proscribed).

Gurmukh Nihal Singh, 'First popular movement in the Punjab', *Punjab Past and Present*, vol. 7, no. 1 (1973).

Gurmukh Singh, *A Brief Account of Military Sikhs' Struggle for Religious Freedom* (Hyderabad, Sind, 1921; proscribed).

Gurnam Singh, *A Unilingual Punjabi State and the Sikh Unrest* (New Delhi, 1960).

Gustafson, W. Eric, and Jones, Kenneth W. (eds), *Sources on Punjab History* (Delhi, 1975).

Gwyer, Maurice and Appadorai, A., *Speeches and Documents on the Indian Constitution, 1921–1947* (Bombay, 1957).

Hamid, Abdul, *Muslim Separatism in India* (Lahore, 1967).

Harbans Singh, *Sikh Political Parties* (New Delhi, undated).

Harbans Singh, 'The Sikh awakening or the Singh Sabha movement', *Sikh Review*, vol. 10, no. 2 (1962).

Harbans Singh, 'Maharaja Ripudman Singh: his involvement in popular causes', *Punjab Past and Present*, vol. 4, no. 2 (1970).

Harbans Singh, *The Heritage of the Sikhs* (Bombay, 1964).

Harbans Singh, 'The origin of the Singh Sabha', *Punjab Past and Present*, vol. 7, no. 1 (1973).

Harrison, Selig, *India, The Most Dangerous Decades* (Princeton, 1960).

Heimsath, Charles, *Indian Nationalism and Hindu Social Reform* (Princeton, NJ, 1964).

Hukum Singh, *The Punjab Problem: An Elucidation* (Amritsar, undated).

Hukum Singh, *The Sikh Problem and its Solution* (Amritsar, 1951).

Hukum Singh, *The States Reorganization in the North* (Delhi, undated).

Hunter, W. W., *The Marquess of Dalhousie* (Oxford, 1895).

Husain, Azim, *Fazl-i-Husain: A Political Biography* (Bombay, 1946).

Indian National Congress, 1917, G. A. Nateson & Company (Madras, 1917).

Iqbal Singh, *Facts about Akali Agitation in the Punjab* (Chandigarh, 1960).

Jagjit Singh, *Singh Sabha Lahar* (Tarn Taran, 1941).

Jaito Affair, SGPC, Amritsar, 1923 (proscribed).

Jaswant Singh, *Facts Without Rhetoric: The demand for Punjabi Suba* (New Delhi, 1960).

Jaswant Singh, *A Plea for a Punjabi State* (Amritsar, 1960).

Jodh Singh, *Some Studies in Sikhism* (Ludhiana, 1953).

Jones, Kenneth W., 'Communalism in the Punjab, the Arya Samaj contribution', *Journal of Asian Studies*, vol. 28, no. 1 (1968).

Jones, Kenneth W., *Arya Dharma* (New Delhi, 1976).

Joshi, Chand, *Bhindranwale, Myth and Reality* (New Delhi, 1984).

Joshi, V. C. (ed.), *Lajpat Rai Autobiographical Writings* (Delhi, 1965).

Kahan Singh, *Ham Hindu Nahin* (Amritsar, 1889).

Karam Singh, *Amar Khalsa* (Amritsar, 1953).

Kartar Singh, *Rekindling of the Sikh Heart* (Lahore, 1945).

Kaur, Amarjit, *et al.*, *The Punjab Story* (New Delhi, 1984).

Khazan Singh, *History of the Sikh Religion* (Lahore, 1914).

Khushwant Singh and Satinder Singh, *Ghadr, 1915* (New Delhi, 1965).

Khushwant Singh, *History of the Sikhs* (Princeton, NJ, 1966).

Khushwant Singh, *The Sikhs* (London, 1953).

Khushwant Singh, *et al.*, *Selections From the Sacred Writings of the Sikhs* (London, 1960).

Khushwant Singh, *The Fall of the Kingdom of the Punjab* (Bombay, 1962).

Khosla, G. D., *Stern Reckoning* (New Delhi, 1949).

Kirpal Singh, 'Some new light on the Gurdwara reform movement', *Sikh Review*, vol. 13 (1965).

Kumar, R. (ed.), *Essays on Gandhian Politics: The Rowlatt Satyagrah of 1919* (Oxford, 1971).

Landau, Henry, *The Enemy Within* (New York, 1937).

Leach, Edmund, and Mukherjee, S. N. (eds), *Elites in South Asia* (Cambridge, 1970).

Loehlin, C. H. 'The History of Christianity in the Punjab', *Punjab Past and Present*, vol. 7, no. 1 (1973).

Low, D. A. (ed.), *Soundings in Modern South Asian History* (London, 1968.

Macauliffe, M. A., *A Lecture on How the Sikhs Became A Militant Race* (Simla, undated).

Macauliffe, M. A., *A Lecture on the Sikh Religion and its Advantages to the State* (Simla, 1903).

Macauliffe, M. A., *The Sikh Religion* (Oxford, 1909).

MacMunn, George, *The Martial Races of India* (London, 1938).

MacMunn, Major L. E., 'The martial races of India', *Army Review*, vol. 1, no. 2 (1911).

Man Singh Nirankari, 'The Nirankaris', *Punjab Past and Present*, vol. 8 (1973).

Marenco, Ethene K., *The Transformation of Sikh Society* (Delhi, 1976).

Maynard, John, 'The Sikh problem in the Punjab 1920–1923', *Contemporary Review* (Sept. 1923).

Mc'Gregor, W. L., *A History of the Sikhs* (London, 1846).

Mennon, V. P., *The Transfer of Power in India* (Princeton, NJ, 1957).

McLeod, W. H., *The Evolution of the Sikh Community* (Delhi, 1975).

McLeod, W. H., *Guru Nanak and the Sikh Religion* (Oxford, 1968).

Misar, Shiv Narayan, *Akali Darshan* (Kanpur, 1922).

Mitra, Nripendra Nath, *Indian Annual Register* (Calcutta, 1919–46).

Mohinder Singh, 'Akali involvement in the Nabha affair', *Punjab Past and Present*, vol. 5, no. 2 (1971).

Mohinder Singh, *The Akali Movement* (Delhi, 1978).

Moon, Penderel, *Divide and Quit* (London, 1962).

Morse, Eric W., 'Some aspects of the Komagata Maru affair, 1914', *Canadian Historical Association Journal* (1936).

Nadis, M., 'Propaganda of the Ghadr party', *Pacific Historical Review*, vol. 20 (1951).

Nahar Singh (ed.), *GooRoo Ram Singh and the Kuka Sikhs, Documents 1863–1871* (New Delhi, 1965).

Nahar Singh Gyani, *Azadi Dian Leharan* (Ludhiana, 1959).

Narain, Brij, 'Eighty years of Punjab food prices, 1841–1920', *Indian Journal of Economics*, vol. 6, pt 1 (1925).

Narain Singh, *Bawa Sikh Hindu Hain* (Amritsar, 1899).

Narang, Gokul Chand, *Transformation of Sikhism* (Lahore, 1946).

Nayar, Baldev Raj, *Minority Politics in the Punjab* (Princeton, NJ, 1966).

Nayar, Baldev Raj, 'Punjab', in Myron Weiner (ed.), *State Politics in India* (Princeton, NJ, 1968).

Nayar, Kuldip, and Khushwant Singh, *Tragedy of the Punjab, Operation Bluestar and After* (Delhi, 1984).

Nehru, Jawaharlal, *An Autobiography* (London, 1936).

Nihal Singh, 'The Sikh struggle against strangulation', *Fortnightly Review*, vol. 97 (1912).

O'Donnel, C. J., *The Causes of Present Discontent in India* (London, 1908).

O'Dwyer, Sir Michael, *India as I Knew It, 1885–1925* (London, 1926).

Pannikar, K. M., *Ideals of Sikhism* (Lahore, 1924).

Parry, R. E., *The Sikhs of the Punjab* (London, 1921).

People's Union for Democratic Rights and People's Union for Civil Liberties, *Report of a Joint Inquiry into the Causes and Impact of the Riots in Delhi from 31 October to 10 November, 1984* (New Delhi, 1984).

Polier, Col. A. L. H., 'The Siques or history of the Sique', reprinted in *Punjab Past and Present*, vol. 4, no. 2 (1970).

Prem Singh Sodhbans (ed.), *Kharak Singh Abhinandan Granth* (Delhi, 1953).

Prinsep, Henry T., *Origin of the Sikh Power in the Punjab and Political Life of Muharaja Ranjeet Singh* (Calcutta, 1834).

Proceedings of the Punjab History Conference, 1968 (Patiala, 1968).

Proceedings of the Punjab History Conference, 1970 (Patiala, 1970).

Proceedings of the Punjab History Conference, 1971 (Patiala, 1972).

Proceedings of the Punjab History Conference, 1972 (Patiala, 1972).

Punjabi Suba: A Symposium (New Delhi, undated).

Rai, Lajpat, *The Arya Samaj, An Account of its Origin, Doctrines and Activities and a Biographical Sketch of the Founder* (London, 1915).

Rai, Lajpat, *The Agony of the Punjab* (Madras, 1920).

Rai, Lajpat, *Young India, An Interpretation and a History of the Nationalist Movement from Within* (New York, 1917).

Ram, Dharamvir, *Punjab Ka Itihas* (Allahabad, 1950).

Ramusack, Barbara N., 'Incident at Nabha: interaction between Indian states and British Indian politics', *Journal of Asian Studies*, vol. 28, no. 3 (1969).

Ratan Singh, *The Revolt of the Sikh Youth* (Lahore, 1943).

Ray, Niharranjan, *The Sikh Gurus and the Sikh Society* (New Delhi, 1975).

Rudolph, Lloyd L. and Herber, Susanne, *The Modernity of Tradition, Political Developments in India* (Chicago, 1967).

Sahni, Ruchi Ram, *Struggle for Reform in Sikh Shrines* (Amritsar, undated).

Sahni, Ruch Ram, *Report of the Guru-Ka-Bagh Congress Inquiry Committee* (Lahore, 1924).

Sampurananand, *Akalion Ka Adarsh Satyagrah* (Benares, 1922).

Sardul Singh Caveeshar, *India's Fight for Freedom* (Lahore, 1936).

Sarsfield, Landen, *Betrayal of the Sikhs* (Lahore, 1946).

Sarup Singh (ed.), *Birth of Khalsa* (Lahore, 1941).

Sarup Singh, *The Forgotten Panth* (Amritsar, 1945).

'Sat Sri Akal', *Blackwoods Magazine*, vol. 213 (1923).

Scott, George Batley, *Religion and Short History of the Sikhs, 1469–1930* (London, 1930).

Seal, Anil, *The Emergence of Indian Nationalism: Competition and Collaboration in the Later 19th Century* (Cambridge, 1968).

Seal, Anil, Johnson, Gordon, and Gallagher, Jack (eds), *Locality, Province and Nation: Essays on Indian Politics, 1870–1940* (Cambridge, 1973).

Sen, S. P. (ed.), *Dictionary of National Biography* (Calcutta, 1974).

Sen, N. B. (ed.), *Punjab's Eminent Hindus* (Lahore, 1943).

Sethi, G. R., *Sikh Struggle for Gurdwara Reform* (Amritsar, 1927).

Sewa Ram Singh, *Report of the Working of the Sikh Deputation to England* (Lahore, 1920).

Sher Singh, *Thoughts on Forms and Symbols in Sikhism* (Lahore, 1927).

Shiromani, Akali Dal, *Punjabi Suba* (Amritsar, undated).

'Sikh situation in the Punjab', *Fortnightly Review*, vol. 119 (1923).

'Sikhs and their shrines', *New Statesman*, vol. 23 (1924).

'*Sikhism and Indian society*', Transactions of the Indian Institute of Advanced Study (Simla, 1967).

Smedley, Agnes, 'Jodh Singh', *Nation*, vol. 114 (Mar. 1922).

Sohan Singh Josh, *Tragedy of Komagata Maru* (New Delhi, 1975).

Sohan Singh Josh, *Akali Morcha Da Itihas* (Delhi, 1972).

Speary, Earl E., *German Plots and Intrigues in the United States During the Period of Our Neutrality* (Washington DC, 1918).

Steinbach Lt-Col., *The Punjab, Being a Brief Account of the Country of the Sikhs* (London, 1846).

Sundaram, G. A., *Guru Ka Bagh Satyagrah* (Madras, 1923).

Swarup Singh Sandhu, *The Sikhs Demand their Homeland* (Lahore, 1946).

Talwar, K. S., 'Early phases of the Sikh renaissance and struggle for freedom', *Punjab Past and Present*, vol. 4, no. 2 (1970).

Tandon, Prakash, *Punjabi Century, 1857–1947* (Berkeley, 1968).

Tara Singh, *To All Men of Good Conscience* (New Delhi, 1959).

Tara Singh, *Meri Yaad* (Amritsar, 1965).

Teja Singh, *Growth of Responsibility in Sikhism* (Lahore 1921).

Teja Singh, *Gurdwara Reform Movement and the Sikh Awakening* (Jullunder, 1922).

Teja Singh, *Sikhism, its Ideals and Institutions* (Calcutta, 1938).

Teja Singh, *Essays in Sikhism* (Lahore, 1944).

Teja Singh and Ganda Singh, *A Short History of the Sikhs* (Bombay, 1950).

Teja Singh, *Guru Nanak and his Mission* (Amritsar, 1963).

The Struggle for Freedom of Religious Worship at Jaito (Amritsar, undated; proscribed).

Thackwell, E. J., *Narrative of the Second Sikh War, 1848–49* (London, 1851).

Trevaskis, Hugh Kennedy, *The Land of the Five Rivers* (Oxford, 1928).

Truth About Nabha (Amritsar, 1924; proscribed).

Thorburn, S. S., *The Punjab in Peace and War* (London, 1904).

Van den Dungen, P. H. M., *The Punjab Tradition* (London, 1972).

'Where the Sikhs worry Britain', *Literary Digest*, vol. 80 (London, 1925).

Woodruff, P., *The Men Who Ruled India* (London, 1954).

Index

Ajnala 135
Akali 167n., 177
Akali Dal xv, xvi, 174, 196; achieve
  Sikh majority in Punjab 216;
  after partition 208–10; agitation
  against central government
  218–19, 228–9; Anandpur Sahib
  resolution 219–21; appeals
  against Akali tactics 198; Azad
  Punjab scheme 205–6; becomes
  dominant Sikh party 196;
  changing views of leaders 221–2;
  coalition with Janata party 218,
  220; critical of communal award
  205; demonstration at Congress
  session 214; during Second
  World War 202; elections to
  SGPC 212, 214; equated with the
  Khalsa *panth* 197–8; factions join
  forces 223–4; forms coalition
  government 217–18; general
  election, 1952 210–11; ideology
  developed 207; leadership contest
  216; loses power 218;
  negotiations with central
  government 229;
  non-co-operation with Indian
  Statutory Commission 203;
  organize general strike 229; plans
  for a separate Sikh state 207, 211;
  publicity campaign 222; relations
  with Indian National Congress,
  200–1; religious appeal 210; seek
  better political leverage for Sikhs
  200–3, 209; separate Sikh identity
  and 199–202; SGPC and 197;
  splits into two factions 218–19;
  'stop the canal' campaign 223;
  submits grievances to central
  government 222–3; traffic
  obstruction campaigns 225
Akali, Phula Singh 92–3
Akalis 92–3, 99–100, 105–7, 116,
  148; *Akali* 167n., 177; Akali

diwans, A's at Janam Ashan 110,
  112, 113–14; Akali *jathas* 100,
  109, 114, 123–4, 125–6, 138, 212,
  222, 223; A's at Nankana 134;
  arrested at Guru-ka-Bagh 155;
  campaigns at Golden Temple
  213–15, 224; concern to district
  officers 128; disarming of A.
  bands 141–2; *Fauj* (army) 139,
  140; government curbs A.
  activity 176–8, 182, 192n.;
  incident at Guru-ka-Bagh 152–5;
  jathas congregate at Amritsar
  133; *jathas* sent to Bhai-Pheru
  178–9, 180; *jathas* sent to
  Guru-ka-Bagh 152–5; *jathas* sent
  to Jaito 176, 177, 178; massacred
  at Janam Ashan 109–10; new
  SGPC and 123–6; occupy Baba
  Budha and Hothian shrines
  128–9; occupy Khadaur Sahib
  gurdwara 106; officers arrested
  177; picket Golden Temple 133;
  reaction to Sikh Gurdwaras Bill
  1925, 190; recruitment for Akali
  Dal 125–8, 179; repression of
  144–9; resurgency of militancy
  176; success of 138; use of
  non-violent civil disobedience
  152–3
All India Muslim League 70, 87, 203,
  205
All-India Sikh Educational
  Conference 221
All World Sikh Convention 222
Amar Das, third guru 2, 5
Amritsar xii, 3, 9, 185; Akal Takht 3;
  A. Mission School 16; founding
  of 2; Harmandir 2; martial law
  declared in 85–6; massacre at
  Jallianwallah Bagh 85; Singh
  Sabha in 17; *see also* Golden
  Temple
Anandpur Sahib 3, 186

Angad, second guru 2, 3
Arjun, fifth guru 2–3, 5
army, Indian: demobilization 84–5;
    importance of Punjab to 61;
    loyalty of Sikhs undermined 137;
    Operation Bluestar xi–xii,
    229–30; recruiting agents 65;
    recruitment 61–2, 63; recruitment
    campaign 64; recruitment of
    Sikhs 24–5; Sikhs in xi, 11, 24–5,
    61, 144, 155; territorial-quota
    system of recruitment 64–5;
    World Wars and 62–3, 202
Arya Samaj xiii, 20–2, 45, 75
Aryan 54

Bedi, Baba Gurbaksh Singh 46, 63
Bedi, Baba Kartar Singh 108, 109, 116
Bedi, Gurbux Singh 95
Bhadaur, Tegh, ninth guru 95
Bhai Pheru 178–9, 180, 182, 185
Bhasaur 18
Bhindranwale, Jarnail Singh xi, xii,
    226–30
Brahmins 20
British administration 9, 38–9, 81
Budge-Budge riots 56, 66, 70, 134

Canada xi, 53–6, 67
caste 2, 4, 6, 45–6; *chuhra* 14, 24; *jats*
    5–6, 50–1, 127; *khatris* 5;
    untouchables 23–4
Central Sikh League *see* Sikh League
Chand, Sri 43
Chelmsford, Lord 69
Chenab Canal Colony 48–9
Chief Khalsa Diwan 18, 39, 45, 47, 48,
    70, 72, 73, 81, 86, 93, 158–60,
    203, 221
Christian missionaries 13–15, 22, 40
civil disobedience xi
colonial authority xiii, xiv
communal consciousness xii, xiii,
    xiv–xv
Communist party 217
constitutional reform 70–1; British
    ministers visit India 206;
    communal award 204–5;
    conference in London 204;
    Congress-League scheme 70–1,
    72, 74, 76, 78–9; Indian Statutory
    Commission 202–5;
    Montagu-Chelmsford report 69,

76–7, 79; Morley-Minto reform
    scheme 71, 78; plans for new
    Indian Union 205; Sikhs and
    71–5, 77; Southborough
    committee 79–81
Criminal Law (Emergency Powers)
    Bill 83
Cripps, Sir Stafford 205

Dalhousie, Lord 8
Dam Dama Taxal 226
Das, Narain 107–11, 146–7
Defence of India Act 67, 83
Delhi 93–4
Dutt, Pandit Guru 21
Dyer, General R. E. H. 85, 89, 98

education 17–18, 41
emigration/emigrants 53–6, 66–70, 91,
    127, 172n.

Ferozepur 17, 81, 185
First World War 61–6; political
    change during 69–79; *see also*
    army
Forster, George 6, 7
fundamentalism xii

Gandhi, Indira xii, 216, 230
Gandhi, Mahatma 83, 85, 87, 90, 94,
    96–7, 112, 201
Ghadr 55, 56
Golden Temple xii, 3, 38, 46, 75, 81,
    186, 207; Akali campaigns at
    213–15, 224; Akali *jathas* at 224;
    Arur Singh 95, 98; Bhindranwale
    seeks sanctuary in 226–7; civil
    suit 136–7; election of
    management committee 99;
    extremists fortify G.T. 229;
    General Dyer invited to 86;
    low-caste Sikhs at 97–8;
    managers of 38, 51, 56–7, 67, 75;
    Operation Bluestar 229–30;
    picketed by Akalis 133; release
    of Sikh prisoners 137; seized by
    Akalis 107; SGPC and 132–3,
    136; Sikh demands for control of
    81, 97–9; Sunder Singh
    Ramgarhia 132
government of India 141, 143–4,
    165–6, 210, 233; Akali Dal
    submit grievances to 222–3,

228–9; Akali leaders resume negotiations 229; *gurdwaras* bill and 160, 164; in favour of action against the Akalis 143–4; Narain Das and 146–8; need for action against the Akalis 145–8; reports on situation in Punjab 144; seals off the Punjab 229; States Reorganization Commission 211
Government of India Act (1919) 69, 70, 79, 87, 202; *Further Rules and Regulations* 94; Indian Statutory Commission 202–5
governor-generals 67
Gujranwala 9
Gurdaspur 9
gurdwaras xiv, 70, 149; Baba Budha and Hothian shrines occupied by Akalis 128–9; Bhai Pheru 178–9, 180; campaign for reform of g's. 97–100, 113, 146, 149; definition of g. 162; drafting of permanent bill 184–5; election of local g. committees 188; forcible takeover of xv; government intervention 110–12; *granthis* (scripture readers) 43; g. at Khadaur Sahib 106; g. at Panja Sahib 44–5; Harmandir 2; Hindu customs in 45; incident at Gur-ka-Bagh 151–6; Janam Ashan g., 107–12, 113–14; Jaita g., 175; management of xiv, 43, 47–8, 75–6, 106, 142, 143, 149, 173; mismanagement xiv xv, 44, 81; occupied by Akali *jathas* 100, 109; Punjab government and 105–6, 115–23, 142; revenues from xiv, 43–4, 125, 195; Rikabganj g. 93–4; settlement at Guri-ka-Bagh 163–5; SGPC's jurisdiction over 194; Sikh Gurdwaras and Shrines Bill (1921) 117–23; Sikh Gurdwaras and Shrines Bill (1922) 156–64; Sikh Gurdwaras and Shrines Bill (1925) 185–91; Udasi sect and 43; used as terrorist bases 229; *see also mahants*
Gurmat Granth Pracharak Sabha 42
Gurmat Granth Pracharak Sabha, Amritsar 20

Gurmat Granth Sudharak Committee, Lahore 20, 42
Guru Granth Sahib 2, 4, 124, 175, 187; English translation of 18–19
Guru-ka-Bagh 155–9, 163–5
Guru-ka-Langar 2
gurus xii, 1–3
Gyani, Gurbax Singh 87

Hailey, Malcolm 160–1, 163–4, 181–2, 183–4, 187–8, 193n.
Ham Hindu Nahin 19
Hardayal, Lala 55
Hargobind, sixth guru 2, 3, 5, 207
Himachal Pradesh 214
Hindus xii–xiii, xiv, 20, 73; after partition 208; Arya Samaj xii, 20–2; campaign against government 91; caste 5–6; converts to Sikh faith 27–8; educated Punjabi society 20–1; H.customs in Sikh worship 45; political representation 203; reaction to Sikh Gurdwaras and Shrines Bill 118, 121, 191; Sikhism and 45–8, 199, 211; Swami Dayanand 20, 21; take Khalsa baptism 23; Vedas 20
Hindustani Workers of the Pacific Coast 55
Hunter Committee report 91
Hunter, Lord 87, 89

Ibbetson, Denzil 24
identity xii; evolving nature of Sikh i. 26; separate Sikh i, xii, xvi, 19–20, 23, 25, 42, 199–202; Sikh and Hindu xii–xiii, 46, 199
Imperial Legislative Council 83
independence 208
India Criminal Law (Amendment) Bill 83
India, President of xi, 196
Indian Mutiny (1857) 10
Indian National Congress 70, 77, 82, 94, 138, 153, 216–17, 218; Akali demonstration at 214; appeasing Muslim League 206; boycotts Hunter committee 87; relations with Akali Dal 200–1; report on disturbances in Punjab 88
Indian Statutory Commission 202–5
Ingress into India Ordinance 67

Jallianwallah Bagh 85, 86, 89
Jan Singh, the 217, 218
Janam Ashan gurdwara 107–12
Janata party 220
jats 5–6, 50–1, 127

Karachi 18
Kartapur 5
Kashmir xi
Khalsa Advocate 44, 47, 72, 77–8, 80
Khalsa Akhbar 22–3, 45, 74
Khalsa Biradri 45
Khalsa brotherhood xii–xiii, 3;
    adoption of surname Singh 4;
    army disbanded 7, 12; five
    symbols 4, 5, 86, 92, 124, 209;
    foundation of 3–5; growth of
    23–4; jagidars 7–8; jats join 5–6,
    12; Khalsa nationalism 92; pahul
    (baptism) 4; Panj Pyaras 3–4;
    results of annexation of Punjab 8,
    12; temporal and spiritual
    authority for 4
Khalsa College, Amritsar 41, 51–3, 70,
    74, 81, 97, 134
Khalsa Diwan Society 53–5
Khalsa Handbill Society 23, 41
Khalsa High School, Lyallpur 74
Khalsa nationalism xiv, 92–4
Khalsa Samachar 23, 44, 75, 78
Khalsa Sewack 43, 44
Khalsa symbols 4, 5, 86, 92, 124, 209
Khalsa Tract Society 23, 42
Khatris 5
Khilafat committee 139
kirpan (sword) 4, 86, 92, 93, 141, 145
Komagata Maru 55–6, 66, 70, 134

Lahore 9; Commissioner of 108, 109,
    112; Deputy Commissioner of
    110, 128; Shuddhi Sabha 22;
    Singh Sabha in 17
Longowal, Harchand Singh 218,
    220–1, 225
Loyal Gazette 80–1, 82, 133
Lyall Gazetter 84

Macauliffe, Max Arthur 25–6
mahants (gurdwara managers) 43, 44,
    51, 100, 106, 116, 165;
    Babe-de-Ber shrine 75–6, 81, 94;
    conference of 107; Guru-ka-Bagh
    150–1; mismanagement by 44–6;

Narain Das, m. at Janam Asthan
    107–11; Nirmala and Udasi m's.
    118; Sadhu Ram's dharamsala
    113; Sunder Das 150–1, 155;
    Udasi Mahamandal 107–8, 109
Majithia, Dayal Singh 19
Majithia, Sunder Singh 18, 100
Malviya, Madan Mohan 87
Moguls 2, 3
Montagu, Sir Edwin, Secretary of
    State for India 69
Muslims 24, 40, 70–1, 72, 73, 89–90,
    91, 201, 203

Nabha 173–83, 191n.
Namdhari (Kuka) sect 15–16, 36–7
Nanak, first guru 1–2, 3, 5, 16, 17, 31,
    32–3n., 43, 46, 107
Nanakpanthis 5, 26, 31
Nankana Sahib 106–14, 134–5, 186
Narain, Lala Jagat 226
National Volunteeers 139
nationalism/nationalists 86, 88, 139;
    alliance between Sikhs and n.
    politicians 69, 70; Khalsa n's. 92;
    n. politicians visit Nankana
    112–13; new phase of 90–1
Nehru, Jawaharlai 91, 201, 215, 216
Nehru, Motilal 201
newspapers 23, 43, 44, 45, 76
Nirankari sect 15, 226
Nirmalas 118
non-co-operation (passive resistance)
    83, 94, 97, 112–13, 123, 128, 137,
    138, 139, 201, 202

O'Donnel, S. P. 143, 145–6, 147,
    165
O'Dwyer, Michael,
    Lieutenant-General of the Punjab
    88, 89

pahul (baptism) 4, 5, 23
Pakistan xi, 205, 208
Panch Khalsa agency 23, 42
Panja Sahib 44–5
panth 197, 207
partition 208, 210
passive resistance see
    non-co-operation
Patiala and the East Punjab States
    Union (PEPSU) 207–8, 214
political representation xiv

Punjab xi, xiii; after partition 208; agrarian disaffection 48–51; agricultural economy 42; annexation of xiv, 7; British administration in 9, 38–9; Budge-Budge riot 56, 66, 70; census, 1868 11–12; central government takes over administration 226; Christian missionaries 13–15; converts to Christianity 14; coalition government 217; decline of Sikhism 13; demand for wheat 62; economic distress 84–5; effects of demobilization 84–5; friction between Hindus and Sikhs 70; general strike 229; growth of political meetings 139; High Court 19; Hunter committee 87, 89; increased literacy 40–1; increased prosperity 28; Indian army 61–2; industry and trade 41–2; influenza epidemic 84; martial law in 85–6, 91; Muslim minority interests 71; power sharing 216; protest meetings 95; protests against Rowlatt bills 83–6; reorganized state of 216; report on disturbances in P. 88; return of emigrants 66–8; sealed off 229; Sikh population in 11–13, 27–9; terrorism in 227–30; war loans 62

Punjab Akhbar 52

Punjab Colonization of Land Act 48–50

Punjab Darpan 81, 82

Punjab government 36; acts to curb Akali activity 176–8, 182, 215; acts cautiously 141–3, 176; acts against the SGPC 179–80; army recruitment and 64–5; arrest of Sikh militants 135; ban on slogan shouting 213–14; civil suit over Golden Temple 136–7; concern over Akalis 140–1; conciliatory attitude 137–8, 224–5; conflict with SGPC 132–8; criticism by government of India 143–4, 147–8; enforces Seditious Meetings Act 135; *gurdwara* bill drafted 117–22, 156; *gurdwara*

management and 105, 110–12, 113, 115–23, 150; incident at Guru-ka-Bagh 151–6; inquiry into Nankana massacre 111–12; Khalsa College and 51–3; *mahants* appeal to 108; management of Golden Temple and 38; memorandum on Sikh politics 57; need for Punjabi clerks 39–40; negotiations with SGPC fail 180; policy over *kirpans* 144–5; postponement of *gurdwara* bill 122; propaganda battle with SGPC 149–50; Punjab Colonization of Land Act 48–9, 50; Punjab Legislative Council 78–80, 96, 114, 177–8, 203; raising of war loans 65–6; rallies public sympathy 166; reaction to Tat Khalsa militancy 105–6; Reforms Advisory Committee 95; reopens negotiations with SGPC 165–7, 180–1, 184; report on Narain Das 147; repression of Akalis 144–9; Rikabganj *gurdwara* 93–4; separate electorates 79; settlement at Guru-ka-Bagh 163–5; SGPC issue ultimatum to 115; Sikh Gurdwaras and Shrines Bill 117–23, 154–64, 185–91; Sikhs and constitutional reforms 72–3; *see also* Sikh Gurdwaras and Shrines Bill

Punjab Hindu conferences 46, 47

Punjab Legislative Assembly 217

Punjab Legislative Council 78–80, 82, 114, 177–8

Punjab Provincial Congress Committee 73

Punjab State Reorganization Bill 216

Punjabee, The 46–7, 73–4

Punjabi *suba* 211–18, 232n.

Rai, Lajpat 49, 50

Ram Das, fourth guru 2

Ram, Lala Munshi (Swami Shradhannad) 21

Ram, Sir Ganga 163

Report on Indian Constitutional Reforms (Montagu-Chelmsford Report) 76–7, 79

Rowlatt Act 82–7

Rowlatt, Justice S. A. T. 83

Samundri, Teja Singh 93, 94
Sant Sewak 107
self-government 69, 70, 78, 203
shahidi dal (band of martyrs) 93, 127–8
shahidi jatha (martyrs' jatha) 214–15
Shiromani Akali Dal 100
Shiromani Gurdwara Prabhandak Committee (SGPC) xv, 100, 118, 141; abdication of Maharaja of Nabha and 173–4, 176, 177; Akali Dal and 197; arrest of officers of 135; Bhai Pheru 178–9; conflict with Punjab government 132–8; control of shrines xv; co-operate with government 142–3; demand for separate state 221; divisions within 123–4; effect of sudhar committee's jatha upon 183; elections 124, 174, 196, 212, 214; elections to Legislative Council 177; establishment of publicity bureau 125; establishment of regular organization 124–6; establishment of shahidi dal 127–8; excommunications 196; Golden Temple and 132–3, 136–8; government and religious demands 142; incident at Guru-ka-Bagh 151–6; increased authority of 194–6; Janam Ashan shrine and 108, 110; jathas and 126; membership of 124; move to Ajnala 135; negotiations with government fail 180; non-co-operation 115, 123; officers arrested 177; propaganda 136–7; propaganda battle with government 149–50; publication of religious tracts 125; quasi-religious authority of xvi, 196; rallies public sympathy 166; recognizes futility of resistance 149; recruitment for the Akali dal 125–8; reopens negotiations with Punjab government 165–6, 180–1, 184; response to Sikh Gurdwaras and Shrines Bill 119, 123, 190; revenue from shrines xv–xvi, 125, 195; shahidi jatha goes to Jaito

179–80; tactics attacked by sudhar committees 183; use of financial resources 195
Sialkot 9; Babe-de-Ber shrine 75–6, 81, 94
Sikh 95
Sikh Gurdwaras and Shrines Bills xv; 1921 bill 117–23; 1922 bill 156–64; 1925 bill 185–91, 193n.; concession to Tat Khalsa opinion 187–8; protests from Sahajdhari Sikhs 188–9
Sikh Hindu Hain 19
Sikh League 82, 87–8, 91, 138–9, 201, 204; abdication of Maharaja of Nabha and 173; adopts policy of non-co-operation 97, 139; district leagues 91–2, 95; forums for nationalist propaganda 92; second session of 96–7
Sikh political leaders xi, xii, xiii, 127
Sikhs xi; admiration for courage of 9–10; after partition 208; agrarian community 28–9; alliance with nationalistic politicians 69, 70; Anglo-Sikh relations 39, 53, 57; apprehension at Christian influence 22; army and xi, 11, 24–5, 61–6, 137, 143, 144, 155; bitterness against the government 136; caste and 5–6; change of nature of community 29–32; conference at Lahore 205; constitutional reform and 71; conversions to Christianity 14–15; decline in numbers 9, 12–13; definition of 11, 26, 27, 121–2, 162, 187; deputation to London 95–6; egalitarianism of 23–4; elections 1923, 177–8; emergence of S. elite 42–3; English-educated xiii; escalation of political activity 139–41; extremists outside India 234n.; First Anglo-Sikh war 11; formation of sudhar committees 182–4; government commission 215; growing disaffection 224; growth of militancy 2, 3, 4–5; Hindu converts 23, 27–8; Hinduism and xii–xiii, xiv, 6–7, 13, 45–8, 199, 211; immigrants in North America 53–6; industry

and trade 42; influence of Akalis upon 140; *jats* 5–6, 50–1, 127; loyalty during First World War 62–3; Montagu-Chelmsford report and 77–9; mutiny and 10; need for reform 15, 18–19, 21–2; non-co-operation 137; persecution of 43; plans for S.majority state 207, 210, 211–12; political representation 202–5, 208; politicization among xiv; population distribution 218; princely states 63; release of prisoners 137; religion 25–6; reports to government of India 144; representation of 79–80, 82, 94–6; repression of 148–9; return of disaffected emigrants 67; rewards for war effort 63–4; schisms among 86; Second Anglo-Sikh war 10, 38; separate community xiii–xiv, 18–20, 71–5, 77, 86–7, 92, 199–202; significance of Sikh Gurdwara Act, 1925, to 190–1; S.aristocracy 14–15; S.elite 70; S.militants 50, 135, 138, 171–2n., 199; S.press 23, 43, 56, 76, 112, 133; Southborough committee and 80–1, 82, 95; spread of literacy 40–1; sympathy for 24; terrorist campaign 226–30; widespread adoption of Khalsa symbols 92

Sikhs, Kesdhari 5, 7, 11, 26, 30, 31–2, 43, 80, 95, 199

Sikhs, Rajput 25

Sikhs, Sahajdhari 5, 7, 26, 30, 31–2, 46, 80, 106, 116, 119, 188, 199

Singh, Ajit 49–50, 52

Singh, Amar 84

Singh, Arur 95

Singh, Baba Dyal 15

Singh, Babu Teja 18

Singh, Bhai Balak 16

Singh, Bhai Ditt 17, 19–20, 45

Singh, Bhai Sahib Arjun 86

Singh, Bhai Takht 17

Singh, Bikram, Maharaja of Faridkot 17

Singh, Chanda 81

Singh, Fateh 215, 216

Singh, Gobind, tenth guru xii, 3, 10, 25, 30–1, 92, 136, 153, 197, 207, 227

Singh, Gurdit 55–6, 134

Singh, Harbans 123

Singh, Jhandra 84

Singh, Kanwar Harnam 14

Singh, Kharak 97, 124, 135, 148–9, 190

Singh, Maharaja Dalip 7, 14

Singh, Maharaja Ranjit 6, 18, 92–3

Singh, Mahtab 124, 135, 190

Singh, Professor Teja 118–19

Singh, Ram 16, 36–7

Singh, Sabhas xiii, 16–18, 22, 37, 40, 41, 42, 43, 50, 75, 119; Chief Khalsa Diwan 18, 39, 45, 47, 48, 63, 70, 72, 73, 81, 86, 93, 158–60, 203, 221; co-operation with government 37–8; emphasis on female education 17–18, 41; Khalsa College 41, 51–3, 74; principles of 16–17; propaganda 22; success of 30; use of the press 22

Singh, Sardar Gajjan 79, 82

Singh, Sardar Tara 74–5

Singh, Tara 200, 201, 206, 207, 210, 211–13, 215, 216

Sri Chand 2

Sri Hargobinpur 5

States Reorganization Commission 211–12, 214

sudhar committees 182–4

Talwandi, Jagdev Singh 218–19, 221, 222, 225–6

Tarn Taran 5, 45, 93, 186

Tat Khalsa xiii, xv, 22, 32, 39, 43, 78, 93, 116, 119, 190–1; concessions in 1922 *gurdwaras* bill 157; elite 74; friction with Arya Samajists 75; growth of militancy 81, 105; involvement in politics 91; perversion of the Sikh faith 45–7; reaction to Sikh Gurdwaras and Shrines Bill 118–22; renewed conflict with government 173; tension with the Hindus 69–70; *see also* Akalis

Teg Bhadur, ninth guru 3

Temple, Sir Richard 8

terrorism xi, xii, 83, 172, 227, 234n.

Tribune 82

Trumpp, Dr Ernest 18–19
Turkey 89–90

Udasi Mahaamandal 107–8, 109, 116

Udasis, 2, 43, 118, 199
United States of America xi, 53–5, 66–7, 68–9